A gift of

John Philip Fayen

DATE DUE

OCT 1 0 1990			
OCT 3 0 1990			
	201-6503		Printed in USA

La Salle and His Legacy

Frenchmen and Indians
in the Lower Mississippi Valley

•

Patricia K. Galloway
EDITOR

UNIVERSITY PRESS OF MISSISSIPPI
JACKSON/1982

Copyright © 1982 by the University Press of Mississippi
All Rights Reserved
Manufactured in the United States of America

Library of Congress Cataloging in Publication Data
Main entry under title:

La Salle and his legacy.

Chiefly papers presented at the 1982 annual meeting
of the Mississippi Historical Society.
Bibliography: p.
Includes index.
1. Mississippi River Valley—History—To 1803—
Congresses. 2. La Salle, Robert Cavelier, sieur de,
1643–1687—Congresses. 3. Mississippi River Valley—
Description and travel—Congresses. 4. America—
Discovery and exploration—French—Congresses. I. Gallo-
way, Patricia K. II. Mississippi Historical Society.
F352.L34 1983 977 82-17498
ISBN 0-87805-171-6

This volume is sponsored by the
Mississippi Department of Archives and History
and the
Mississippi Historical Society

Contents

Introduction

With 1982 marking the tricentennial of the exploration of the lower Mississippi Valley by the expedition led by René-Robert Cavelier de La Salle, it was thought fitting that the occasion should be commemorated by a variety of observances in the states bordering the river along the expedition's route. In the state of Mississippi a Governor's Commission was appointed and the Mississippi Historical Society proposed to contribute to the scholarly aspect of the observance by devoting its annual meeting of 1982 to papers related to the theme of early French exploration and settlement. The papers in this volume include eight that were presented at that meeting, plus an additional six especially written. The Mississippi Historical Society and the Mississippi Department of Archives and History have both lent their support to the dissemination of this research through publication.

Although to most people it probably seems that La Salle and his men, permanently fixed in the pantheon of explorers of the North American continent, need little further introduction, the fact is that this whole early period of exploration and colonization by the French in the southeastern United States has received far less scholarly attention than the corresponding activities in the same area by the English and the Spanish. Even the figure of La Salle himself, as Brasseaux' work shows, has been variously portrayed through historical research, and arguably never with complete accuracy. Nor, in spite of the existence of many narrative retellings of the events of the journey, have the sources ever been studied with an eye to the reliability and independence of their observations. Indeed, a new source was first made public just last year, and Galloway's study incorporates it in a reexamination of the sources.

Probably the most important accomplishment of La Salle's journey was the establishment of peaceful relations with the

Native American groups the party met along the way; yet ethnohistorical research has never dealt in a comprehensive way with the evidence provided to it by this early contact. Stubbs' paper shows that even a fleeting contact with the expedition left valuable traces for the study of an individual group, while Brain's shows how archaeology and history may cooperate to illuminate events that occurred before Europeans ever entered the scene.

One measure of the success of La Salle's exploration was the contribution it made to the cartography of the Southeast. De Vorsey reexamines the early French cartography of the area, before and after 1682, to argue from the evidence conveyed by La Salle to European cartographers that La Salle's motivation to return and establish a colony may have led him to a stratagem that in fact impeded accurate cartography for several decades. The paucity of modern studies of the French cartography of the period makes this examination of the evidence particularly valuable.

But La Salle was one actor on a larger stage: French colonization around the world. Cooke offers a consideration of New World colonialism as one example of the Gallic attitude toward colonial ventures in general, while Conrad traces La Salle's exploration and the subsequent creation of the Louisiana colony as they fit into France's strategy in North America. Nor did the movement to establish the colony on the lower Mississippi occur in a vacuum. Holmes and Coker examine, respectively, aspects of the Spanish and English reactions to what those countries perceived as French intentions on the Mississippi and in the Gulf of Mexico.

Native American observations of the intruding Europeans come down to us for the most part indirectly, but we may be sure that word of the newcomers spread rapidly along the trail and river networks and careful consideration of their potential threat or usefulness took place in the tribal councils of the many and populous Indian groups along the lower Mississippi and the Gulf of Mexico. York reexamines the case for the existence of a common trade language in the area that would have aided such rapid communication, and argues that the evidence for its existence before the coming of Europeans and for its origin from the Choctaw language may be stronger than linguists have previously thought. It is certain that the title of first Indian diplomatist of the lower Mississippi Valley must be awarded to La Salle's partner, Henri de Tonti; Galloway studies two documents which record his early negotiations with the two tribes that were to shape the Louisiana colony's Indian policies throughout its history: the Chickasaw and Choctaw. Brown outlines an ongoing study of the interaction between the French and the only group they actually settled among, the Natchez, using the evidence of archaeology to discover what actual influence the cultures of the two peoples had on each other.

European colonies in the New World required fortification against two perceived dangers: the possibility of native uprising and the certainty of eventual challenge from other European powers. Wilson's interesting study examines the history of Fort Rosalie at the Natchez settlement, which was eventually poor protection against the former threat; Ekberg takes a look at the fortifications eventually erected at the spot where Bienville first turned the English back from the Mississippi River—never used in fact for defense, it was perhaps their very existence that assured the safety of New Orleans.

Useful as these papers are, and the reader familiar with this field of research will discover that each makes a new contribution to our knowledge of the French colony and its Indian neighbors, they and all the research which has preceded them only begin to scratch the surface of a very rich treasure of source materials. To date the most thorough exploitation of these materials has been by Marcel Giraud, the distinguished French scholar whose multi-volumed history of French Louisiana examines them in exhaustive detail. But Giraud's published work so far reaches only to cover a little more than a third of the colony's history, and its emphasis falls on the political and economic history of the colony, not its social history or the ethnohistory of its native peoples. For the time being it is safe to leave Giraud to the completion of his excellent work, but for the latter two fields there is much to be done and much to be learned.

It is true that the culture of the French in Louisiana remained distinctly Gallic in flavor and the ruling circles in New Orleans did everything they could to create a little Paris on the Mississippi. But environmental and social conditions were very different in the Southeast from those in France or Canada, and their subtle influence pervaded the new Louisiana culture as the colony took hold and colonists began to commit themselves to the lands they held. They learned many of the adaptations they had to make from the country's natives, who had long since mastered all the factors in their environment, and additional adaptations in the background of their lives were made by their African slaves. This mixing of cultures is most evident in creole cuisine, but it was far more pervasive than that, extending to clothing and shelter as well. The social environment also was subtly changed. Penniless younger sons of minor nobility and even petty thieves and smugglers founded fortunes, families, and respectability in the more open atmosphere of the New World; though this sounds like simply another truism of American colonial life, the fact was that though the names were changed, social stratification still remained, not as a precise model of what was found in France but as a loose analogy. All of these changes in French lifeways that made the colonists distinctly *Louisianais* have been noticed by scholars in passing; however, except for Samuel Wilson's series of studies of architecture and building, none have been studied systematically.

There has been a great deal of interest in the past in the "Great Men" of the Louisiana colony's history: La Salle, Iberville, Bienville, Cadillac, Vaudreuil. But all of these men and most others whose motivations and role in the colony's history have been thought of interest never committed themselves to Louisiana; in the end, they all returned to France. Many colonists, however, did not. The salutary attention that the new social history is paying to merchants, artisans, women, and slaves deserves to be directed toward the history of those groups in the

Louisiana colony; so far the only such nonpolitical group to be studied in detail—and that because its influence was far greater than its numbers—is that of the colony's religious personnel. Yet French colonists were the first to exploit the lumber industry in south Mississippi; thriving Louisiana sugar and rice plantations were first established by Frenchmen; the commerce that made New Orleans a great port city was founded in the colonial period; fine furniture was crafted in imitation of eighteenth century French styles, using the new woods found in the colony; the shortage of women gave them a *de facto* independence that they never let go of; blacks, whether through manumission or mestizo birth, formed a free society of their own from surprisingly early in the colony's history. All of these topics await further in-depth study from specialists in the various subfields that apply; all would richly reward such study.

The interaction of the French in the Louisiana colony with their Native American neighbors was, as we have suggested, exceptionally fruitful and nonexploitative by colonial standards. But that is not to say that there were not inequities and terrible cruelties on both sides. The whole story of the Natchez uprising, its causes and results both for the colony and the Natchez themselves, has not been told: the fate of those Natchez deported as slaves to Santo Domingo, of those who fled to dubious sanctuary with the Chickasaw, of those who fled even further to take refuge in a small settlement in South Carolina—for years these questions have languished unanswered under the supposition that the Natchez were wiped out by the French in 1730. And the histories of the so-called "small tribes" on the lower Mississippi—Chouacha, Bayougoula, Acolapissa, Chitimacha—have only recently begun to come to light, as the remnants of some of these tribes have struggled for official recognition by the government of the United States. Even those tribes that figured importantly in the colony's history—the Quapaw, Tunica, Natchez, Chickasaw, and Choctaw—have been neglected by historians while archaeologists alone attempted to piece together the story of their development out of the great Mississippian chiefdoms of prehistory. Yet there is a great deal of inferential evidence about this very tantalizing aspect of ethnohistory to be gathered from the French colonial documents, as John R. Swanton, the first ethnographer of the Indians of the Southeast, was very well aware. His success in using the limited number of documents available to him has led to the impression that he saw them all, when in fact he exploited only a tiny fraction of them. A reevaluation of the ethnography and ethnohistory of the Native Americans of the Louisiana colony is in order, using *all* the documents. This too represents a sizeable challenge to researchers working in the new paradigm of the history of those who write no history.

The foregoing suggestions and recommendations represent only an idiosyncratic gleaning. The whole of not one but many cultures remains to be reconstructed. The present volume represents some contributions to this effort; it is to be hoped that it may encourage others to "go and do likewise."

Patricia Galloway

PART I

La Salle's Expedition of 1682

The Image of La Salle in
North American Historiography

CARL A. BRASSEAUX

•

HISTORY, like journalism, is transformed by the popular biases and world views of successive generations. Individuals reflect their environment, and their writings mirror their personal realities. This psychological phenomenon—a subconscious process, resulting from years of internalization of prevailing values—is most evident in the major schools of American historiography.

Living in an era in which individual initiative, unabashed imperialism, and the white man's burden were the hallmarks of western society, nineteenth-century historians were understandably preoccupied with personalities and events which seemed to exhibit these values. Consequently, their works are replete with accounts of intrepid European and Anglo-American adventurers who braved overwhelming odds to impose their own civilization upon an often reluctant aboriginal society.

Many twentieth-century historians have been no less guilty of presentism. Profoundly influenced by the rejection of Victorian values and the economic and social dislocation so pervasive *entre deux guerres*, historians of the 1920s and 30s placed greater emphasis upon economic questions and examined more critically the ostensibly selfless motives of the nation's heroic figures. The historical criticism of the post-World War I historians was refined by their successors in the aftermath of the century's second global conflict. In an era when public figures have been consistently unable to bear unblinking public scrutiny, modern American historians have been fascinated with the flaws and failures of their subjects.

Over the years, therefore, prominent figures in American history have gradually slipped from the pinnacles upon which they

3

had been placed by the country's pioneer historians. The great men of one age are the butt of criticism for another. Such is the case with René-Robert Cavelier de La Salle.

La Salle was enshrined in the American pantheon by the nationalist American historians of the pre-World War I era. In his landmark *History of the United States from the Discovery of the Continent*, George Bancroft portrays the French explorer as a fearless adventurer who faithfully carried his monarch's standard across the North American interior.[1] Bancroft, however, merely echoed the findings of his less illustrious Louisiana counterparts. As early as 1827, New Orleans jurist and historian François-Xavier Martin had noted in the first volume of his history of Louisiana that La Salle was passionately consumed by his interest in "discoveries."[2] Charles-Étienne Arthur Gayarré, in his somewhat later history,[3] expands upon Martin's conclusion, suggesting that the French adventurer had imposed upon the Canadian government

> his views and projects for the aggrandizement of France, and suggested to . . . Governor Frontenac . . . the gigantic plan of connecting the St. Lawrence with the Mississippi by an uninterrupted chain of forts.[4]

Gayarré's view of La Salle was complemented by that of fellow creole Alcée Fortier.[5] Fortier, the last major Louisiana historian of the pre-World War I era, indicated in his four-volume history of the Pelican State that the Frenchman "intended to hold the whole country for the French king, from the Great Lakes to the Gulf of Mexico."

The prevailing American view of La Salle was shared by early European students of Mississippi Valley history. Gabriel Gravier, most prolific of the French *américanistes*, affirmed the conclusions of his American predecessors in a full-length biography of La Salle and in a summary article.[6] The American view of La Salle as an intrepid adventurer and selfless agent of the French crown was shared by Paul Chesnel, professor of history at the Sorbonne, whose *Histoire de Cavelier de La Salle* became

4

the most influential European work in this formative stage of La Salle studies.[7]

Throughout the nineteenth century René-Robert Cavelier de La Salle was portrayed by Mississippi Valley historians as a benign agent of French imperialism in the North American interior. This interpretation was embellished significantly in the post-Civil War era by Francis Parkman. An independently wealthy scion of an old New England family, Parkman devoted his life to a multi-volume history of the Franco-British struggle for supremacy in North America. This historiographically significant series embodies the poorly veiled anglophile bias of its author, with one notable exception: *La Salle and the Discovery of the Great West*.[8] Hampered by failing vision and thus limited to an hour or two of writing per day, Parkman often despaired of success for his project, which he deemed of national importance. In La Salle the New Englander saw a man who, like himself, possessed great ability, but whose achievements were limited by nagging, often crippling problems. Parkman consequently portrayed the Frenchman as the greatest French explorer and colonizer in early North America, claiming that La Salle failed to realize his full potential because of the sinister machinations of his detractors and rivals and the unrelenting demands of frontier life.

Parkman's *La Salle* enjoyed immediate success and wide circulation: twelve editions of the work appeared within twenty years of its initial publication. The psychological transposition manifested in the historian's image of his subject, so vividly analyzed by William R. Taylor,[9] had a lasting impact upon American historiography. From 1869 to the present, Parkman's work has been the principal force in shaping the popular conception of the French explorer.

After the appearance of Parkman's *La Salle*, popular writers and historians rushed to incorporate the New Englander's thesis into their works. Superlatives soon punctuated their normally pedestrian prose, and with each retelling La Salle garnered new accolades. By World War I, the Frenchman's image had become distorted to such an extent that it bore little resemblance to historical reality. Indeed, La Salle had emerged as a folk hero whose adventurous spirit and fearlessness had acquired legendary proportions. John S. C. Abbot's *The Adventures of Chevalier de La Salle and His Companions* is perhaps the best example of this new wave of La Salle literature. In the preface Abbot states that

> There is no one of the Pioneer[s] of this continent whose achievement equals those of the Chevalier Robert de la Salle . . . Fear was an emotion La Salle never experienced. His adventures were more wild and wondrous than almost any recorded in the tales of chivalry.[10]

Equally unrestrained in their praise are a host of other American authors down through the 1930s.[11] Unqualified praise for La Salle also marked early twentieth-century French works, such as Maurice Constantin-Weyer's *Life and Exploits of La Salle*.[12] Shortly before World War II, Le Mission "Cavelier de La Salle" of the Institut des Études Américaines published a volume of essays to eulogize the Rouen native.[13] In the chapter entitled "La Découverte et la prise de possession de la Louisiane,"[14] André Chevrillon, a member of the French Academy, characterized La Salle as an unsung French national hero, adding chauvinistically that his "life and actions brought greater honor to our race." A larger-than-life figure, Chevrillon's La Salle was the personification of the Neitzschean superman.[15]

Such intemperate prose, which typified the La Salle literature of the early twentieth century, became progressively uncommon after World War II. The last works of this genre appeared more than a decade ago[16] and have happily been supplanted by more balanced works which have looked beyond the explorer's glittering popular image.

This more objective view of La Salle resulted from greater historical criticism of extant primary source materials. This increasingly scientific historical methodology reflected the growing interest of serious scholars in the exploration and early development of the Mississippi Valley. By 1920, professional historians had replaced laymen and journalists at the cutting edge of La Salle studies, and their meticulous scholarship quickly invalidated the unscientific methodology of their predecessors.

The first skeptic was Justin Winsor,[17] whose *Cartier to Frontenac* was a commendable attempt to separate fact from fiction. Winsor's book profoundly influenced the next generation of American historians, who no longer accepted with blind trust the findings of their predecessors. Building upon the foundation laid by Winsor, Frederick Austin Ogg at Indiana University set the tone for this intellectual movement in *The Opening of the Mississippi*,[18] which, for the first time, examined in depth La Salle's business dealings as motivation for his exploration of the Mississippi Valley.

Just as Ogg questioned La Salle's ostensibly honorable and completely patriotic motives for charting the mid-American wilderness, the Indiana historian's successors carefully examined the questionable and often fantastic claims of La Salle's late nineteenth- and early twentieth-century apologists. The leading debunker of the La Salle myth is unquestionably Jean Delanglez, whose *Some La Salle Journeys*[19] has become the standard reference work on the explorer's many lengthy voyages. Other skeptics include Lionel Groulx[20] and G. L. Jaray.[21] Their findings have been popularized by Pierre Lephoron[22] and John U. Terrell.[23]

While many modern historians were engaged in removing La Salle's controversial mantle of virtue, other scholars labored to fill the rather significant gaps in the existing career biographies of the French adventurer. Although a few articles focused upon specific incidents in La Salle's career in Lower Canada and the Mississippi Valley,[24] the bulk of the new research centered upon the ill-fated Matagorda Bay colony.

Because of the role of the Matagorda Bay colony as a catalyst in the Spanish occupation of Texas and reexploration of the Gulf Coast, this aspect of La Salle's career quickly became the domain of the Spanish borderlands historians. Herbert Eugene

Bolton, father of Spanish borderlands studies in the United States, broke new ground with his article on the location of the colony.[25] Bolton's study was followed by William Edward Dunn's article on the Spanish efforts to find it.[26] Dunn's dissertation, subsequently published as a monograph entitled *Spanish and French Rivalry in the Gulf Region of the United States, 1678–1702,*[27] was the standard work on this subject for over half a century. Also useful are works on related topics by Folmer, Hoese, Leonard, Moraud, O'Donnell, and du Terrage.[28]

The vast amount of new material generated by such twentieth-century scholars laid the foundation for several books which are now generally considered the standard works on La Salle. E. B. Osler's *La Salle,*[29] based upon extensive primary and secondary research, is a penetrating biography which explodes the La Salle legend and reveals the explorer as "a very vulnerable, courageous, ambitious, difficult man whose failure sprang from his own strange, withdrawn personality." Osler's concluding chapters on La Salle's tragic attempt to colonize the lower Mississippi Valley, though sound, have been supplanted by the research of Robert S. Weddle, whose *Wilderness Manhunt: The Spanish Search for La Salle*[30] offers much new information regarding the final chapter of La Salle's life.

The Weddle and Osler books represent the best efforts to date to document the long and turbulent career of René-Robert Cavelier de La Salle. But as we have seen, history is dynamic, constantly changing its perception of the past, and many questions regarding the controversial explorer remain unanswered. For example, to what extent did La Salle's activities alter France's long-term goals and aspirations for North America? To what extent did he alter French Indian policy? How extensively was the material culture of the Ohio and upper Mississippi Valley Indian tribes altered by La Salle's Illinois settlement? Did La Salle intentionally avoid the mouth of the Mississippi River and sail toward the Mexican mines, as modern research implies? Is the critical tone of modern La Salle historiography justified; or, does the explorer merit the accolades once accorded him; or, should this explorer be seen in a more balanced light, in which his personality flaws are not given preeminence? These questions must be addressed before René-Robert Cavelier de la Salle can assume his rightful position in American history.

Notes

[1] George Bancroft, *History of the United States from the Discovery of the Continent,* 2, 160–174.

[2] François-Xavier Martin, *The History of Louisiana from the Earliest Period.*

[3] Charles-Étienne Arthur Gayarré, *History of Louisiana,* 4 vols.

[4] Ibid., 1, 24.

[5] Alcée Fortier, *A History of Louisiana,* 4 vols., 1, 17–18.

[6] Gabriel Gravier, *Découvertes et établissements de Cavelier de La Salle de Rouen dans l'Amérique du Nord;* idem, "René-Robert Cavelier de La Salle."

[7] Paul Chesnel, *Histoire de Cavelier de La Salle.*

[8] Francis Parkman, *La Salle and the Discovery of the Great West.*

[9] William R. Taylor, "A Journey into the Human Mind: Motivation in Francis Parkman's *La Salle.*"

[10] John S. C. Abbot, *The Adventures of Chevalier de La Salle and His Companions* (New York, 1898).

[11] Representative examples are: Katherine Coman, "La Salle's Ill-Fated Enterprise," in Coman, *Economic Beginnings of the Far West,* 2 vols. (New York, 1912), 1, 66–81; John Finley, *The French in the Heart of America* (New York, 1915), 55–64; James K. Hosmer, *A Short History of the Mississippi Valley* (Boston, 1901), 35–50; J. V. Jacks, *La Salle* (New York, 1921); Lyle Saxon, *Father Mississippi* (New York, 1927), 85–101; J. H. Schlarman, *From Quebec to New Orleans: The Story of the French in America* (Belleville, Illinois, 1930); William Dana Orcutt, *Robert Cavelier, The Romance of the Sieur de La Salle* (Chicago, 1904); Clifford Smith, *La Salle and the Pioneers of New France* (New York, 1931); Joseph Wallace, *Illinois and Louisiana Under French Rule* (Cincinnati, 1893), 71–74.

[12] Maurice Constantin-Weyer, *The Life and Exploits of La Salle* (New York, 1931).

[13] Institut des Études Américaines, *Louisiane et Texas* (Paris, 1938).

[14] Ibid., 13–33.

[15] Ibid., 31.

[16] Robert Viau, *Cavelier de La Salle* (Tours, 1960); John Anthony Caruso, *The Mississippi Valley Frontier: The Age of French Exploration and Settlement* (Indianapolis, 1966), 159–224.

[17] Justin Winsor, *Cartier to Frontenac.*

[18] Frederick Austin Ogg, *The Opening of the Mississippi: A Struggle for Supremacy in the American Interior.*

[19] Jean Delanglez, *Some La Salle Journeys.*

[20] Lionel Groulx, *Notre Grande Aventure: L'Empire français en Amérique du nord, 1535–1760.*

[21] G. L. Jaray, "Cavelier de la Salle, Founder of the French Empire in America."

[22] Pierre Lephrohon, *Le Destin Tragique de Cavelier de la Salle* (Paris, 1969).

[23] John U. Terrell, *La Salle: The Life and Times of an Explorer* (New York, 1968).

[24] Louise Kellogg, "Wisconsin Anabasis;" C. H. Prator, "La Salle's Trip across Southern Michigan in 1680;" Marc de Villiers du Terrage, "La Salle Takes Possession of Louisiana."

[25] Herbert Eugene Bolton, "Location of La Salle's Colony on the Gulf of Mexico."

[26] William Edward Dunn, "The Spanish Search for La Salle's Colony on the Bay of Espiritu Santo, 1685–1689."

[27] William Edward Dunn, *Spanish and French Rivalry in the Gulf Region of the United States, 1678–1703: The Beginnings of Texas and Pensacola.*

[28] Henry Folmer, *Franco-Spanish Rivalry in North America, 1524–1763;* H. Dickson Hoese, "On the Correct Landfall of La Salle in Texas, 1685;" Irving A. Leonard, "The Spanish Re-Exploration of the Gulf Coast in 1686;" M. Moraud, "Last Expedition and the Death of Cavelier de La Salle, 1684–1687;" Walter O'Donnell, *La Salle's Occupation of Texas;* Marc de Villiers du Terrage, *L'Expédition de Cavelier de La Salle dans le golfe du Mexique, 1684–1687.*

[29] E. B. Osler, *La Salle.*

[30] Robert S. Weddle, *Wilderness Manhunt: The Spanish Search for La Salle.*

Sources for the La Salle
Expedition of 1682

PATRICIA GALLOWAY

•

THERE IS NO DOUBT that La Salle's exploration of the
lower Mississippi Valley in 1682 was at least equal in importance
to Soto's "discovery" of the river, both to Indians and Europeans; La Salle's journey and his later attempt at a Gulf Coast
colony resulted in sufficient French interest to stimulate the
later settlement effort under Iberville, and it was La Salle's efforts, not Soto's, which motivated the Spanish to establish their
outpost in Pensacola. But due to the fantastic interest stirred by
the information brought back by the earlier Spanish expedition
as well as the "first" in European exploration that it represented,
the route of the Soto expedition has received—and is still receiving—sustained and at times nearly fanatical attention. The same
has not been the case of the La Salle expedition of 1682, although the identities of all the peoples and places he encountered along the way are far from certain. No complete reexamination of the evidence has been attempted with these questions
in mind for nearly forty years, yet until such a review is carried
out, any attempts to correlate the evidence of the narrative accounts with the archaeological evidence will be futile. It is the
purpose of this paper to help lay the foundations for such a
reexamination by looking at the narratives themselves with a
critical eye in order to judge their reliability as sources.

As a preface to this review we may sketch in broad lines the
relevant part of the expedition. La Salle and his party started
down the Mississippi from its confluence with the Illinois in
February of 1682, stopping at several points on the way down to
the sea to obtain provisions and to establish peaceful relations
with the Indians encountered along the way. The party explored
the passes at the mouth of the Mississippi and then formally
took possession of the whole watershed for the King on April 9,

1682. Then they proceeded to return the way they had come, as before stopping along the way. La Salle himself fell ill and stayed with part of the party for several months at Fort Prudhomme on the Chickasaw Bluffs, but he had returned to Canada by the autumn of 1682.

The accounts of the trip are replete with interesting details about landscape, fauna, and especially about the Indians that the Frenchmen met. The special value of this last set of information lies in the fact that it offers a group of observations of the political environment along the river which is potentially of extraordinary usefulness, when taken in comparison with the similar observations made by the Spaniards of a hundred and forty years before, in gauging the social change and population movement that had taken place in the interim. It is not, however, simply a matter of welding a group of harmonious sources into a single narrative, for the sources do not always agree, nor are they all worthy of equal confidence. There has been a great deal of scholarship directed at unraveling the relationships among the extant sources,[1] but the recent discovery of a new source, together with the age of most of the scholarship, warrants a new and comprehensive look at the documents.

There are several issues to be considered in evaluating the evidential value of any single narrative account of the expedition. A first set may be called the "codicological" issues, or the information that we can obtain from the physical appearance of the sources themselves and other external evidence of their dates, authorship, and possible relationships with one another. A second set must be derived from a close study of the texts and other sources, since they pertain to the identities and viewpoints of the witnesses themselves—including their physical viewpoints during the course of the exploration. Only after considering all these issues can we say which of the sources may be considered most reliable for any given aspect or segment of the events which they portray, since in several cases attribution of authorship is even uncertain.

To cover the major codicological issues briefly, we list a capsule bibliography for each source together with appropriate commentary in chronological order:[2]

Procès verbal accounts, March 13 and 14 (Arkansas) and April 9 (mouth of Mississippi), 1682. Translated in B. F. French, *Historical Collections of Louisiana*, 1, 45–50; French text in Pierre Margry, *Découvertes et établissements*, 2, 181–92; MS in Archives des Colonies (AC), série F 3, fol. 241.

These are the official sworn testimonies of the members of the expedition, taken down following each of the two acts of taking possession at the mouths of the Arkansas and Mississippi rivers to serve as legal instruments recording those claims. The account of the journey in these documents describes only the trip south and ends with the formal claim of the Mississippi watershed for Louis XIV on April 9. They were drafted by the expedition's official notary, Jacques de La Metairie, and signed by important members of the expedition. The extant manuscripts are the original documents. According to a letter of La Salle, probably written to Frontenac, La Salle sent these two accounts to Quebec from Michilimackinac in October of 1682.[3] They are primary manuscripts whose purpose, to document official claims, dictated both their brevity and, within the limitations of the report format, their veracity; the two reports may be seen as the communal sworn testimony of their signers.

Membré to Le Roux, June 3, 1682. Translated in Marion A. Habig, *The Franciscan Père Marquette*, 207–214; French text in Margry, *Découvertes et établissements*, 2, 206–212; MS in Bibliothèque Nationale (BN), MSS Clairambault 1016, fols. 163–165v.

This is a letter written from Fort Prudhomme on the return journey by Father Zenobius Membré, the expedition's Franciscan Recollect missionary priest, as he prepared to stay behind with La Salle while the latter recovered from illness. It is a brief summary of the journeys out and back, and does not claim to be a complete account but rather a hurried report of the highlights of the trip for Membré's superior in Quebec, Father Le Roux. It was given to Tonti to forward to Quebec as Tonti departed with a small party for Michilimackinac. The extant manuscript is not the original, but a copy found among the papers of the Abbé Claude Bernou.[4] We are assured to a certain extent of its authenticity, however, since a summary version of it was made in Canada and sent to France by August 14, 1682.[5] Delanglez thinks that this letter was used as one source, not the most important, for the anonymous *Relation* to be discussed presently.[6]

Tonti to _____, July 23, 1682. Translated in Habig, *Franciscan Père Marquette*, 215–29; French text in Habig, ibid.; MS in BN, MSS Clairambault 1016, fols. 165v–168v.

This letter is written from Michilimackinac after Tonti had left the party of La Salle and Membré at the Prudhomme Bluffs. The letter contains a fairly detailed summary of the complete voyage of exploration, though it is more detailed for the southward journey than for the return and it mentions few dates. It was sent to Quebec with Membré's letter, but we do not know to whom it was actually addressed. The manuscript copy which survives, in the same hand as the copy of the Membré letter and forming a single document with it, is also found among Bernou's papers.[7] Delanglez considers this letter to be the primary source for the anonymous *Relation*.[8]

Anonymous, *Relation de la découverte de l'embouchure du Mississippi, faite par De La Salle, en 1682.* Translated in Melville B. Anderson, *Relation of the Discoveries and Voyages of Cavelier de La Salle from 1679 to 1681;* French text in R. Thomassy, *De La Salle et ses Relations inédites,* 1–8, reprinted in Jean Delanglez, "La Salle's Expedition of 1682," 28–35, also in Margry, *Découvertes et établissements,* 1, 535–44; MSS in Archives du Service Hydrographique, carton C.67[2], No. 15, pièce no. 4, and BN, MSS français, nouvelles acquisitions 7485, fols. 170–175v.

This "official" report of the journey offers no clear statement of authorship, but the concluding paragraphs contain claims of surpassing the Spanish and of having suffered considerable financial loss in the process, suggesting to several investigators that it may have been at least partially attributable to La Salle himself.[9] The original manuscript is lost, and of the two copies that survive, one of them (in the Renaudot collection at the Bibliothèque Nationale) was made by a copyist who worked regularly for Renaudot, a close colleague of Bernou.[10] This fact, along with a host of internal textual comparisons, led Delanglez to assert that in spite of Habig's stout defense of Membré's authorship,[11] the report was instead drawn up using the Membré letter of June 3, 1682, and the Tonti letter of July 23, 1682, plus a few additions from a letter of La Salle[12] also found among Bernou's papers, and that the author was none other than the Abbé Claude Bernou himself.[13] The French text as printed by Delanglez from Thomassy's text of the ASH version uses typographical variation to show how the sources were interwoven to make the completed whole, indicating that to the three sources mentioned additions were minimal and consisted mostly of transitional phrases and sentences.

If the authorship of this account is to be ascribed to Bernou, who was in Rome at the time of the expedition, it is obvious that we cannot consider it as a unified eyewitness account and should prefer the sources which were demonstrably used in its composition. It is true, however, that both Bernou and Renaudot could have had access both to other letters from La Salle himself and to verbal information from Membré, and one cannot rule out the possibility that the tiny amount of material not accounted for by the known sources may have come from these.

Tonti memoir of November 4, 1684. Translated in Melville B. Anderson, *Relation of Henri de Tonty;* French text in Margry, *Découvertes et établissements* 1, 573–616; MSS in BN, MSS Clairambault 1016, fols. 220–266v and 267–279.

This memoir was the first detailed account of the expedition that Tonti seems to have written. It was sent to his protector the Abbé Renaudot in Paris[14] at a time when promotion of a colony on the Mississippi was vital to the plans of both La Salle and Tonti himself. Because it was written reasonably soon after the events it narrates and at a time when Tonti had more leisure to write at length, it contains a great deal more circumstantial detail than the earlier 1682 letter. In this memoir the dates for the downriver journey agree point for point with those in the anonymous *Relation* and the Le Clercq-"Membré" account, which is not surprising if both of them depend upon Tonti's 1682 letter, but this is not the case with the return journey, for no dates are given in this memoir. This version also disagrees with Tonti's later 1691 memoir on several points, which will be taken up when we describe that work.

This account represents the observations of La Salle's partner, second-in-command, and chief negotiator with the Indians. It is possible that it could have been based upon notes taken at the time by Tonti, since in the 1691 memoir Tonti mentions keeping notes on his 1689–90 explorations. The precise agreement of dates for the downstream journey, however, suggests that he had kept a copy of at least part of his 1682 letter or notes that served as its source.

Minet journal, *Voiage fait du Canada par dedans les terres allant vers le sud, dans l'anne 1682,* 1684–85. No printed version. MS Public Archives Canada MG18 B19.

This journal was written down by the engineer and cartographer Minet, who was meant to have served La Salle's second expedition of 1684/85 in that twin capacity but returned to France with Beaujeu after disagreements with La Salle and was subsequently imprisoned briefly for desertion.[15] The journal recounts the events of the first expedition, in which Minet did not participate. He says that he has his information from Nicolas de la Salle and Gabriel Barbier,[16] and that he has heard what La Salle, Tonti, and Membré have to say about it as well. He also claims to have written the journal during the 1684–85 voyage to the Gulf of Mexico, to pass the time. These claims are quite possible, since Minet states that La Salle brought Nicolas, Barbier, and one L'Esperance back to France with him in 1683, and La Salle himself in a memoir to the Minister of Marine and Colonies, Seignelay, states that one of the proofs of his exploration claims is the witness to them borne by "three of those who followed him on it, whom he has brought to France, and who are in Paris."[17] Since Barbier, Nicolas, and Minet were all present on the voyage from France to the Gulf, and since Barbier remained on the Texas coast[18] while Nicolas and Minet returned to France,[19] Minet obviously had much time to consult repeatedly with Nicolas. Minet claims that he chose to record the stories of Nicolas and Barbier because in their youth and frankness and in the agreement of their accounts he felt they had the ring of authenticity, so that he took them aside and had them tell him their stories. There is a good possibility that Minet did not actually put his notes together into the existing account until after the departure for France of Beaujeu's ship from her intermediate stop in Virginia, since in his memoir on the search for the Mississippi mouth, presumably finished in May of 1685, Minet mentions Nicolas' journal but not his own memoir incorporating it.[20]

The manuscript itself, acquired from private ownership by the Public Archives Canada in 1981,[21] is plainly not a completely finished work but some stage of a draft, since it is full of crossings-out and alterations and includes a few addenda at the end. The primary dependence upon Nicolas de la Salle that Minet claims is certain, since the account is very similar to Nicolas', but the two accounts are by no means identical, and indeed Minet probably received, as he claims, an independent oral account from Nicolas—perhaps one referring to Nicolas' own notes. The totally independent observations of Barbier as an experienced *voyageur,* especially evident in the Chickasaw incident,[22] are probably the source for the occasional insightful observations and descriptions not recorded by Nicolas. There is some additional matter in this version which may have been taken from the Tonti memoir of 1684, especially for the events of 1678–81 preceding the actual trip down the Mississippi and for certain incidents, such as the Quinipissa attack.

Nicolas de la Salle Account, 1685. Translated by Melville B. Anderson in Nicolas de la Salle, *Relation of the Discovery of the Mississippi River;* French text in ibid. and in Margry, *Découvertes et établissements* 1, 547–70; MS existence unknown (see discussion below).

This account as published by Margry purports to have been written down by an anonymous collector of exploration accounts on the basis of some sort of narrative given to him by young Nicolas de la Salle, a member of the expedition though no relation to its leader, in 1685. Margry says that he obtained the account from a collection of travel descriptions,[23] but beyond what Surrey refers to as "papers in the possession of M. Leon Techener,"[24] we know very little else about Margry's source, and its whereabouts are presently unknown. The original source, that is Nicolas' diary mentioned by Minet,[25] also seems to be lost, since it is not the document calendared by Surrey for 1678–1685, an "Account . . . by La Salle, clerk of the Marine, of what he knows of the discoveries in N. Am. made by the Sieur de la Salle, 1678–1685."[26] This document is only seven pages long, and it is a general recital of the material advantages offered by the lands bordering the Mississippi both as seen by Nicolas and as reported by the Indians. Nicolas did sail in 1678 to join La Salle's company, he did sail back from the Texas coast with Beaujeu in 1685, and he was employed as a naval clerk in Toulon in 1698, which is the dateline of the document.[27] There is good reason that Nicolas would wish to bring his knowledge to light at this time, when the foundation of a colony was finally to be commenced, since his subsequent commitment to that colony—he founded a family and died there—attests to the sincerity of his interest in the New World. But by no stretch of the imagination could this brief document be the source of Nicolas' journal account.

In the journal we have the closest thing to a day-by-day description of the journey that we are likely to find. Although cast by its editor in the third person, with frequent reference to what "little La Salle" says, in substance the text makes no egotistical claims to special knowledge or close connection with the leaders of the expedition, and indeed the importance of the events is clearly not always understood by the observer, as would be likely from this young man, accustomed to the ways of the

French military hierarchy[28] but nevertheless new to the scenes of the American wilderness. This very limitation of the point of view of the teller vouches for the sincerity of his narrative, which was ostensibly what attracted Minet to it also, but the reader must not forget the fact that the diary has in fact been recast, since for example the numbering of the days seems to have been done without regard for the fact that Nicolas seems to have written at each halt, not just at the end of the day, and there are far too many days in this version of his diary. This fact, however, argues even more strongly for the nearness of this version to its original source.

It will doubtless be suggested, as the Minet journal receives more attention, that Minet may have been the author of this anonymous retelling of Nicolas' story. Without further study this point cannot be decided definitively, but my collation of the two versions has suggested that not only the circumstances suggested for the creation of the two versions—why would one write down a single account when one had access to the information in both?—but substantial differences in style and diction tend to argue against this possibility.

Account of "Father Membré," first published in 1690. Translated in J. G. Shea, *Discovery and Exploration of the Mississippi Valley*, 165–84; French text in Chrétien Le Clercq, *Premier établissement de la foi dans la Nouvelle France* 2, 209–64; no MS extant.

It is quite certain that Hennepin's claim to the authorship of the original journal on which this account is based is spurious.[29] Habig's comparison of this account to that of the anonymous *Relation* just discussed proves rather conclusively that the former is dependent upon the latter,[30] but if that is the case and in turn Delanglez' identification of the author of the *Relation* as Bernou is correct, then this account must be ascribed to much the same source.[31] Thus in spite of Joutel's observations on the journal-keeping proclivities of Membré and the other Recollects on La Salle's Texas expedition,[32] it seems clear that what was printed ostensibly by Le Clercq as the journal of Membré contained nothing of Membré's save that part of his 1682 letter that

19

had been used in the *Relation,* and since Membré himself had died in the 1689 Karankawa massacre of the remnants of La Salle's colony on Matagorda Bay, that missionary, whose integrity while he lived was never in question, did not live to refute the attribution.

The rewriting that was done to transform the *Relation* into the "Membré" account had mainly to do with recasting the narrative in the first person, with the priest telling the story and putting himself forward constantly as having been closely involved with the most important events of the trip, though we know from Habig's biography that Membré himself was far more modest than he is made to seem here.[33] One example can be cited to demonstrate the contradictions into which the revisor has been led by the use of a source itself based on several sources. At one point the narrator puts himself in the company of Tonti when the latter went to visit the chief of the Taensa Indians and to fetch him back to meet La Salle. Yet the narrator also gives a detailed account, as though he were an eyewitness, of the elaborate preparations for the visit which were made in La Salle's camp *after the departure of Tonti's party.* Nor does the narrator mention anything of that extraordinarily interesting Taensa society described so fully in Tonti's longer accounts, though if he had accompanied Tonti he would have been unlikely as a missionary to neglect such a description, particularly of the "temple" Tonti saw and described in his longer memoirs. In the anonymous *Relation,* since no particular persona is established for the narrator and the events are described in the third person, these flaws are not obvious. It seems, therefore, that this narrative, inserting the figure of the priest, was part of a propaganda effort to assert the prior claims of the Recollects to the mission in the lower Mississippi Valley.[34]

One should not forget, however, that well before the time this account was published, Renaudot had received Tonti's 1684 account of the expedition; Nicolas de la Salle's independent account and even Minet's version could also have been in circulation. Thus the composer of this account potentially had at hand not only the *Relation* but these three other important sources as well.

Tonti memoir, 1691. Translated in B. F. French, *Historical Collections* 1, 52–98; MSS in BN, MSS français, n.a. 7485, fols. 103–108, and AC, série C13C, 3, fols. 128–141v.

This later memoir by Tonti is actually a summary of his whole career in the New World from 1678 to 1690, written apparently to demonstrate his loyalty to La Salle and his goals and to show that Tonti had done everything he could to aid La Salle's final colonizing attempt. Presumably one reason for this was to prove that Tonti deserved to be recognized as La Salle's successor, since the original document was sent to Tonti's friend and protector Renaudot, who had copies made for Villermont and Pontchartrain.[35] It offers an account of the La Salle journey of 1682 in the context of the long recital of Tonti's services. It is safe to assume that the account is authentic, if perhaps padded a little with heroics given its purpose, but since it was written ten years after the expedition, and Tonti had made a second trip to the sea by that time, there is generally more circumstantial detail than is to be found in Tonti's earlier narrative, but we cannot be sure that such detail was actually observed in 1682. The contradiction of his own earlier accounts in attributing a threatened attack to the Natchez rather than the Koroas may not be due to the fact that he did not have a copy of the 1684 memoir, but rather to an equivalence in the two names[36] or to changed conditions observed by Tonti on his 1686 journey down the Mississippi.[37] In general the memoir is vague as to distance and times, again implying that Tonti was referring to memory rather than notes or other documents. The brief *procès verbal* of Tonti's 1686 journey is far too summary an account to have made any contribution[38]

The problems of ascribing authorship to these accounts are many, making it particularly hard to decide to what extent they may be considered independent observations. The attentive reader will have noticed that the Hennepin account, now universally accepted as entirely spurious,[39] has been omitted. On the other side of the coin, the authenticity of the brief *procès verbal* accounts has never been questioned, and we are safe in relying on them as far as they go.

But in the case of the remaining "authentic" narratives, prior scholarship has produced considerable evidence that they are not all independent. Examination of the anonymous *Relation* and the Membré accounts in Membré's early letter and as published by Le Clercq shows, as we have seen, that these three are quite closely related and share not only chronology but even word-for-word identity at many points. That the Membré letter comes first chronologically makes it certain that it is a partial source for the other two. These questions have been treated at some length by the Jesuit scholar Jean Delanglez in his discussion of the authorship of the anonymous *Relation*,[40] and this work has shown not only that they are related but that the anonymous and Le Clercq versions may have been part of the propaganda efforts of Bernou and Renaudot in favor of the granting of all Indian missions in North America to the Recollects.[41] Membré's Franciscan biographer Habig had demonstrated the relationship of the two longer accounts to Membré's early letter on the basis of parallel passages,[42] and Delanglez has shown their additional dependence on Tonti's letter of the same period.[43] Hence of these four related sources, only two, the Tonti and Membré letters, may be considered as independent witnesses, and both are unfortunately brief.

The situation with respect to the two other more lengthy memoirs attributable to Henri de Tonti (a third, which was printed in France and disowned by Tonti himself,[44] is not listed here) is less complex. The discrepancies between the accounts of 1684 and 1691 seem to be of a kind easily attributable to the probabilities that Tonti did not have the 1684 account to hand when he composed that of 1691, and that with the passage of ten years, during which time he had made another trip over the same route, his memory of the original events had altered to fit what he learned at a later date. If this is true, given Tonti's tendency as a keen-eyed trader and Indian diplomatist to record much detail about the Indians met along the way, the two accounts may preserve two "snapshots," four years apart, of the native polities of the lower Mississippi, so that it would be advantageous for the two accounts to be compared carefully.

The Nicolas de la Salle and Minet journals should be considered together, since it is only by comparison with the former that we can determine what portions of the latter came from other sources and hence hope to winnow out the testimony of our fourth actual witness, the elusive and possibly illiterate Barbier.

It may seem odd that once Delanglez and Habig had disposed of the myth of La Salle's authorship of the anonymous *Relation*, we were left with no surviving complete account of the journey certainly by La Salle, nor any clear reference to the existence of one.[45] The answer to this enigma may simply be that La Salle had no need to record such a memoir nor any time to do so. One letter, a fragment without beginning or end, recounts the events of the first part of the journey from late December until the expedition reached the confluence of the Missouri with the Mississippi.[46] This fragment appears to be a sort of journal, with detailed descriptions of topography, flora, and fauna of the Illinois country where La Salle had built his main outpost in the west, and although it is possible that the complete document did continue to describe the whole journey, it is equally possible that La Salle was simply describing his main base of operations. We know that the duties of commander of the expedition kept him intensely occupied throughout the voyage, so it may be that once past the mouth of the Missouri La Salle did not have time to record anything more. During his illness on the return journey, and for some time afterwards, he felt himself too weak to attempt such a composition, although he did write one letter to Father Le Fevre which now seems to be lost.[47] Having rallied his spirits, he was then too busy with the poor state of his business affairs and the enmity of La Barre to have much time for writing lengthy memoirs,[48] and once he had sailed to France to obtain the king's support for a second expedition in late 1683, there was no need for him to do so—his supporters Renaudot and Bernou had already supplied the "official" anonymous *Relation,* Father Membré had been in France since the end of 1682, and La Salle himself with several of his men would then have been on hand to supply any lacunae that the court felt needed filling. La Salle also seems to have been a reluctant writer when deeply involved in his projects; in the French archival records during the period when he was preparing for his second expedition, we find repeated complaints from Bernou to Renaudot that La Salle has not written supplying needed information.[49]

However disappointing the facts may be, then, for the study of La Salle's 1682 expedition we have only five first-hand witnesses whose testimony we can use: the notary Metairie, Father Membré, Henri de Tonti, Nicolas de la Salle, and Gabriel Barbier, and of these only Tonti and Nicolas have actually been responsible for full-length detailed accounts, and only Tonti's accounts are certainly from his hand alone. In describing each of the documents I have alluded to something of the characters of the writers and the purposes for which the documents were prepared, as far as that may be ascertained. But it is also necessary to evaluate the extent to which the reasons for the compositions may have influenced their truthfulness.

Metairie we need doubt not at all for intention, since he was the government's official witness on the journey. Membré had every reason to communicate honestly with his superior in the brief letter he wrote from the Chickasaw Bluffs, and we know that he was given a trustworthy character by all who knew him; our only reservations about his testimony are the other face of its potential great value: his experience as a missionary among the Illinois[50] and his mission itself may have biased him toward close observation of Indian lifeways on the journey, while at the same time they may have urged him to seeing what he wanted to see.

Tonti's accounts were all written more or less overtly for the purpose of gaining favor. The first, the short letter, may have been sent in the first place to Frontenac,[51] who had a financial interest in the projects of the partnership, but in any case it eventually probably reached Renaudot—it is to be remembered that Frontenac travelled on the same ship as Membré—Tonti's protector at court, and through him got to Bernou to serve as the most important source for the official *Relation*. Tonti's first report, brief as it is, casts no particular color on the events of the journey but instead gives the brisk and factual account that one would expect of his experience as explorer and Indian diplomatist. It is the most immediate and least considered of Tonti's narratives.

Tonti's second account, written expressly for Renaudot while Tonti spent the winter in Montreal after having been displaced by La Barre's man at the Illinois post,[52] was written ostensibly both to "occupy you during your hours of leisure" and to "satisfy your curiosity, which is very wide-ranging regarding foreign lands."[53] It is a complete account of his enterprises with La Salle from the time Renaudot's recommendation caused him to throw in his lot with the explorer in 1678 until Tonti received the news that La Salle had carried the day in France and that he, Tonti, had been restored to control of the Illinois post. Thus this letter, written to thank a partisan and to justify his continued confidence and support, does not alter facts substantially but amplifies the narrative considerably with many more details on Indians, especially the government and religion of the sedentary agricultural tribes of the lower Mississippi; comments on the natural resources of the country and their abundance; and a great deal of information on the motivations for decision-making by himself and La Salle and much more detail on their actions. And since the account of the return journey is very abbreviated in both the 1682 letter and the 1691 account after the encounter with the Quinipissa, this is the only extended account of the threatened Koroa/Natchez attack that Tonti wrote.

Tonti's third memoir of 1691[54] was written under less auspicious circumstances. It covers the years 1678 to 1690, ending with Tonti's return from an unsuccessful overland journey west of the Mississippi in quest of La Salle's lost colony. At the close of the narrative he states that it would have been more complete (presumably for this last journey) had he not lost his notes, so it seems that he must have written it shortly after his return. At this time, though Frontenac had been restored to power, Tonti and La Forest did not yet know that they had succeeded to La Salle's rights in the Illinois country. The heavy expense of the fruitless 1689–90 trip was another burden on Tonti's mind, and since he now knew with certainty that La Salle was dead and the attempt at a colony a likely failure, he must also have known that a recital of the history of his loyalty to La Salle would argue that he should rightfully become La Salle's successor. The memoir was thus sent to Renaudot in Paris, where copies were made for Villermont and Pontchartrain, the new Minister of Marine and Colonies. Differences between this account and the one of 1684 do tend to bear out the assumption that in this one Tonti was trying to present himself as the most qualified person to carry on La Salle's plans. There is additional description of Indian lifeways among the Chickasaw and Arkansas—and some of this information doubtless had come through his involvement with the Arkansas trading post he established in 1686—and especially among the Taensa, whose religious practices and redistributive chiefdom system of government are described in much more detail than before, perhaps from information he learned on his 1686 trip down the river. The untoward incidents with the Quinipissa and the Koroa/Natchez, on the other hand, are greatly minimized, and the second is even much softened, with the Natchez chief helping to protect the French.[55] Another incident that has nothing to do with the exploration of the Mississippi shows an even more telling alteration of fact: Tonti and a few men, having left La Salle with most of the party at the Prudhomme Bluffs, met four Iroquois warriors who said they were a part of a band of 100 men; in the 1684 account, the Iroquois were fleeing from a drubbing by the Sioux, and Tonti shared his supplies with them, while in the 1691 version he suspected immediate attack and departed at speed—in the interim, part of Tonti's responsibility to the crown in holding the Illinois post had been to form a barrier against the Iroquois, while at the earlier period it was still felt that they might be won to the French alliance.

We know less of Nicolas de la Salle than of Tonti, since his not particularly exciting career has attracted far less research. Margry says that he was related to the naval commissioner who in 1687 became Commissioner General of the galleys.[56] Certainly the young man was destined for a military career, and he was first attached to La Salle's company of explorers in 1678.[57] He may have had some official role of minor importance in the 1682 trip, for it is to be noted that though Tonti lists him in his 1684 memoir as simply among the company, he did sign both of the *procès verbaux,* in each case next to last, before the notary Metairie.[58] La Salle, as we have seen, took him along with Barbier and another man back to France in 1683 to serve as a witness for the truth of his claims, perhaps in Nicolas' case because he had kept a journal of the trip. When those claims were accepted and La Salle set out for the Gulf in 1685, again Nicolas was present, but this time it seems assigned to naval duty under Beaujeu's command, returning with the ship to France. He must have been continuing his journal at this time, since Minet was able to see it, and it must have created some contemporary interest to have been included in such a collection as Margry alleges and to have been taken over into Minet's composite work. In any case, after the return from the Gulf he pursued a naval career which moved toward administrative assignments—by 1698 he was naval clerk in the port of Toulon, a married man with several sons—but with the reawakening of interest in a Gulf colony it was doubtless a thought of opportunities there that caused him to put the brief outline of his experiences in America into the summary form that is the only manuscript we have definitely written by Nicolas, and he probably sent it along with his request to Pontchartrain for a good post in the new colony. Both his naval experience and his administrative record secured him such a post, as naval commissioner for the colony under Iberville and then Bienville.[59] We need not really be concerned with the rest of his career, though he was involved in opposition to Bienville and died at the first settlement on Mobile Bay in 1710. We cannot discount the possibility that Nicolas hoped his journal would attract attention to himself when he first kept it, but what we can see of the original through the edited version in Margry and through the Minet composite does not lend this possibility much support, although certainly the 1698 summary *was* written to obtain preferment.

Gabriel Barbier remains an even more shadowy figure; he is referred to as a Canadian by Joutel and seems to have been among the experienced *voyageurs* recruited in Canada by Tonti for the 1682 expedition, but he too was taken back to France by La Salle in 1683 to testify to the truth of his claims, and when we see him next with the Texas colony he seems to be a man of some military rank, since Joutel refers to him as *Sieur* and since he was appointed commandant of the small garrison left behind at Matagorda Bay by La Salle.[60] Yet there is no evidence that he wrote anything at all; only dimly can we discern what must have been an oral account to Minet.

Thus finally we must consider Minet himself briefly, since he at least made apparently valid attribution of his sources. As the official engineer/cartographer of La Salle's colonial venture he bore important responsibility, and his later imprisonment, as a result of what he felt were unfair representations by La Salle, must have rankled a great deal, to say the least; so our major concern with him must have to do with just exactly when he composed the extant manuscript journal. We have suggested that this must have taken place on the return voyage with Beaujeu, but this should not argue for any undue bias, since he did not know that he would be condemned until well after his arrival in France, and if that is true then he would simply have been fulfilling the cartographer's function of gathering explorers' memoirs—as did the more famous Delisles—which would serve for the making of maps. Indeed in Minet's case these memoirs did so serve, since he prepared a map of the Mississippi Valley with their aid as well as a detailed portrayal of the delta at the mouth of the Mississippi, which latter map appears at the very end of the 1684/85 manuscript describing the 1682 expedition and could not possibly have had another source of information, since of course La Salle never found the Mississippi Delta from the Gulf.[61] Chabot has remarked upon the bitterness obvious in the second part of the journal manuscript which describes the later expedition, at least part of which must have been prepared during his month-long imprisonment,[62] but this tone is not present in the Nicolas / Barbier compilation. Nor is it surprising that Minet might have had access to Tonti's 1684 memoir, as we have suggested; as an engineer and cartographer he might well have had it given to him to aid his work before departing from France.

Delanglez, in his examination of the sources for the anonymous *Relation*, set a helpful example for all who wish to make comparative source studies by demonstrating the usefulness of itinerary diagrams. In that article he included such diagrams for three of the sources that we wish to consider here: *procès verbaux*, Membré 1682 letter, Tonti 1682 letter.[63] Diagrams taken from these of Delanglez are shown in Figs. 1 and 2, with similar drawings prepared for the two Tonti memoirs, Nicolas' account, and Minet's compilation in Figs. 2 and 3. The comparative simplicity of the first three short accounts is obvious at a glance, as is the difficulty of preparing such diagrams for the more lengthy and complex narratives. But most important, the diagrams show the narratives in such a starkly skeletal form that the relationships among them are abundantly obvious. Hence we see, for example, that it was indeed Tonti who was responsible for the notion of another river whose mouth was near that of the Red River and which led to the sea; Nicolas, indeed, has his "Rivière aux Risques," but he makes no such claim for it. And it is clear that in both Tonti 1684 and Nicolas there is some notion of the hydrographic complexity of the Yazoo Basin.

The most striking feature, however, has been mentioned earlier in passing but becomes much more obvious when exposed thus in graphic form: the extraordinarily minute details of distances recorded by Nicolas and taken over virtually without alteration by Minet. Nicolas records a total of 292 leagues (730 miles, if a league is taken as 2.5 miles) from the junction of the

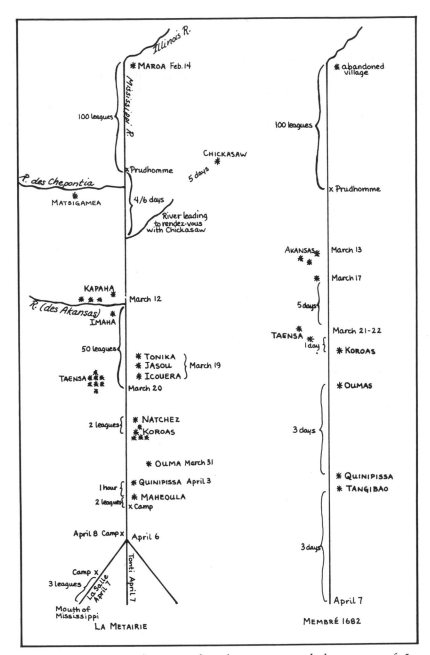

Figure 1. Itinerary diagrams for the *proces verbal* account of La Metairie (left) and the Membre letter of 1682 (right). After Delanglez, "La Salle's Expedition," 36.

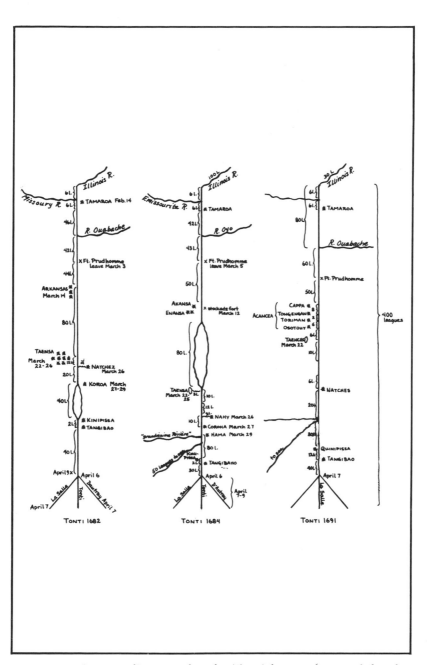

Figure 2. Itinerary diagrams for the Tonti letter of 1682 (left; after Delanglez, "La Salle's Expedition," 37), the Tonti memoir of 1684 (center), and the Tonti memoir of 1691 (right).

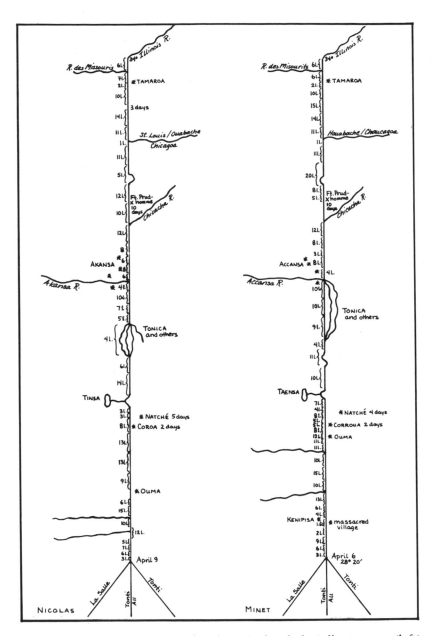

Figure 3. Itinerary diagrams for the Nicolas de la Salle account (left) and the Minet journal (right).

Illinois with the Mississippi to the delta at the river's mouth; in two instances he fails to record a distance, but at most this would probably add only sixty miles or twenty-four leagues for a total of 352 leagues or 880 miles. This agrees amazingly well with the total from Tonti 1684, 370 leagues or 927 miles, especially when we consider how Tonti tended to deal in sweeping chunks of thirty, fifty, even eighty leagues at a time. It also means that the two figures, seemingly arrived at in such different ways, validate each other. But it is still obvious, as we have said, that Nicolas' account and hence also Minet's have too many days indicated, since a departure on February 6 (as per *procès verbal*, Tonti 1682, and Tonti 1684) and arrival at the three Mississippi mouths on April 6 (*procès verbal*, Tonti 1682, Tonti 1684, and Minet) comes to fifty-nine days, but Nicolas records sixty-five, even though in the chart we have combined his records of more than one short distance in a day. This fact suggests strongly both that Nicolas did in fact record distances between halts and also that his editor must have misunderstood this in several instances.

Another kind of assistance is offered by the diagrams in making comparisons between accounts attributable to the same source. Thus in the case of Nicolas and Minet, discrepancies of distance can point to one of two possibilities: Minet's use of another source, perhaps Barbier; or Minet's recording a distance closer to Nicolas' original observation than the version that we have from the hands of an anonymous editor. Where such discrepancies coincide with noticeable textual differences that are caused by addition or substitution of different content, we can be certain that we are dealing with information taken from another source than that represented by Nicolas' journal.

Tonti's estimations of distance are more generalized, but in comparing his three accounts we can observe several things. First, he is consistent in using this kind of estimation. In addition, although there are enough discrepancies to suggest that the three accounts are not so closely related to one another as to indicate such direct borrowing as seems to be the case with Nicolas and Minet, a closer relationship between Tonti 1682 and Tonti 1684 is indicated (especially by the 80 leagues between the

Arkansas and Taensa and the about 50 leagues between the Missouri and Ohio river mouths), whereas a refinement of knowledge due to Tonti's constant further involvement in the Mississippi Valley and his additional travels there is indicated by the changes in those distances seen in Tonti 1691. This, too, confirms suggestions that we have made.

When we wish to examine the discrepancies that exist between same-source groups of narratives, however, it is necessary to resort to a different kind of internal evidence. The issue of physical point of view is a complex one, for it is a factor that was not purposely recorded, and yet it may go some distance in helping us explain these variations among the itinerary diagrams. The expedition proceeded down the Mississippi River in several canoes—we do not have a certain number, but it probably varied from twelve to fifteen[64]—and its personnel consisted of twenty-three Frenchmen and eighteen Indian hunter/guides plus ten of their wives and even three children. No source gives us passenger lists for the various canoes, and although there is some indication that the Indian hunter/guides mostly traveled together,[65] it is reasonable to assume that the passenger groups changed slightly from time to time, perhaps as often as daily in some instances. The canoes proceeded sometimes in file and sometimes in a more bunched group, as the vicissitudes of river conditions or considerations of safety dictated. In addition, frequent side-trips were made by one or more canoes in order to investigate something more closely or to seek game to feed the explorers. Given these varying conditions, it is obvious that even leaving the issue of personal bias aside, observers in different canoes would be likely to view an event or a feature of the passing scene differently, because what they saw *was* in fact different.

Side-trips on land are especially important, since few were made by the entire exploration party and frequently only a few men were sent inland to hunt or to visit Indian groups. If the observer were not with such a party, he could not report what they saw from first-hand knowledge and would have to have obtained his information from someone who could. But it is only by careful comparative reading of the texts that we can hope to reconstruct any of this detail.

In the accompanying table an attempt has been made to list the major events and visitations along the route and to indicate, for each one and where possible, who could have been the prime observers; the names of those who subsequently wrote or contributed to memoirs are underlined. The usefulness of a table such as this is that it establishes as far as may be known who were in fact the eyewitnesses at many important points. Several examples may be cited to show what kind of value this has. In the Minet journal one finds the only description of the capture of the two Chickasaws by Barbier, and since this is the only source which claims to use Barbier's information, we may be confident that the ruse by which the capture was made is faithfully described. Here we can also find the explanation for the placement of descriptions of Taensa society: in the Tonti memoirs of 1684 and 1691, the detailed descriptions are presented for the downstream journey, while in Nicolas and Minet they occur for the upstream journey. The explanation is now clear—Tonti had no one else who contributed to a memoir with him on the downstream trip, but on the return trip Nicolas was with his party. A third example is the occurrence in Nicolas' and Minet's accounts of a rather more complex picture of the exploration of the three outlets of the Mississippi than we see in any other primary account. We can understand this from the observation in Minet that after the first day's explorations, Nicolas, Barbier, and Membré remained at the forks, so that they were in a position to receive the reports of all parties and to observe the composition and destination of the several groups,[66] and we in turn may have confidence in this description of the exploration of the birdfoot delta. There are a number of finer points that could be pursued further through the use of this information, but what we have seen should suffice to show the usefulness of such an approach in establishing the evidential value of a set of descriptions of the same events.

Though we began this essay by reviewing the scholarship that eliminated some of the sources favored in the past, I think we

Events and Prime Observers

Major events/ visitations	Member(s) of French party present	Sources
Tamaroa village (deserted)	All	
Fort Prudhomme	La Salle and half of party (24) go east.	T1, T2 (PV)
	Gabriel Barbier* *dit* Minime + 2 Loups bring in Chickasaws.	T1, T2, PV, N, N/B
Chicacha R.	Tonti* and party sent ahead to explore.	N, M
Arkansas villages Cappa Tongengan Toriman Osotouy	All All	
River branch to Tunica Taensa village	Tonti*, Prudhomme, ?Clance, 2 Arkansas.	T1, T2, T3, PV, N, N/B
Natché	Tonti* chases in canoe (Nicolas* in canoe), La Salle and (8) men sleep at village.	T1, T2, T3 (N, N/B)
Coroa	All	
Quinipissa	Membré* boat first sees.	T2
	D'Autray, Haisnault, Migneret, Brossard scout.	T2
	Mixed French and Indian party scouts.	PV, N
Tangipahoa	Empty canoe w/barbecued human ribs found by scouting party.	N/B
Mouths of Mississippi	Nicolas, Barbier, Membre stay at confluence.	N/B
Right (west)	La Salle and party (10).	T1, T2, PV, (N, N/B)
Center	Tonti*	T1, T2, T3, PV, N, N/B
	La Salle and all.	T3, N, N/B
Left (east)	D'Autray.	T1, T2
	Tonti*.	N, N/B
Tangipahoa	All	
Quinipissa	Hostages: Andre Haisnault + 1 Loup.	T1, T2, N, N/B
	Scouts: Haisnault, D'Autray, Brossart, 4 Loups.	T2
	Destroy canoes: La Salle and party.	T1, T2
Coroa	All	
Natché		
Taensa	Tonti* with party (including Nicolas) return a Taensa.	T2, (N)
Arkansas	La Salle with 3 canoes in advance party.	T2
	Tonti* with rest of party behind.	T2, N, N/B
Fort Prudhomme	La Salle ill, remains with most of company (including Nicolas*, Membré*).	T1-3, (N), N/B, (M)
	Tonti* sent on with Brossard, Cauchois, Massé, 1 Loup.	T2

Tonti letter = T1; Tonti 1684 = T2; Tonti 1691 = T3; Membre letter = M; proces verbaux = PV; Nicolas = N; Minet = N/B

Names of individuals who later wrote, or contributed to, reports of the journey.

have been amply recompensed by the addition of the newly-discovered Minet source, which not only reinforces the authenticity of Nicolas de la Salle's account, but which also introduces a new witness, Gabriel Barbier, whose testimony we have not had before. Or rather, that we have not known we had before. In Minet there is a passage that is not in Nicolas, which describes how, after having left the massacred Tangipahoa village and before arriving at the river's delta branching, the observer's party met with three Indians in a canoe, who fled through the reeds and canes and abandoned their canoe:

> We went to the canoe and found there some smoked cayman and a side of human ribs that we took, leaving a piece of cloth [?] for payment. Since hunger was pressing us, having had only a little corn each day, we fell upon this meat. When we had eaten it we realized it was human by the bones and from the taste, that was better than the cayman.[67]

Now let us compare a passage from the Le Clercq–"Membré" narrative, a passage which does not appear in the anonymous *Relation:*

> We were out of provisions, and found only some dried meat at the mouth [of the Mississippi], which we took to appease our hunger; but soon after perceiving it to be human flesh, we left the rest to our Indians. It was very good and delicate.[68]

Even did we not now know that this narrative by "Membré" is a composite work, the final remark above would have seemed rather odd coming from the missionary, though the handing over to the Indians does fit. With the new source, however, we know not only that this did happen and something more about it, but that with the aid of the kind of analysis we have been doing it may even be possible to rehabilitate portions of the discredited Bernou-Renaudot compilations.

Notes

[1] Pierre Margry's publication of many of the sources and Parkman's use of them in *La Salle and the Discovery of the Great West* led to much critical examination of the sources, particularly by John Gilmary Shea (see his *Discovery and Exploration of the Mississippi Valley*), Marion A. Habig (*Franciscan Père Marquette*), and in many articles

and monographs by Jean Delanglez, whose works will be referred to repeatedly in this essay.

[2]We have attempted to list here only a printed translation, printed French text, and original manuscript provenience for each source. For a much more detailed bibliographic essay, see Habig, *Franciscan Père Marquette*, 258–78. Habig does not, of course, mention the Minet manuscript found in 1981.

[3]La Salle to Frontenac, October 1682, Bibliothèque Nationale (BN), MSS Clairambault 1016, fol. 148. According to a later memoir of La Salle addressed to Seignelay, Frontenac had delivered them to Colbert; see Margry, *Découvertes et établissements* 3, 19.

[4]Habig, ibid., 207n; Delanglez, "La Salle's Expedition of 1682," 18. Delanglez, as we shall see, feels that the letter was not in the possession of Bernou by accident.

[5]BN, MSS Clairambault 1016, fol. 169—thus also among the papers of Bernou.

[6]Delanglez, ibid.

[7]Ibid.

[8]Ibid.

[9]Thomassy, Gravier, Harisse, and Villiers du Terrage thought La Salle was the author; see Delanglez, ibid., 8–9 and 12, n. 44.

[10]Delanglez, ibid., 8.

[11]Habig, ibid., 234–38.

[12]La Salle to Frontenac, October 1682, BN, MSS Clairambault 1016, fol. 148.

[13]Delanglez, ibid.

[14]Edmund R. Murphy, *Henry de Tonty: Fur Trader of the Mississippi*, 29.

[15]Habig, ibid., 151.

[16]The identity of Nicolas will be discussed presently. Gabriel Barbier (sometimes *dit* Minime) was one of Tonti's Canadian *voyageurs* who met and brought back two Chickasaws from a hunting expedition on the Chickasaw Bluffs near Memphis.

[17]Minet journal, 55; Margry 3, 17–28. *l'ouest et dans le sud de l'Amérique Septentrionale*, 3, 17–28.

[18]Eventually remaining as commander of the small force left behind by La Salle as he set off on his final fatal attempt to find the Mississippi, Barbier was doubtless killed with Membré in the Karankawa massacre.

[19]Margry 2, 601.

[20]Ibid.

[21]See Victorin Chabot, "Journal inédite relatant les expéditions de Cavelier de la Salle." I am indebted to M. Chabot and the Public Archives Canada for making a microfilm copy of the Minet journal available for this study.

[22]See John Stubbs, "Chickasaw Contact with the La Salle Expedition in 1682," this volume.

[23]Margry 1, 547n.

[24]Although Surrey, *Calendar of Manuscripts in Paris Archives and Libraries* 1, 6 wrongly calendars Nicolas' account as printed by Margry as a version of the anonymous *Relation*, she does give the information about the Techener papers as Margry's source for Nicolas' journal; one can no longer determine where she obtained this information.

[25]See Margry 2, 601.

[26]Surrey, ibid., 1, 4.

[27]From ASH 67, no. 15.

[28]Margry 1, 547n.

[29]See Delanglez, ibid., 26–7.

[30]Habig, ibid.

[31]Delanglez, ibid., 18.

[32]Cited in Habig, ibid., 174.

[33]Habig, ibid.

[34]See Shea, *Discovery and Exploration*, 78–82

[35] Tonti to Villermont, September 2, 1693, BN, MSS français 22803, fols. 285–285 bis.
[36] See Jeffrey Brain, "La Salle at the Natchez," this volume.
[37] Jean Delanglez, "The Voyages of Tonti in North America, 1678–1704."
[38] Margry 3, 554–58
[39] See Shea, ibid., 104–105.
[40] Delanglez, "La Salle's Expedition."
[41] Idem, *The Journal of Jean Cavelier: The Account of a Survivor of La Salle's Texas Expedition*, 17.
[42] Habig, ibid.
[43] Delanglez, "La Salle's Expedition."
[44] This is the *Dernières découvertes dans l'Amérique septentrionale de Monsieur de la Salle par Chevalier de Tonti*, published in 1697. See Habig, ibid., 278.
[45] Delanglez, ibid., 3.
[46] La Salle to———, ca. 1682, in Margry 2, 164–80.
[47] La Salle to Frontenac, October 1682, in Margry 2, 288–301.
[48] Of the documents written by La Salle during this period, all are arguing the reasons why more expeditions are needed (see references in Habig, ibid., 272–5). La Salle does mention several events of the expedition in support of his argument (see La Salle to Frontenac, October 1682).
[49] See Surrey, *Calendar* 1, 8–18.
[50] Habig, ibid.
[51] Habig, ibid., 215n.
[52] Delanglez, "Voyages of Tonti," 273.
[53] Margry 1, 574.
[54] For this date and the evidence for it see Delanglez, ibid., 259–60
[56] Margry 1, 547n says the son of this man; Nicolas de la Salle to Pontchartrain, July 22, 1700 (AC, C13B, 1, no. 4) suggests that he was his brother.
[57] Minet journal, 4.
[58] Margry 1, 594 and Margry 2, 185 and 193.
[59] Jay Higginbotham, *Old Mobile*, 35 and 35n.
[60] Henri Joutel, *Joutel's Journal of La Salle's Last Voyage, 1684–7*, 116; Margry 3, 258.
[61] The manuscript map is in Minet journal, 59 (reproduced in Chabot, ibid., 9). The cuts reproduced in Thomassy, *De La Salle et ses relations inédites* (Fig. 2) are taken from Minet's large Carte de la Lovisiane (Bibliothèque du Service Hydrographique C 4044-4), where one appears on a flap covering the other. This map was drawn on the return journey to France; see Sara Jones Tucker, *Indian Villages of the Illinois Country: Atlas*, Plate VII and notes to that plate. It is interesting to note that the Franquelin fragment shown by Thomassy as Fig. 1 and taken from a tracing of Franquelin's "lost" 1684 map, almost exactly reproduces the sketch from Minet's journal. For Minet to have copied it, he would have to have seen it before leaving France.
[62] Chabot, ibid., 9.
[63] Delanglez, "La Salle's Expedition," 36–7
[64] This is a very rough estimate assuming that at least at the beginning most of the canoes in use were bark canoes and that they were not heavily loaded, carrying an average of four to five people. This estimate may be quite wrong, of course, since La Salle's party may have had one or more of the so-called "canots maîtres," which could carry some fourteen people (see Surrey, *The Commerce of Louisiana during the French Regime*, 56; cf. Margry 1, 608–609), and we know that on the lower river they were able to acquire Indian-made pirogues, which also had greater capacity than this.
[65] This is suggested by the fact that the Indians brought along for the journey, having come overland, made bark canoes for themselves as the exploration party waited for the spring thaw: see Margry 1, 549.
[66] Minet journal, 40.

[67] Ibid., 37–8. The word translated as "piece of cloth" is *haleine* in the text, but Minet's terrible phonetic spelling is evident throughout the journal, so the word has been taken as *haillon*.

[68] Shea, ibid., 175.

The Chickasaw Contact
with the La Salle Expedition in 1682

JOHN D. STUBBS, JR.

•

LA SALLE'S EXPEDITION down the Mississippi in 1682 was indeed a significant historical event. To claim the lower Mississippi was strategically important for the French, for not only would the French be able to tap the natural resources of the area, thereby competing with the English, but they would also be able to utilize the natural water route between their northern and projected southern settlements. Further, a powerful French presence in the lower valley would deter the English from continuing their westward expansion.

The accounts of the expedition provide us with a brief glimpse of life along the river, a life that had significantly changed from the time of the first European penetration into the area by Soto 142 years earlier. The so-called "Mississippian decline," the decline of the great mound-building cultures, had left a diverse group of native peoples in the area. This diversity can easily be illustrated by noting the different sociopolitical organization of various tribal groups in the region. The Natchez, Koroa, and Taensa, for example, retained some Mississippian characteristics with their centrally organized chiefdoms,[1] while the Chickasaw and Choctaw were organized as egalitarian societies with autonomous village groups.[2] The observations made by the members of La Salle's expedition are particularly important in view of the profound changes that would soon take place as European contact with these tribal groups became more regular and indeed continuous.

Because of their significance, the observations made by the expedition members should not be passed over too quickly no matter how incidental they may seem. The bits of information in the accounts pertaining to the Chickasaw are few, but they hint at the location of Chickasaw settlements and give some

41

indication of Chickasaw movement and political relations. The objective here is to examine the circumstances surrounding the Chickasaw contact with the expedition and to discuss their implications. Later events will be used to supplement this discussion.

To place the Chickasaw contact in proper perspective it is necessary to outline the course of the expedition in broad terms. La Salle descended the Mississippi from its confluence with the Illinois in early February, 1682. In late February he stopped for ten days and erected Fort Prudhomme on the Chickasaw Bluffs near present-day Memphis, Tennessee. From there he continued to descend the river, stopping for food and supplies and to meet with Indians he encountered along the way. He reached the mouth of the river in early April, 1682, and formally took possession for France on April 9, 1682. Shortly thereafter he returned by the same route he had come, stopping once more at Fort Prudhomme to recuperate from a severe illness that caused him to remain there for almost two months.

The portion of the descending voyage from Fort Prudhomme to the Natchez villages on the lower part of the river is of particular importance here, for it was during this part of the journey that the expedition came in contact with the Chickasaw. The various accounts generally agree on the course of events, but there are some differences, and these are noted in the discussion below.

It is necessary to note here that eight accounts were used as the basis for this discussion; they are referred to below as the Membré letter, the anonymous account, the Membré narrative, the account of Nicolas de la Salle, the Minet journal, the Tonti memoir of 1684, the Tonti memoir of 1691, and the *procès verbal* account.[3]

Sometime in late February, February 24 according to the Membré narrative and February 16 according to the *procès verbal* account, a member of the expedition, gunsmith Pierre Prudhomme, became lost while hunting. The expedition party immediately began to search for him the following day. It became evident during the early stages of the search that Indians were present in the area. All accounts except for the Membré letter and the Tonti memoir of 1691 note that many Indian paths were seen. The Tonti memoir of 1684 and the *procès verbal* account both claim that Indians themselves were seen in the woods, and both Nicolas de la Salle and Tonti 1684 record that members of the search party discovered a recently vacated wooden lodge. These concrete signs of Indians in the area induced La Salle to construct a fort, naming it Fort Prudhomme after the missing gunsmith.

All accounts agree that two Chickasaw Indians were brought in during the search. Minet, who states that Barbier, the Frenchman who brought them in, was one of his informants, reports the circumstances of the encounter:

> While searching for him [Prudhomme], Sieur Barbier found two savages who made as if to flee; Barbier threw his gun to the ground, making them sign of peace; they approached, he pulled out a pistol from behind his back and took them by force to M. de La Salle, who took them with him.[4]

The *procès verbal* and anonymous accounts and the Membré narrative further state that five Chickasaws were encountered and only two of the five were taken back to the fort. La Salle and his party soon learned that their village was only a short distance off. The Tonti memoir of 1684 and the *procès verbal* both record the village as being two days' travel away, while the Membré narrative and anonymous account set the distance at one and a half days' distance. Membré makes an additional note that the Indians generally count ten to twelve leagues per day.

Four accounts record that La Salle and half the party set out with the two Chickasaws toward their villages in hopes of learning some news of Prudhomme. The Nicolas de la Salle account, the Tonti memoir of 1691, and the Membré letter all fail to mention that anyone accompanied the Chickasaws, while Minet states only that one Chickasaw was sent with presents to ask for Prudhomme's release. The confusion is understandable, however, since we learn from the four other accounts that after travelling the distance stated, La Salle found that the village was still another three days off (four days according to the *procès verbal* account). At this point one of the Chickasaws continued on to the village laden with presents and assertions of good faith from La Salle. The other Chickasaw accompanied the party back to the fort. The plan was for La Salle to meet the Chickasaw elders further down the river on the bank (four days downstream according to the *procès verbal* account). Prudhomme was found shortly after the party returned to the fort, and the expedition continued. The anonymous account states that the other Chickasaw was sent back to his village with presents at this point, but four other accounts clearly state that the Chickasaw accompanied them down the river; thus we can disregard this statement.

From all accounts it is clear that they never met any additional Chickasaws on the banks of the river. The accounts of Nicolas de la Salle, Minet, and the Membré letter made no mention of the missed meeting, but the *procès verbal* account says that they missed the channel that would take them to the meeting place because of fog. The Tonti memoir of 1684 also mentions the supposed rendezvous location, and contends that they took a wrong turn and ended up on the wrong side of an island that he estimated to be eighty leagues in length. It is interesting to note that the *procès verbal* account records the missed meeting place before mentioning the Arkansas encounter, implying that the meeting was to have been to the north of the Arkansas. The Tonti memoir of 1684 clearly records the meeting point as being below the Arkansas.

There are only four additional references to the Chickasaw. Nicolas de la Salle, Minet, and Tonti all remark that the Arkansas did not mistreat the Chickasaws accompanying the party, significant because they all mention that the Chickasaw and Arkansas were continually at war. The only further mention of the Chickasaw is from the Membré narrative, which notes that the Chickasaw (plural in his reference) chose to depart from the expedition at the Natchez or Koroa villages—it is ambiguous as to just where he (or they) left.

We can now turn to the locational hints about the Chickasaw.

The distance from the Chickasaw Bluffs area to the Chickasaw villages was unfortunately measured in travelling days. The estimates made by the Chickasaw Indians themselves vary in the accounts from four and a half days, this according to both the Membré narrative and the anonymous account, to five days according to the Tonti memoir of 1684 and six days according to the *procès verbal*. Fortunately the Membré narrative has provided us with an estimate of how many leagues are generally travelled in a day, and his estimate of ten to twelve will have to suffice for our purposes.

At the very best we can only guess at the location of the Chickasaw villages. The smallest distance estimate (four and a half days at ten leagues per day) would place the Chickasaw settlements just to the south of present-day Tupelo, Mississippi, a location where Chickasaw settlements are known to have existed for later periods, and could possibly have existed for the time period in question.[5] Using the rate of ten leagues per day the other estimates would indicate that the Chickasaw were located further away, probably to the south in present-day Clay County, Mississippi. There seems to be some plausibility to this latter location, for the evidence from two letters by Tonti written while on tour among the Choctaw and Chickasaw in the late winter of 1702 would indicate a more southern location.[6] Recent site survey in Clay County has also verified the presence of Chickasaw settlements in the area.[7]

If we estimate conservatively at 12 leagues per day, the meeting point would almost certainly be to the south of the Arkansas villages. Further, since the Chickasaw were continually at war with the Arkansas, we would expect them to choose a more southern meeting point. This would suggest, when combined with the evidence presented in the Tonti memoir of 1684, that the meeting place was to have been somewhere between the Arkansas and Taensa villages, the next major stop for the expedition.

Given the large distance the Chickasaw had to cover and the limited time which they had to cover it, it seems likely that they would have taken a water route rather than travel over land. The most likely candidate for a water route to the south is the Yazoo River. This route would probably have been preferable to following the Big Black River, which enters the Mississippi further south than the Yazoo. The Big Black also cuts through what was then Choctaw territory, making it less safe for the Chickasaw, who were traditional enemies of the Choctaw. One drawback to this hypothesis, however, is that the Yazoo enters the Mississippi slightly further south than is reasonable to expect for a four-day trip downriver from Fort Prudhomme, even at twenty leagues per day. But further supporting evidence for the use of the Yazoo comes from its proximity to the Chickasaw settlements in either location mentioned above. Also, later historic evidence indicates that the Yazoo provided good accessibility to the Chickasaw and could be used effectively as an approach to them, thus indicating its importance.[8]

Indications of the intertribal political relations of the Chickasaw come from the Arkansas and the Natchez encounters. Tonti 1684, Minet, and Nicolas de la Salle indicate that the Chickasaw and the Arkansas were constantly at war. This would be true in later times as well. The De Batz map of 1737, copied from a map drawn by Mingo Ouma, a Chickasaw war chief, indicates that the Arkansas were still considered enemies at that time.[9] The fact that the Chickasaw chose to leave the expedition while at the Natchez villages is particularly telling. This action would suggest friendly relations between the Natchez and the Chickasaw at the time. The possibility that there was some sort of alliance between the Natchez and the Chickasaw is further strengthened by the fact that the Natchez later sought refuge among the Chickasaw in 1731 when they were driven from their land by the French.

The Chickasaw contact with the expedition also gives us a sense of the freedom of movement enjoyed by the Chickasaw. We know from these accounts that they were ranging some 120 to 150 miles from their villages in northeast Mississippi. Their meeting with the expedition clearly illustrates that they had frequent access to the Mississippi River. And further, they seem to have thought nothing of travelling as far south as the Natchez

villages, over 200 miles to the southwest. This freedom of movement certainly did not change in later times, for the Chickasaw
later became a major threat to French shipping on the Mississippi, a threat noted as early as 1721.[10]

One can only guess at the activities of the Chickasaw in the
lower Mississippi Valley, but it would seem unlikely that they
would range that far south for the purposes of hunting, especially with the vast resources to the west of their settlements.
One possible explanation for the Chickasaws' appearing that far
south is for slave raids. The accounts of the Soto expedition
describe a slave raid by the Chickasaw on the Chakchiuma,
suggesting that such raids were not out of the ordinary.[11] There
are numerous accounts of the Chickasaws' raiding other tribes
in later years. The presence of a Choctaw slave in New England
before 1700 suggests that the Chickasaw-English slave trade,
later a big business, was well under way by that time.[12] In 1702
Tonti noted two Chickasaw-Chakchiuma raiding parties while
making his way northward from the Choctaw to the Chickasaw
settlements. He further notes the presence of an Illinois among
the Chickasaw, most likely a slave.[13] Later accounts by Bienville
in 1708 note Chickasaw raids on the Choctaw and Tohome.[14]
But it was the tribes of the lower Mississippi Valley that were
especially hard hit.[15]

The probable scenario for such activities would be to enter the
lower valley by way of the Yazoo River, to conduct the raid,
and then to return northward via the Natchez Trace. If such a
scenario is plausible, having the Natchez as allies would be extremely important, since they could provide sanctuary for the
Chickasaw and were on the main path leading to the Chickasaw
villages.

Although we gain very little cultural information about the
Chickasaw from the various accounts of the La Salle expedition
in 1682, we can extract a broad sense of place for the Chickasaw
in Mississippi. Not only do we have some indication of where
their villages were, but we also come away with a sense of their
relationship to the tribes of the lower Mississippi Valley. Perhaps the most striking implication from these few facts is the

freedom of movement the Chickasaw seem to have enjoyed. Brief as it is, this early glimpse of the Chickasaw has generated hypotheses which can be strengthened or amended by further archaeological research and a fuller exploitation of documents of the period.

Notes

[1] Jeffrey P. Brain, "The Natchez 'Paradox,'" 215-11; idem, "Late Prehistoric Settlement Patterning in the Yazoo Basin and the Natchez Bluff Regions of the Lower Mississippi Valley."

[2] John R. Swanton, "Social and Religious Beliefs and Usages of the Chickasaw Indians," 190-216; also see Patricia Galloway, "Henri de Tonti du Village des Chacta, 1702," this volume.

[3] For full references see Galloway, "Sources for the La Salle Expedition of 1682," this volume.

[4] Minet journal, 15.

[5] Jesse Jennings, "Chickasaw and Earlier Indian Cultures of Northeast Mississippi," 155-226; John D. Stubbs, Jr., *Archaeological Survey of Lee County, Mississippi*, (Jackson: Mississippi Department of Archives and History, forthcoming).

[6] Galloway, "Henri de Tonti," this volume.

[7] Samuel O. Brookes and John Connaway, "Archaeological Survey of Clay County, Mississippi."

[8] Patricia Galloway, "La Salle in Mississippi, 1682: An Investigation of the Itinerary," 6, report on file, Mississippi Department of Archives and History.

[9] Bienville and Salmon to Maurepas, December 22, 1737, Archives des Colonies, série C13A, 22, fols. 61-64; in Dunbar Rowland and A. G. Sanders (ed. and trans.), *Mississippi Provincial Archives: French Dominion* 1, 357-60.

[10] De Batz, September 7, 1737, AC, C13A, 22, fol. 67; in Rowland and Sanders, *MPA:FD* 1, 355-6.

[11] Norman W. Caldwell, "The Chickasaw Threat to French Control of the Mississippi in the 1740s," 467.

[12] John R. Swanton, *Final Report of the United States De Soto Expedition Commission*.

[13] A. W. Lauber, *Indian Slavery in Colonial Times Within the Present Limits of the United States*, 54.

[14] Galloway, "Henri de Tonti," this volume.

[15] Bienville to Pontchartrain, February 25, 1708, AC, C13A, 2, fols. 89-117; Rowland and Sanders, *MPA:FD* 3, 113.

[16] Arrell Gibson, *The Chickasaws*, 40.

La Salle at the Natchez:
An Archaeological and
Historical Perspective

JEFFREY P. BRAIN

•

IN MARCH, 1682, during his epic voyage of discovery down the Mississippi River, La Salle visited the Natchez Indians near the modern city bearing their name. The Natchez were one of the most powerful and interesting of the lower Mississippi Valley tribes, and for this reason scholars value every scrap of information about them contained in the records of the early explorers. Unfortunately, the geography of that first known contact by literate Europeans[1] is clouded by apparent confusion in the historical documents. The first to call attention to the problem was John R. Swanton, who, more than seventy years ago, declared that it was "almost impossible to reconcile" the details in the various accounts of the expedition;[2] the problem was compounded when these accounts were compared with the early eighteenth-century documents pertaining to the Natchez. Swanton was confused because the explorers themselves were somewhat confused by the people they met and because his archaeological (and therefore geographical) perceptions were naive. It is the purpose of this paper to suggest a reconciliation of the documentation and add the perspective of recent archaeological research.

The historical documentation of the La Salle expedition consists of seven primary accounts; supporting textual and cartographic evidence also are available. The primary accounts were recorded by members of the expedition: these include a *procès verbal* notarized by La Metairie on April 9, 1682;[3] a letter written by Father Zénobe Membré on June 3, 1682; a letter by Henri de Tonti written on July 23, 1682;[4] an account by Nicolas de la Salle which was given to an unknown author who wrote it down in 1685;[5] and a similar manuscript recorded by Minet in 1685[6] from the descriptions of Nicolas de la Salle and a Sieur Barbier.[7] Tonti also wrote a relation dated November 14, 1684,[8] and a memoir in 1691[9] which is very important for the additional information it contributes from the perspective of later explorations by the author.

An official account of the expedition was drawn up in Paris primarily from the Membré and Tonti letters in 1683, and a related document exists under the presumed authorship of Father Chrétien Le Clerq. These two reports must be discounted for the purpose of this paper since they are secondary sources and in any case do not contain reliable new information about the events under consideration. Also to be ignored in this study are two of the primary accounts, unfortunately the two earliest: the *procès verbal* and the Membré letter. Since they were the first records of the expedition, it could be expected that these might be the most accurate, but they are so condensed that some events are glossed over, and these include the first meeting with the Natchez—or perhaps it should be called the first meeting with the Koroa, for that is the identification given in both La Metairie and Membré, but more of this later.

We are left, then, with the following accounts which offer some detail about that first meeting with the Natchez: the Tonti letter of 1682 (supplemented by the later writings), the account attributed to Nicolas de la Salle, and the record of Minet. The Tonti and younger la Salle documents have long been acknowledged as reliable, if occasionally contradictory, sources of information. The Minet account is a recent acquisition by Public Archives Canada. It is an exciting and important discovery since it appears to be a hitherto unknown record by members of the expedition. This version of the expedition is very similar to the Nicolas de la Salle account, but there are differences in details, some of which are quite germane to the present discussion. It is necessary, therefore, to consider further the relationship of these two documents.

Minet attributes his own compilation to the stories of Nicolas de la Salle and Barbier, yet in another instance he admits to the existence of a journal by Nicolas.[10] Curiously, both the Minet and the published Nicolas de la Salle accounts are written in the third person. It is possible, under the circumstances, that Minet was the unknown author[11] of the published account as well as the new testament. It is not reasonable, however, to suggest that he simply plagiarized from one to the other. While a comparison of the two documents reveals many similarities which demonstrate an affinity of information, the differences in detail are sufficient to ascribe a new input for the Minet document. Presumably the source was Barbier, although we cannot be certain until the manuscript is subjected to more thorough historiographic analysis. With this caveat, the new information will be presented as prima facie evidence.

To return to Swanton's problem, and the subject of this paper, the following documents are determined to be the most relevant and in the pages below will be referred to by the parenthetical designations: the Tonti letter of 1682 (Tonti I), supported by his later 1684 relation (Tonti II) and 1691 memoir (Tonti III); and the accounts written in 1685, one attributed to Nicolas de la Salle (Nicolas), the other derived from Nicolas de la Salle and Barbier (Minet).

All of these documents agree that La Salle's party left the Taensa in late March and, after they had descended eleven (Nicolas and Minet) or twelve (Tonti I-III) leagues, a canoe was sighted crossing the river. Some of the French who were in the advance party (Tonti claims the honor) gave chase and followed the canoe to the left bank, where they were confronted by a large number of armed warriors. Discretion being the better part of valor, they did not land, but quickly withdrew to the right bank where La Salle had landed with the main party. After a council, Tonti recrossed the river bearing a calumet, which was honored by the Indians. Assured of peace, La Salle crossed over and then was invited to visit the village of these Indians. The invitation was not to a local encampment on the river, where the natives had been fishing when encountered, but to a more important village which, according to all five accounts, was three leagues inland from the river.

It is in the description of the next sequence of events that the major discrepancies among the accounts are found. Tonti (I-III) consistently records that La Salle stayed only one night at the village, which is identified as "Nahy" or Natchez, and that he returned with a chief the next day. In the earlier relations (I, II), Tonti identifies this Indian as the chief of the Koroa who had been sent for by the Natchez and came to the village during the night, while in his later memoir (III) this same person is said to be the chief of the village they had been visiting and brother of the Great Sun Chief of the Natchez. Accompanied by the chief (whoever he was) and his retinue, the expedition then embarked in their canoes and paddled downriver: ten leagues to the Koroa village in the earlier accounts, six leagues to the principal (i.e., Great Chief's) village of the Natchez in Tonti III, which describes this village as being on a hillside near the river.

The discrepancies in the events are even greater when the Nicolas and Minet accounts are considered, although they compare favorably with each other. Both agree that La Salle visited three days at the first village. According to Nicolas, the chief asked La Salle to stay while he sent for other chiefs to talk to him; Minet is more specific in identifying the chiefs as the "*chefs de leur autres vilages.*"[12] The former says the nation is called the "Natché;" the latter acknowledges that the village is called "Natché," but that the nation is known as the "Corroa" or "Corroua" (Koroa). After three days—during which time a worried Tonti is said to have inquired after La Salle's good health, an anxiety curiously unreported by Tonti himself—the chiefs still had not arrived, and La Salle returned to the river camp. The French stayed there two more days before finally giving up hope of the promised visitation. Taking to their canoes with an Indian escort (four "Natché" according to Nicolas, and two unidentified Indians per Minet), they travelled eight leagues downriver to the Koroa—another village of the "Corroa" in Minet's account—who lived on a hill near the river.

Thus, although they clearly describe the same event, there would appear to be some considerable contradictions reported in the accounts of the first meeting with the Natchez. The desscriptions of times, distances, and peoples differ markedly, and one can sympathize with Swanton's confusion. For present purposes, however, some of the discrepancies can be ignored. For example, the question of how much time La Salle stayed at the first village is a very interesting conundrum, but one for which no explanation is possible from the information available since we are totally dependent upon the idiosyncrasies of the reports themselves. On the other hand, the questions of distances and peoples can be considered from a broader perspective of knowledge, and they are the only crucial questions for reconstructing the geography of that first meeting with the Natchez. In fact, a reconsideration of the details pertinent to these questions may not be as discordant as perceived by Swanton.

To summarize, then, the apparent facts contained in the five accounts that are important for this study: the French left the Taensa, who are believed to have been residing in the vicinity of Lake St. Joseph[13] (Fig. 1), and paddled downriver eleven to twelve leagues where they made first contact with Indians called the Natchez; La Salle went to their village three leagues inland; the expedition then continued by water six to ten leagues to a second village situated on a hillside near the river which was identified as Koroa, or possibly also Natchez. It was this last confusion that caused the greatest problem for Swanton. The confusion was compounded by his reliance on the eighteenth-century documents which placed the Natchez only one league from the river, and did not mention the Koroa at all. Resolution of Swanton's problem depends upon the identification of peoples, and then a reconsideration of distances with the help of archaeological evidence.

According to the above accounts, between the Taensa on the north and the Red River on the south there was on the east bank of the Mississippi River only one major community of Indians. Whatever they were called, they must have been closely related, for they lived in close, and from all accounts friendly, proximity. Who, indeed, were these Indians? In an earlier paper,[14] I proposed that the people known as the Natchez were already a hybrid group by the time of first European contact. The

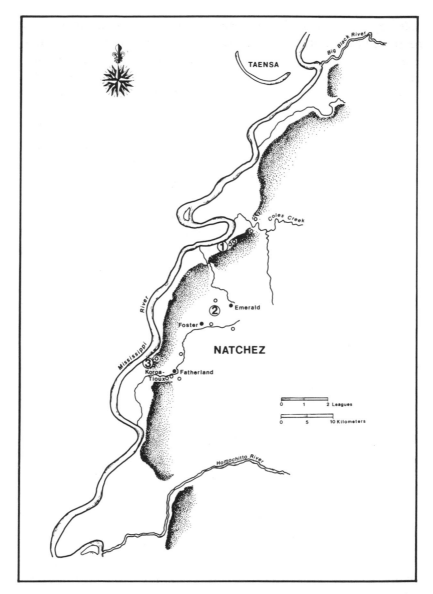

Figure 1. Settlement pattern of the Natchez Bluffs region during the time of La Salle, as reconstructed from archaeological and historical evidence. The numbers refer to the sequence of events discussed in the text.

majority, to be sure, were descendants of a native tradition that can be traced far back into prehistory, but ethnohistorical evidence supported by recently gathered archaeological data indicate that other groups had been accepted in their midst. In eighteenth–century documents, these immigrants were identified by such names as the Grigras and Tioux. The latter are of particular interest since there is circumstantial evidence that this is another name for, or a branch of, the Koroa.[15] Both of these peoples had their roots in the Yazoo country, yet both are associated with the Natchez. At the time under discussion, the Koroa are identified as being with the Natchez, but in 1690 they are placed by Tonti (III) on the Yazoo,[16] where they remain for the next forty years. From the time of Iberville on, however, it is the Tioux who are consistently mentioned as being with the Natchez in the same general venue accorded the Koroa earlier: in both cases they are located near the Natchez, but closer to the river.[17] Throughout the first half-century of French contact it seems that a branch of the Koroa-Tioux resided among the Natchez on a permanent basis, but that they were identified by different names at different times.

The prominence of the name Koroa in the La Salle accounts requires some further discussion. Both of the earliest descriptions of the expedition, those of La Metairie and Membré, refer only, or primarily, to the Koroa (La Metairie mentions the Natchez, but only in relation to the Koroa).[18] Clearly, the highlight of this part of the expedition was the visit to the Koroa village, as described in more detail by Nicolas, Minet, and Tonti. Both Nicolas and the early Tonti (I, II) accounts refer to the first village as Natchez and the second as Koroa. Minet agrees, but provides further insight by referring to all as the Koroa nation, thus confirming that they are one people.

A fuller perception of the situation is later given by Tonti, who was the only one to experience repeated contacts with these peoples. His next visit was in 1686,[19] during which he stopped at only one village and upbraided the Indians for the bad reception they had given the French when they returned upriver four years before. This village was the same one referred to earlier as the Koroa, but in 1686 Tonti called them, too, the Natchez (thus the source of Swanton's confusion). That this was not an error on Tonti's part would seem to be substantiated by his 1691 memoir (III), in which he again refers only to the Natchez at this location and, moreover, refers to the village as being that of the "Great Chief." Tonti's correction is still not quite accurate, for it is necessary to distinguish between the satellite Koroa village (presumably used as a front by the protective Natchez in 1682) and the principal Natchez village, residence of the Great Sun Chief, farther inland. Nevertheless, it may be argued that he came to the same conclusion as reported by Minet: i.e., whatever the name, these people all constituted the same "nation," and the power was concentrated in this second locale.

This brings us to the critical consideration of where exactly the peoples corporately known to history as the Natchez actually resided in 1682, and how that settlement is to be reconciled with the accounts of the first meeting. The general territory of the Natchez nation is not in question, since during the fifty-year period between La Salle's visit and the forced exodus from their homeland that territory clearly included the east bank of the Mississippi River between Coles Creek on the north and the Homochitto River on the south (Fig. 1). The question to be confronted is where the village areas were located during the visit of La Salle and how these relate to the later descriptions of Natchez settlement from the time of Iberville onward. Swanton's basic problem as compounded by the apparent discrepancies are not so great as they seem once our perspective is enlarged by archaeological evidence that was not available to Swanton.

Recent archaeological investigations of the Natchez region have concluded that the protohistoric Natchez nation was centered around the impressive mound sites of Emerald and Foster,[20] which were located some distance northeast of the famed Fatherland site (Fig. 1). Fatherland was also occupied during the late prehistoric-protohistoric periods, but it was a modest mound group compared to Emerald and Foster. The preeminence of the latter two sites, however, apparently declined during the late protohistoric period, and political power had shifted to Fatherland by the time of the full historic period after 1700.[21] Nevertheless, the northern fringe, including Emerald and Foster, continued to be inhabited—if not the actual sites, then certainly the vicinities, which are probably to be correlated with the eighteenth century Natchez villages of Jenzenaque and White Apple respectively.[22] These polities are notable for the considerable influence they were able to exert during the troubled decades of the 1710s and 1720s, when they often seem to have been barely under the control of the Great Sun Chief at Fatherland. In fact, during the entire half century of French contact, beginning with La Salle, the northern fringe had remained an important component of the Natchez, as befits the archaeological evidence which describes the area as the ancestral hearth of the nation.

Swanton's problem can now be recognized as one of perspective. The apparent contradictions of peoples and places in the La Salle accounts can be reconciled, and his confusion is really to be attributed to his reading of the eighteenth-century documents, which emphasize the importance of the Fatherland nucleus.[23] This importance may even have been true in La Salle's time, but cannot be assumed. In any case, the new archaeological evidence indicates the broader geographic dimensions of the protohistoric-historic Natchez, and this evidence integrates well with the details recorded in the historic accounts of La Salle's visit.

A revisionist history, therefore, would propose the following account (Fig. 1). Since he was descending the river, La Salle logically made first contact with the northern fringe of the "Natchez nation." This is indicated by the (1) on the map, a point approximately eleven to twelve leagues below the Taensa according to the reconstructed river route of the period. He then visited far inland to either Foster or Emerald or a related site (2), in any case an important village of the Natchez. While there, he heard of, or was visited by, one or more other important chiefs of the nation. Identified as Koroa by some of the accounts of the expedition, Tonti provides the clue in his sequence of documents that they were representatives of the Fatherland nucleus some distance away. La Salle returned to the river (1) and the expedition then proceeded by water some six to eight leagues[24] to the latter settlements (3). Six to eight leagues would have brought them to the Natchez landing of the eighteenth-century descriptions. Although they apparently visited only the allied Koroa (-Tioux) village, ironically they actually had finally arrived at the principal location which thenceforward would be identified as the Natchez.

It is one of those little misfortunes of history that La Salle, himself not a memoirist, did not take such a perceptive chronicler as Tonti, nor apparently Nicolas or Barbier, with him on that visit to the first Natchez village—for Swanton's confusion might have been alleviated, and our understanding of the seventeenth-century Natchez enhanced.

Notes

[1] The ancestors of the Natchez were encountered by the De Soto expedition. De Soto exchanged messages with their chief, one Quigualtam, in 1542, and the following year the retreating army fought desperately with Quigualtam's warriors while descending the Mississippi River in its escape to the Gulf of Mexico. But De Soto did not visit Quigualtam, nor did any others who left records of the expedition.

[2] John R. Swanton, *Indian Tribes of the Lower Mississippi Valley and Adjacent Coast of the Gulf of Mexico*, 187; see also Andrew C. Albrecht, "The Location of the Historic Natchez Villages," for a more recent discussion of the problem.

[3] For formal citation of this account and others not noted, see Patricia Galloway, "Sources for the La Salle Expedition of 1682," this volume.

[4] M. A. Habig, *The Franciscan Père Marquette*, 215–29; Jean Delanglez, "La Salle's Expedition of 1682," 28–35. It will be noted that in the spelling of "Tonti" I have chosen to follow the orthography of Delanglez, "The Voyages of Tonti," 257.

[5] Pierre Margry, *Découvertes et établissements des français dans l'ouest et dans le sud de l'Amérique septentrionale* 1, 545–70.

[6] Minet, *Voiage fait du Canada par dedans les terres allant vers le Sud dans l'anne 1682*, 1–45.

[7] Sieur Barbier is presumably the Gabriel Barbier listed as a member of the expedition by Tonti: Margry 1, 594; Melville B. Anderson, *Relation of Henri de Tonty, Concerning the Explorations of La Salle from 1678 to 1683*, 61.

[8] Margry 1, 573–616; Anderson, ibid.

[9] Thomas Falconer, *On the Discovery of the Mississippi, and on the South-Western, Oregon, and North-Western Boundary of the United States*, 49–96; B. F. French, *Historical Collections of Louisiana* 1, 62–78; Isaac J. Cox, *Journeys of La Salle* 1, 1–58.

[10] Margry 2, 601.

[11] Ibid., 1, 547n.

[12] Minet, ibid., 33.

[13] Stephen Williams, "On the Location of the Historic Taensa Villages."

[14] Jeffrey P. Brain, "The Natchez 'Paradox'." See also George I. Quimby, "Natchez Social Structure as an Instrument of Assimilation."

[15] Swanton, *Indian Tribes*, 327, 329, 335; idem, *The Indians of the Southeastern United States*, 195.

[16] There is even a strong suggestion by La Metairie, in Falconer, 39, that the main component of the tribe had never left the Yazoo.

[17] Compare the ca. 1685–1688 maps of Minet, Franquelin, and Coronelli (see Louis De Vorsey, "The Impact of the La Salle Expedition of 1682 on European Cartography," this volume) with the various eighteenth-century maps of Diron, Dumont de Montigny and Broutin.

[18] It could be argued that the prominence is due to the fact that only part of the expedition accompanied La Salle to the first village, while all visited the second (*le dit* Koroa) village. The problem with this argument is that Membré, according to Le Clercq's version, may have gone with La Salle to the first village, and certainly some of the signatories to the La Metairie document did.

[19] Margry 3, 556.

[20] Jeffrey P. Brain, "Late Prehistoric Settlement Patterning in the Yazoo Basin and Natchez Bluffs Regions of the Lower Mississippi Valley;" Ian W. Brown and Jeffrey P. Brain, "Hypothesized Cultural and Environmental Factors Influencing Local Population Movements in the Natchez Bluffs Region;" Jeffrey P. Brain, Ian W. Brown, and Vincas P. Steponaitis, *Archaeology of the Natchez Bluffs.*

[21] Robert S. Neitzel, *Archeology of the Fatherland Site.*

[22] Jeffrey P. Brain, Ian W. Brown, and Vincas P. Steponaitis, *Archaeology of the Natchez Bluffs;* Ian W. Brown "The Archaeological Study of Cultural Contact and Change in the Natchez Region," this volume; Ian W. Brown and Stephen Williams, "Archaeological Investigations at Seven Historic Sites in the Natchez Bluffs Region." Of historical note, Daniel G. Brinton, in "On the Language of the Natchez," 2, states that La Salle visited the Natchez village of the Apple. Neither in that article, nor in any other of his available writings does he substantiate that identification. It is to be supposed that he relied upon the Le Clercq version of Membré's account and later eighteenth and nineteenth-century documents which give prominence to the White Apple village. His scholarship might be in question, but his identification would seem to be remarkably accurate.

[23] Swanton, *Indian Tribes*, 45. Swanton reconciles the problem that Fatherland is only one league from the river by suggesting that La Salle must have made first contact with the Natchez near the mouth of St. Catherine Creek, which at the time was many leagues below its present confluence with the Mississippi. While such a postulated first landing would indeed have been approximately three leagues from Fatherland, it would also have been about twice the distance of eleven to twelve leagues from the Taensa cited in the accounts.

[24] The total distance from the Taensa to the second landing—the "real" Natchez landing from then on—is thus computed at 18–19 leagues (Tonti first reckons 22 leagues, then 16 leagues in his 1686 expedition, finally 18 leagues in his memoir). This agrees favorably with Iberville's estimate of 17.5 leagues in Richebourg G. McWilliams, *Iberville's Gulf Journals*, 75.

The Impact of the La Salle Expedition of 1682 on European Cartography

LOUIS DE VORSEY, JR.

•

In the very first sentence of his book *A History of Geographical Discovery and Exploration*, J. N. L. Baker pointed out that "the history of geographical discovery tells of the evolution of the map of the world from its simplest and most elementary beginnings in antiquity to the highly specialized form which is known today."[1] This brief essay will direct attention to the belated manner in which European maps of the New World came to reflect René-Robert Cavelier de La Salle's momentous exploration of the lower Mississippi River and delta in 1682.

This is not a simple story of yet another New World region explored and quickly portrayed cartographically for the eyes and minds of an eager European audience. To the contrary, the first reasonably accurate depiction of La Salle's discovery was not published until 1703 when Claude Delisle produced his seminal "Carte du Mexique et de la Floride" (Fig. 1).[2] By that date a full two decades had elapsed since La Salle's return to France to report the news of his findings to Louis XIV. Why did it take twenty years for European cartographers to depict correctly the true nature and location of the Mississippi's lower course and deltaic mouth projecting into the Gulf of Mexico? Certainly some time lag between an important geographical discovery and the appearance of good published maps depicting it is to be anticipated. Twenty years, however, was an inordinate lag for even the more leisurely pace which often surrounded the events of the seventeenth century and requires explanation. Before examining La Salle's exploration of the lower Mississippi it will be useful to review the general state of geographical knowledge of the Mississippi River and interior of North America which existed in New France during the decades which preceded his discovery.

Figure 1. Claude Delisle, "Carte du Mexique et de la Floride," 1703. Published courtesy of Mississippi Department of Archives and History.

61

In 1634-35 Jean Nicollet returned from a sojourn among the Green Bay, Wisconsin, Indians and fired Quebec imaginations with vague references to a great river down which a three day voyage would carry one to the sea and "from this sea there would be an outlet towards Japan and China."[3] Following Nicollet's route to establish a mission among the Green Bay Indians, Father Allouez learned of the Mascouten Indians who lived along the upper Fox River. In a letter describing his experiences he noted, "these people are settled in a very attractive place, where beautiful Plains and Fields meet the eye as far as one can see. Their River leads by a six days' Voyage to the great River named Messi-Sipi."[4]

The superb map of Lake Superior, which appeared with the Jesuit Relations for 1670 and 1671, represents the westernmost extent of confirmed geographical knowledge of New France for that date.[5] In his discussion of this map Father Claude Dablon, the Superior of the Jesuit Missions in New France, mentioned "the great river called by the natives Missisipi" which took a southward course and "must empty somewhere in the region of the Florida sea, more than four hundred leagues hence." In his description of the Illinois Indians who came to trade at the mission located near the western extremity of Lake Superior, Dablon drew further attention to the legendary 'great river' of the Indians. The Illinois, he wrote, were:

> situated in the midst of that beautiful region . . . near the great river named Missisipi, of which it is well to note here what information we have gathered. It seems to form an inclosure, as it were, for all our lakes, rising in the regions of the North and flowing toward the south, until it empties into the sea—supposed by us to be either the vermillion or the Florida Sea, as there is no knowledge of any larger rivers in that direction except those which empty into these two Seas. Some Savages have assured us that this is so noble a river that, at more than three hundred leagues' distance from its mouth it is larger than the one flowing before Quebec, for they declare that it is more than a league wide. They also state that all this vast stretch of country consists of nothing but treeless prairies,—so that its inhabitants are all

obliged to burn peat and animal excrement dried in the Sun,—until we come within twenty leagues of the sea when Forests begin to appear again. Some warriors of this country who tell us they made their way thither, declare that they saw there men resembling the French, who were splitting trees with long knives; and that some of them had their houses on the water,—for thus they expressed themselves in speaking of sawed boards and of Ships. They state further that all along that great river are various Tribes of different nations of dissimilar languages and customs, and all are at war with one another.[6]

To appreciate Father Dablon's analysis of the Indian accounts of the great river which framed the Great Lakes to the west and flowed to either the Gulf of California or Gulf of Mexico (his vermillion and Florida seas), consideration should be given to one of the most influential maps of his period. Doubtless this would have been Nicolas Sanson's "Amérique Septentrionale," which first appeared in 1650.[7] One of the most prominent features of this map is the range of mountains which extends from east to west cutting the Gulf of Mexico off from the northern interior of the continent, an error probably derived from the earliest known map showing topographic detail in this region—the De Soto Map, ca. 1544.[8]

Only lakes Ontario and Erie were in place on the Sanson map. Furthermore, Dablon's Indian informants were telling him about a great river, larger even than the mighty St. Lawrence before Quebec, which framed or "inscribed" all of the Great Lakes to the west and flowed for a great distance to a southern sea where Europeans and their ships or "houses on the water" had been observed. It is easy to understand Dablon's conclusion that either the Gulf of Mexico or Gulf of California was the recipient of this flow when the Sanson map is in view. Dablon's speculation represents a process vital in all early New World geographical discoveries, an attempt to fit geographical intelligence gained from Indian informants into the prevailing and accepted geographic patterns of his day and culture.

The next phase in the discovery of the Mississippi River was a direct result of the policy of Canadian westward expansion initiated by the aggressive Intendant Talon. Writing in 1670 Talon stated, "I have dispatched persons of resolution, who promise to penetrate farther than has ever been done; the one to the West and to the Northwest of Canada, and the others to the South-west and South. Those adventurers are to keep journals in all instances . . . in all cases they are to take possession, display the King's arms and to draw up proces verbaux to serve as titles."[9] The following year Daumont de Saint-Lusson convened a great meeting at Sault Ste. Marie with representatives of some four-teen western Indian nations. During the ceremonies the Indians were informed that Louis XIV was taking possession of lands lying from Montreal on the east to the South Sea on the west "covering the utmost extent and range possible."[10]

In the continuing thrust of French expansion to the west, Louis Jolliet was assigned to confirm the location of the Missis-sippi River. In 1673 Jolliet and Jesuit missionary Father Jacques Marquette with five *voyageurs* traveled up the Fox River to Lake Winnebago and portaged to the Wisconsin River, then followed it down to the Mississippi. Their route can be followed on the sketch map prepared by Marquette preserved in the ar-chives of St. Mary's College, Montreal. Marquette's "R. De La Conception" is the Mississippi River. From approximately its juncture with the Wisconsin near Prairie du Chien, where they first entered it, down to the Arkansas River, it is reasonably represented. Near the mouth of the Arkansas, local Indians told them that they were close to the sea.[11] Believing the reports that they were dangerously close to Spanish settlements on the Gulf of Mexico, the small party of Frenchmen decided to return to New France. On the return trip they wisely followed Indian recommendations concerning a short-cut up the Illinois River to the Chicago and Lake Michigan. Thus Marquette's remarkable manuscript map shows the route later chosen by La Salle in traveling from the Great Lakes to the Mississippi.

In Marquette's account he told of how he and Jolliet held a council to decide whether they should push on to the Mississip-pi's mouth or return "with the discovery which we had made." He wrote:

After attentively considering that we were not far from the Gulf of Mexico, the basin of which is at the latitude of 31 degrees 60 minutes, while we were at 33 degrees 40 minutes, we judged that we could not be more than 2 or 3 days' journey from it; and that, beyond a doubt the Mississippi river discharges into the florida or Mexican gulf, and not to the east in Virginia, whose sea-coast is at 34 degrees latitude—which we had passed, without, however, having as yet reached the sea—or to the west in California, because in that case our route would have been to the west, or the west-southwest, whereas we had always continued it toward the south. We further considered that we exposed ourselves to losing the results of this voyage, of which we could give no information if we proceeded to fling ourselves into the hands of the Spaniards who without doubt, would at least have detained us as captives. Moreover, we saw very plainly that we were not in a condition to resist Savages allied to the Europeans, who were numerous, and expert in firing guns, and who continually infested the lower parts of the river. Finally, we had obtained all the information that could be desired in regard to this discovery. All these reasons induced us to decide upon Returning; this we announced to the savages, and after a day's rest, made our preparation for it.[12]

In the spring of 1674 Jolliet parted company with Father Marquette at the mission of St. François Xavier on Green Bay, to carry his own report and map to Governor Frontenac in Quebec. Disaster struck when, in Jolliet's words, "in sight of and at the doors of the first French house that I had left nearly two years before . . . my canoe was overturned and I lost two men and my chest. Nothing is left to me but my life."[13] Working from memory, the resourceful Jolliet drew his colored manuscript map titled "Nouvelle Decouverte de Plusieurs Nations Dans Nouvelle France En l'annee 1673 et 1674," now one of the most esteemed cartographic treasures in the collection of the John Carter Brown Library (Fig. 2). In the western extremity of the map Jolliet included a boldly outlined letter addressed to Count Frontenac which described the highlights of his expedition with Marquette down the Mississippi. Distorted though it is, this map represents an exciting new image of the interior of the continent. The Mississippi is shown beginning near the

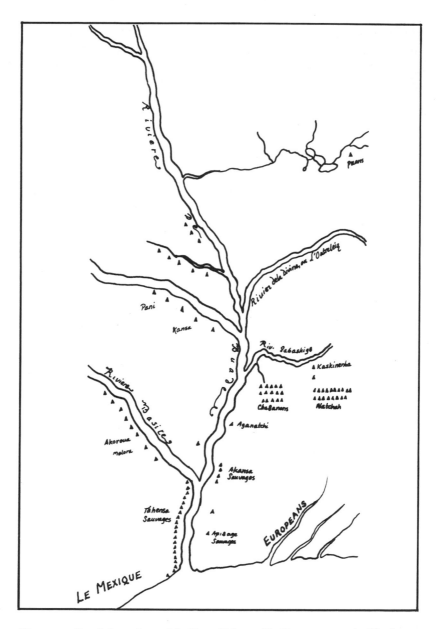

Figure 2. Partial tracing of Jolliet, "Nouvelle Decouverte de Plusieurs Nations Dans Nouvelle France En l'annee 1673 et 1674."

northern extremity of the map close to the "Mer Glaciale" or
Arctic Ocean. A tentative link to that northern sea is even suggested. The Wisconsin and Illinois River routes to Lake Michigan followed by Jolliet and Marquette are shown, with obvious
emphasis being given to the Illinois. The manner in which the
lower Mississippi is shown to follow an almost due south course
to empty into the western end of the Gulf of Mexico at approximately 29 degrees of latitude is perhaps the most notable feature
of this map. Two large tributaries entering the Mississippi from
the west probably represent the Missouri and Arkansas Rivers.
In his letter to Frontenac, Jolliet drew attention to the fact that
"One of the great rivers running into the Mississippi from the
west gives a passage into the Gulf of California (*Mer Vermeille*)." He added, "I saw a village which is only five days'
journey from a tribe which trades with the natives of California.
If I had arrived two days earlier I could have talked to those who
had come and brought four hatchets as a present."[14] The in-
scription "Mer Vermeille ou est La Califournie par ou on peut
aller au Perou au Japon et ala Chine" found in the lower left
corner of Jolliet's map doubtless created excitement in Frontenac and other officials who studied it. Perhaps to further justify returning upriver before reaching the Gulf because of a fear
of capture by the Spanish or their Indian allies, Jolliet included
the caption "Europeans" with small orb and cross symbols
along a river to the east of the Mississippi. There is, of course,
no record of any European settlements in this area at so early a
date as 1673–1674.

A deliberate change of imperial policy on the part of Louis
XIV had the effect of terminating further government–sponsored
explorations in Western Canada. In 1676 Governor Frontenac
was admonished by the king that "concerning these discoveries,
you must on no account encourage them unless there be a great
need and some obvious advantage . . . it is far more worthwhile
to occupy a smaller area and have it well populated than to
spread out and have several feeble colonies which could easily be
destroyed by all manner of accidents."[15] Colbert's faction,
which had consistently espoused a compact colony philosophy

for Canada at court, clearly influenced the king's judgment during this period. As a result, the Jolliet-Marquette probe to the Mississippi was not followed up until René-Robert Cavelier de la Salle convinced the king to grant him royal permission to establish a trade monopoly in the Illinois country in return for finding the mouth of the Mississippi River and establishing a harbor there for French ships.

La Salle returned to Canada with his royal privilege in September 1678 and began to lay the foundation of a trading empire which he hoped would extend from Lake Ontario to the Gulf of Mexico. During 1679–1680 he built his sailing ship *Griffon* on the Niagara River to provide the Great Lakes link in his grandiose scheme. The story of the building and loss of the *Griffon* is well known, as is La Salle's building of Fort Crevecoeur near what is today the city of Peoria, Illinois, and will not be recounted here.

It was not until the winter of 1681–1682 that La Salle was ready to lead his small flotilla of bark canoes down the Illinois and Mississippi. Like his predecessors, Jolliet and Marquette, La Salle made abundant use of Indian informants in gaining a detailed appreciation of what to anticipate en route. Father Louis Hennepin provided an intriguing glimpse of just how meticulously this had been done. He wrote:

> A young Illinois warrior who had taken some captives in the territory to the south was coming back ahead of his comrades and when he passed our stocks, was given corn to eat. Since he was returning from the lower part of the Colbert [Mississippi] River, with which we pretended to be acquainted, the young man made us a fairly exact map of it with charcoal. He assured us he had followed its course in his pirogue and there were no falls or rapids all the way to the sea which the Indians call the great lake. Since the river became extremely broad, there were in places sand bars and mud which partially obstructed it. He also told us the names of the tribes living on its banks and of the rivers emptying into it. I wrote them down . . . The next morning after our public prayers, we went to the village, where we found the Illinois assembled in the wigwam of one of the most important Indians. He was

feasting them on bear meat, a food of which they are very fond. They made room for us in the center of a fine rush mat which they laid for us. We had one of our men who knew their language say that we wished to inform them that the Maker of all things, whom they call the great Master of Life, takes particular care of Frenchmen and had revealed to us the condition of the great river we named Colbert, concerning which we had been at a loss to know the truth ever since they had told us the river was not navigable. We then repeated to them what we had learned the preceding day.

The Indians believed we had learned all this by some extraordinary means . . . They told us their only reason for hiding the truth was their desire to keep our chief and the gray-gowns or bare-feet (as all the American Indians call Franciscan monks). They admitted everything that we had learned from the young warrior and since they have not denied it.[16]

Hennepin himself was sent by La Salle to reconnoitre the Mississippi upstream of the Illinois River and did not actually share in the discovery of the great river's mouth. The map which accompanied the original edition of his *Description of Louisiana* carefully omitted any detail in the area of the lowermost Mississippi. Only a dotted line is included to suggest where Hennepin assumed it to flow and join the Gulf of Mexico.

La Salle began his voyage down the Mississippi on February 13, 1682, with twenty-two Frenchmen and eighteen Indians accompanied by several of their squaws. In the words of La Salle's *procès verbal*, which was solemnly read and signed somewhere near the Mississippi's mouth:

We continued our voyage till the 6th, when we discovered three channels by which the River Colbert discharges itself into the sea. We landed on the bank of the most western channel, about three leagues from its mouth. On the 7th M. de la Salle went to reconnoitre the shores of the neighboring sea, and M. Tonty likewise examined the great middle channel. They found these two outlets beautiful, large and deep. On the 8th we reascended the river a little above its confluence with the sea, to find a dry place, beyond the reach of inundations. The elevation of the North Pole was here about 27 degrees. Here was prepared a column and a cross, and to the said column were affixed the arms of France. . . .[17]

La Salle and his party returned up the Mississippi to consolidate the Illinois country positions as a base for his new trading empire. Ill health and Indian wars prevented his immediate return to Quebec, where the recall of Count Frontenac to France had placed La Salle's archenemy, La Barre, in charge of the government of New France. When in October 1683 La Salle finally left the Indian country for Quebec, La Barre was actively assuming the control of his posts and assets. Rather than tarry in Quebec and risk the winter freeze-up he embarked for France almost immediately.

La Barre's calumnies against La Salle had been relayed to the king by Colbert's powerful son and successor, the Marquis of Seignelay. The king was so thoroughly taken in by the anti-La Salle faction that he wrote to Seignelay as follows:

> I am convinced like you, that the discovery of the Sieur de la Salle is very useless, and that such enterprises ought to be prevented in the future, as they tend only to debauch the inhabitants by the hope of gain, and to diminish the revenue from beaver skins.[18]

Exactly when La Salle was apprised of the king's antagonistic attitude toward his scheme of extending French settlement and control down the Mississippi Valley cannot be determined.[19] By the early Spring of 1684, just months after his hurried return to France, La Salle sent an ingenious "Memoir" to Seignelay which effectively countered the harsh criticism of the La Barre-led faction and placed his plan for a Mississippi Valley colony high on King Louis' list of imperial priorities.

La Salle accomplished this turnabout by launching the greatest geographical hoax in the history of North American exploration, a hoax which, among other things, had the effect of arresting European cartography of the continent for twenty years. What La Salle did was to make it appear that the mouth of the Mississippi River was on the western coast of the Gulf in Texas rather than in present-day Louisiana where he had placed the king's arms and read his *procès verbal* in April of 1682. By this stratagem he made his planned colony appear to be an ideal staging point for an aggressive attack on the fabled mines of New Spain. It would seem certain that La Salle was well aware of the favorable reception which Seignelay and the king were extending to the plan for a similar attack then being promoted by the Spanish exile Peñalosa. If the Peruvian turncoat could find royal support for his invasion scheme, why shouldn't he, La Salle, present his own plan in similar terms?

In 1684 La Salle outlined his accomplishments, including his discovery of the mouth of the River Colbert, as he termed the Mississippi, to Seignelay. He stressed further that "very important conquests" could now be made "for the glory of our King." These conquests were "provinces . . . very rich in silver mines—they adjoin the River Colbert—they are far removed from succour—they are open everywhere on the side on which we should attack them, and are defended only by a small number of persons, so sunk in effeminacy and indolence as to be incapable of enduring the fatigue of wars of this description."[20] Needless to say a due south flowing lower Mississippi such as had been suggested by the maps of Jolliet and Hennepin and found in fact by La Salle could not be made to fit the description which La Salle was promoting to Seignelay and Louis XIV. As Henry Folmer pungently observed, "if the Ministry of the Navy wanted a harbor close to New Spain, La Salle was going to give it to them."[21] And give it to them he did. The enormity of La Salle's hoax can be seen on the maps of two of the best informed cartographers in the French Empire, Vincenzo Coronelli and Jean-Baptiste Louis Franquelin.

Coronelli was in Paris constructing the gores of his famous globe for Louis XIV when the news of La Salle's descent of the Mississippi to the sea reached the French court. On his map "America Settentrionale," a variant of the gores, he showed the Mississippi River displaced far to the west and emptying into the Gulf of Mexico only a short distance north of the mouth of the "Rio Bravo," as the Rio Grande was named (Fig. 3). Thanks to the exhaustive research of Jean Delanglez we can be certain that

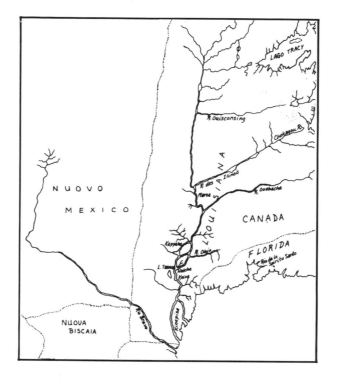

Figure 3. Partial tracing of Coronelli, "America Settentrionale."

Coronelli's hand in this part of his map was guided by La Salle's own *Relation des descouvertes.*[22]

On the elegantly embellished "Carte De l'Amerique Septen-trionnalle . . . En l'Annee 1688," Franquelin, the hydrographer royal in Quebec, showed the Mississippi making a sharp turn to the west to actually join with the Rio Grande before turning sharply to the east and emptying through an intricate delta into the western extremity of the Gulf of Mexico (Fig. 4). Like Coronelli, Franquelin had access to La Salle's account and map of his 1682 Mississippi voyage of discovery.[23] King Louis and his ministers, contemplating the possibility of an attack on the Spanish mines in New Mexico, were, like these cartographers,

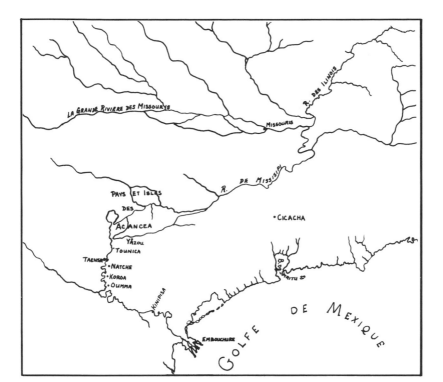

Figure 4. Partial tracing of Franquelin, "Carte de l'Amerique septen-
trionnalle . . . En l'Annee 1688."

duped by La Salle into believing that the Mississippi River found
its way to the sea in Texas, more than 600 miles from its actual
mouth in Louisiana. As Folmer has pointed out, there could
hardly have been a more complete merger of Peñalosa's and La
Salle's plans than by simply uniting the Rio Grande and the
Mississippi.

It is interesting to observe that Louis Hennepin had already
resisted the impulse to connect the Mississippi to the Rio
Grande. It will be recalled that his map of 1683 suggested the
lower course of the Mississippi by a line of dots running due
south. On his map published in Amsterdam in 1697, "Carte
d'un tres grand Pais Nouvellement decouvert dans l'Amerique

Septentrionale," Hennepin chose to follow the Coronelli model and displaced the Mississippi to the west, but did not have it join with the Rio Grande. Like Hennepin's, the maps attributed to the engineer named Minet avoided linking the Mississippi and Rio Grande. Minet did, however, follow the Franquelin model and showed the Mississippi taking a huge swing to the west to enter the Gulf of Mexico in the area of present-day Matagorda, Texas. The fact that Minet had been with La Salle at the outset of the abortive Matagorda Bay settlement must have lent great weight to the hoax.[24]

When France's ambitions finally shifted from the comic opera-like invasion scheme epitomized by Peñalosa, Le Moyne d'Iberville was dispatched in 1698 to found a colony on the Gulf Coast. La Salle's hoax had been so effective, however, that Iberville encountered serious problems in getting his advance geographical intelligence to coincide with what he found when he arrived off the Gulf of Mexico's north coast. In a letter he wrote to Pontchartrain in 1698 he admitted being unable to gain any information about the mouth of the Mississippi at Santo Domingo because "no one has any precise idea" of its location.[25] Later in 1699, after he successfully rediscovered the river's mouth, Iberville wryly remarked that La Salle's mistaken location probably derived "from the great desire he had to locate himself close to the mines of New Mexico" and "to influence the court by this means to make settlements in Louisiana."[26]

Iberville's rediscovery and accurate positioning of the Mississippi's deltaic mouth wrote finished to La Salle's amazing hoax. Cartographer Claude Delisle's careful research for his 1703 "Carte du Mexique et de la Floride" included Iberville's journals, maps, and correspondence describing his voyages to the Gulf coast and Mississippi.[27] This 1703 map and one published by his son Guillaume under the title "L'Amerique Septentrionale, dressee sur les Obervations de Mrs. de l'Academie Royal des Sciences et quelques autres et sur les Memoires les plus Recens," appear to be among the earliest printed maps to show the mouth and course of the Mississippi River with reasonable accuracy.[28] In 1718 Guillaume Delisle incorporated his

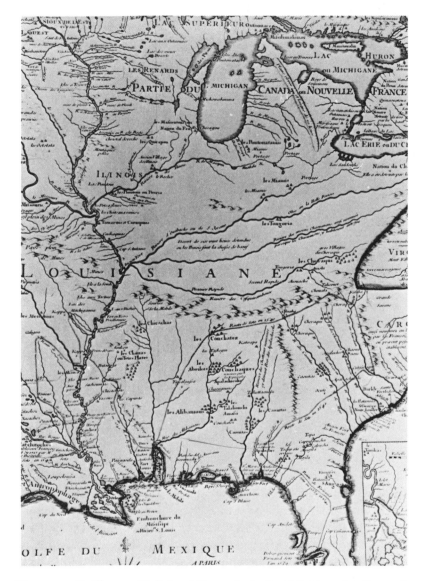

Figure 5. Guillaume Delisle, "Carte de la Louisiane et du Cours du Mississippi," 1718. Published courtesy of Mississippi Department of Archives and History.

father's meticulous research in the map titled "Carte de la Louisiane et du Cours du Mississippi" with its large-scale inset "Carte Particuliere Des Embouchures De La Riviere . . . " (Fig. 5). As William Cumming has pointed out, "this is one of the most important maps of the Mississippi Valley. Quickly copied, widely referred to, it was the chief authority for the Mississippi River for over fifty years."[29]

In writing of La Salle's hoax, historian Henry Folmer provided an excellent summary conclusion for this essay:

> Thus began a series of lies and deceptions, misrepresentations, and fantasies which were ultimately to lead to La Salle's ruin and violent death and that of most of his companions. Had he remained faithful to his original plan of founding a colony on the Mississippi, La Salle would probably not have ended his life in tragic failure. The colonial rivalry between his country and Spain ensnared La Salle into an adventure of conquest that was no longer suited to his times. The days of Cortes were definitely passed in 1682.[30]

My own conclusion would include a correction to the many historical accounts and studies which have argued that La Salle attempted to found his colony on Matagorda Bay in Texas because he was unable to determine his longitude accurately and missed the true mouth of the Mississippi. To arrive at such a conclusion is to misjudge completely the abilities and motives of the gifted former Jesuit teacher of mathematics, and genius of North American exploration, René-Robert Cavelier de La Salle.

Notes

[1] J. N. L. Baker, *A History of Geographical Discovery and Exploration*, 17.

[2] In his essay on the sources of the 1703 Delisle map, Jean Delanglez makes the point that this and other maps which are attributed to Guillaume were, in fact, authored by his father Claude. See Delanglez, "The Sources of the Delisle Map of America, 1703."

[3] William P. Cumming, S. E. Hillier, D. B. Quinn and G. Williams, *The Exploration of North America*, 32.

[4] Reuben Gold Thwaites, *The Jesuit Relations and Allied Documents* 54, 231. John Gilmary Shea states that Allouez was the first European to use the name "Missisipi." See his *Discovery and Exploration of the Mississippi Valley*, xxiv.

[5] "Jesuit Map of Lake Superior, and Parts of Lake Huron and Michigan" facsimile

facing page 94 in Thwaites, *Jesuit Relations*, 55. For a discussion and facsimile of this map see Emerson D. Fite and Archibald Freeman, *A Book of Old Maps Delineating American History*, 154–58.

[6] Thwaites, ibid. 207–209.

[7] For a discussion of the significance of Nicolas Sanson's maps in shaping the geographical perceptions of the Jesuits in Canada see Jean Delanglez, *El Rio Del Espiritu Santo*, 96.

[8] Barbara Boston has developed a convincing set of arguments to prove that Alonso de Santo Cruz was the author of this map. Her work can be consulted in "The De Soto Map."

[9] Quotation from Cumming, *et al.*, ibid., 35.

[10] Ibid.

[11] For a detailed account of Jolliet and Marquette's expedition see Thwaites, *Jesuit Relations* 59, 89–163.

[12] Ibid., 159–61.

[13] Ibid., facsimile of Jolliet's Map with letter to Frontenac facing p. 87. Translation from Fite and Freeman, *A Book of Old Maps*, 161.

[14] Ibid.

[15] Cumming *et al.*, ibid., 36.

[16] Marion E. Cross (trans.), *Father Louis Hennepin's Description of Louisiana*, 80–81.

[17] Theodore C. Pease and R. C. Werner, *French Foundations, 1680–1693*, 110–111.

[18] Quoted in John Anthony Caruso, *The Mississippi Valley Frontier*, 180.

[19] Folmer suggests that he learned this as early as the autumn of 1682. See Henry Folmer, *Franco-Spanish Rivalry in North America 1524–1763*, 143.

[20] Pease and Werner, ibid., 118.

[21] Folmer, ibid., 146.

[22] Jean Delanglez, *Hennepin's Description of Louisiana: A Critical Essay*, 114.

[23] Sara Jones Tucker (comp.) *Indian Villages of the Illinois Country, Atlas*, 4.

[24] Minet's manuscript journal with an included sketch map of the mouth of the Mississippi was recently acquired by the Public Archives Canada. For published versions of his more general maps, see Justin Winsor, *Narrative and Critical History of America* (Boston, 1884) 4, 237; also Gabriel Gravier, *Decouvertes Et Etablissements De Cavelier De La Salle de Rouen dans l'Amérique du Nord*.

[25] Folmer, ibid., 204.

[26] Ibid., 147.

[27] Jean Delanglez, "The Sources of the Delisle Map of America, 1703," 289–91.

[28] For a photographic reproduction of a 1700 Delisle map showing the influence of Iberville's rediscovery of the Mississippi's mouth see C. O. Paullin, *Atlas of the Historical Geography of the United States*, plate 22A. The 1703 map is an improved depiction and can be found in Cumming *et al.*, ibid., 155.

[29] Cumming *et al.*, ibid., 156.

[30] Folmer, ibid., 144.

Maps Mentioned in the Text

1. *Carte du Mexique et de la Floride*, by Guillaume Delisle, 1703. Reproduced in William P. Cumming *et al.*, *The Exploration of North America 1630–1776*, 155; Figure 1, this essay.

2. *Lac Superieur Et Autres Lieux Ou Sont Les Missions Des Peres De La Compagnie De Jesus Comprises Sons Le Nom D'Ontaouacs*, anonymous, 1672. Original in *Relation*

de ce qui s'est passé de plus remarquable en la Nouvelle France 1670 et 1671, 1672. Reproduced in Cumming *et al., The Exploration of North America,* 34.

3. *Amerique Septentrionale,* by Nicolas Sanson d'Abbeville, 1650. Reproduced in Cumming *et al., The Exploration of North America,* 47.

4. [Sketch of the de Soto Expedition], anonymous, ca. 1544. Reproduced in William P. Cumming, R. A. Skelton and D. B. Quinn, *The Discovery of North America* (New York: American Heritage Press, 1972), 121.

5. [The Marquette Map], by Jacques Marquette, S. J., ca. 1674. Reproduced in Sara Jones Tucker, *Indian Villages of the Illinois Country,* plate V.

6. *Nouvelle Decouverte de plusieres Nations Dans la Nouvelle France en l'année 1673 et 1674,* by Louis Jolliet, 1674. Reproduced in Cumming *et al., The Exploration of North America,* 17; Figure 2, this essay.

7. *Carte De La Nouvelle France et de la Louisiane Nouvellement decouverte, dediee Au Roy,* by Louis Hennepin, 1683. Reproduced in Cumming *et al., The Exploration of North America,* 39.

8. *America Settentrionale,* by Vincenzo M. Coronelli, 1690. Reproduced in Cumming *et al., The Exploration of North America,* 148; Figure 3, this essay.

9. *Carte de l'Amerique septentrionnalle . . . ,* by Jean Baptiste Louis Franquelin, 1688. Reproduced in Cumming *et al., The Exploration of North America,* 41; Figure 4, this essay.

10. *Carte d'un tres grand Pais Nouvellement decouvert dans l'Amerique Septentrionale,* by Louis Hennepin, 1697. Reproduced in Cumming *et al., The Exploration of North America,* 54.

11. *L'Amérique Septentrional, dressée sur les Observations de Mrs. de l'Academie Royale des Sciences et quelques autres et sur les Memoires les plus Recens,* by Guillaume Delisle, 1700. Reproduced in C. O. Paullin, *Atlas of the Historical Geography of the United States,* plate 22A.

12. [Minet Map of the Mouth of the Mississippi]. Reproduced in Victorin Chabot, "Journal inédite relatant les expéditions de Cavelier de La Salle," 9.

PART II

The Beginnings
of French Colonialism
in the Southeast

France, The New World, and Colonial Expansion

JAMES J. COOKE

•

IN 1962 the Franco-Algerian war came to an end when representatives of those two peoples decided that an eight-year slaughter had to cease. A colonial war, just as costly as the Indochinese War which had preceded it, this war left France drained of treasure, with many thousands of her sons dead or maimed. In the context of her imperial system, which sons was she to mourn: those that were French or those that were Algerian? Charles de Gaulle had called the struggle for *Algérie française* a "sterilizing obsession," and it had been just that, as other colonial enterprises had been for several hundred years before.

The French never understood imperialism as other Europeans saw it. Scholars, diplomats, bureaucrats might have talked in terms of trade, commerce, markets, raw materials, and belatedly discussed *mise en valeur,* but they seem never to have had full faith in these terms. For France, colonialism was glory, the most consistent theme running through her expansionistic experience. It was glory—for the king, the emperor, for the Republic—that brought into being New France, Louisiana, Algeria, the Ivory Coast, Madagascar, and Indochina. It was glory, translated at times into grim determination, that brought her to the Plains of Abraham, to Mexico, to Dien Bien Phu, to Evian sur Bains. It was never glory for the lands of the empire itself, but for France. As one of France's leading colonialists shouted to the Chamber of Deputies in the 1880s, "By her empire will France be great again!"

Another consistent theme occupying a role in French colonial history is the constant problem of getting French people to leave France and go to the colonies. Certainly, there is enough evidence to convince us that life for the peasantry in France under Louis XIV and Louis XV was grim, with a mere subsistence level in food and housing,[1] but would one trade off the village or the town for the unknown wilds of a New France or a Louisiana? If it is true that Jean-Baptiste Colbert first saw expansionism as a reflection of the glory of the king of France, it is doubtful that those who would populate the New World shared so lofty a concept. In a series of papers given before the French Colonial Historical Society in April, 1978, Glenn Conrad, Mathé Allain, and Carl Brasseaux argued convincingly that a combination of such factors led to a policy of forced emigration to the Louisiana colony in the late seventeenth and early eighteenth centuries, forcing Governor Jean Baptiste Le Moyne de Bienville to lament that the royal policies left him with "a bunch of deserters, contraband salt dealers, and rogues."[2] Philip Boucher, in a paper delivered before the Western Society for French History in 1978, explores problems in dealing with French migration in the *Ancien Régime.* He discusses all of the old arguments for the failure of emigration policies: Frenchmen loved the homeland too much, there was a failure of the absolutist state to limit governmental interference in the mercantile adventure, there was under-population, etc., etc. Boucher then offers another intriguing view:

> These incomplete or inadequate explanations of French reluctance to inhabit the American wilderness rarely address the crucial question of French images of the New World. Any plausible analysis of the Old Regime's colonial difficulties should emphasize French impressions of this "strange new land" and their relationship to emigration patterns.[3]

The persistence of this problem of migration continues under the Republic, suggesting that it sprang from some deeply embedded failure to conceptualize empire in terms of French-populated colonies. In the Archives Nationales, Section d'outre-mer, in Rue Oudinot in Paris, are hundreds of cartons of documents and papers known as the collection of the Comité française pour l'outre-mer. In working in this collection, I ran across many letters from French persons, in the late nineteenth and early twentieth centuries, seeking information on emigration to Africa, both north and subSahara. Many were written in poor French, telling tales of hardship in France, looking for a new life in the colonies. The response from Joseph Chailley was always direct, cold, and discouraging. Frankly put, there was little encouragement for French people to settle in these new lands, and the official and unofficial voices of expansionism saw the New Imperialism as not for the colonist. To be sure, there was always interest on the part of some colonialists in the colonies as a possible outlet for the impoverished of France; many were intrigued by America's westward expansion and equally fascinated by the system of Indian Reservations. But for the bulk of those French persons interested in a brave new world, there were bewildering reports of a new paradise which was at the same time a savage land filled with physical and moral dangers. Like the Old Empire, the New Imperialism never presented a consistent view of the empire to would-be settlers or investors. This seems to be true for the whole fabric of French imperial expansion from the *Ancien Régime* to the twentieth century.

Many French writers, from Marc Lescarbot in his *Histoire de la Nouvelle France* (1609) to Pierre Loti portraying Morocco in *Le Roman d'un Spahi* (1881), consistently employed the motif of exoticism in describing these acquired territories. *Exotisme* sold books, and many Frenchmen eagerly bought up the travel tales, and later the novel, because of the setting. The Fleur de Lys or the Tricolor surely amassed more glory for waving over these strange, perfumed lands filled with whirling tribesmen or enticing veiled women. Martine Astier Loutfi, a leading scholar in the field of French colonialism and literature, has written:

> The fear that colonization would destroy the natural paradisiac world, combined with strong nationalist sentiments, gave to French colonization some of its peculiarities—its paternalistic naiveté, its moral concerns and its ostentatious contempt for economic profits.[4]

If this is the case, and it appears to be one of the most constant threads in the tapestry of colonialism, then it may explain why the French empire was never really painted as a very hospitable place for a New France to be established.

Scholars in recent years have apparently become skeptical of the traditional explanations for imperialism in general, and it follows that these same writers have brought into doubt some long-held assumptions about France's lack of enthusiasm for colonization. Carl Brasseaux has said of Louisiana's image in the late seventeenth and early eighteenth centuries:

> The failure of voluntary emigration was largely the product of Louisiana's stereotype in France. Seventeenth century explorers Hennepin and La Hontan had forged the initial stereotype by consistently depicting the province as a wilderness inhabited by redmen who were paradoxically barbaric, yet noble, but always dangerous.[5]

One finds here the reason for the dilemma of colonial emigration in the metropole's view of the new world, New France as well as Louisiana. Travel accounts and other works written about the New World were meant to excite and to tantalize, but they did both too well. Cornelius J. Jaenen has made it clear that writers such as Lescarbot constantly contradicted themselves in their accounts of New France and rose to the heights of expression in indicating that with the Indians France had an opportunity to perhaps find the lost tribes of Israel, convert the heathen, and really see something unusual, something never heard of in France before.[6]

Writing in the *Revue française d'histoire d'outre-mer,* Olive Dickason has stated that

> Europe's discovery of the Amerindian is usually represented as being her first large-scale encounter with man living in a state of nature. According to this view, it was that experience which was largely responsible for the development of the European idea of *l'homme sauvage,* the savage who could be either noble or debased, but who in any event was not civilized.[7]

If this was the Savage Man, living without laws, without the trappings of civilization as Europeans knew it, and without the True Religion, then it followed that it fell to Europe to bring the benefits of legal systems, clothes, and Christian salvation to the

New World. It also followed, as Jaenen, Boucher, and Brasseaux suggest, that while it was perfectly all right for Jesuits and *coureurs de bois* to go among them, the "average" French person would not really want to try to settle in a land inhabited by men and women who were savage. Thus the various accounts of New France and Louisiana backfired in France.

To reinforce the reluctance of imperialist effort in France, two stereotypes developed, one applicable in large measure to New France and the other to Louisiana. It appears that the description of the Indians in New France, while inconsistent, tended to paint a rather frightening view, one which would make a metropolitan French person think twice about migration to North America. Louisiana, on the other hand, soon became known as a dumping ground for the worst and the most unfortunate in French society, and a policy of forced migration, drawing from the prisons and the impoverished areas of France, was the only solution to the problem of a colony which was seen as one vast swamp, inhabited by huge alligators and fierce Indians. After the 1713 Treaty of Utrecht brought a period of peace to Europe, interest was revived in settling Louisiana, and the program proposed by the Comte de Pontchartrain's project was bitterly opposed by some of Louis XIV's advisors, who saw little good in a program which brought ne'er-do-wells, thieves, and other drains on French society to the colony at the mouth of the Mississippi.[8]

Regardless of the pictures painted by returning colonists, travelers, and administrators, interest in the new lands remained. Explorers such as Cartier reported seeing hairy beings with one leg hopping through the forests of New France, and Champlain stated that he had been forced to stop an exploratory mission because of a monster he called the *Gougou*.[9] Cornelius Jaenen has cited the passage as explanation of France's failure to discover a rumored vast horde of gold and silver in the interior of New France:

> The great horrible frightful monster is on the passage leading to this mine, some savages call him Gougou, others the evil mother; because he has the face of a woman and eats all those he can catch.

He is of such frightening height that the top of the highest masts of the tallest ships would not come up to his waist, also having a pouch where he could put a whole ship.[10]

Lescarbot did state that if one was in poverty in France, then New France offered untold opportunity for a life of some comforts. But was this adequate hope when placed against the many accounts of unicorns, unipeds, hairy men, *Le Gougou,* and other sorts of monsters and savages? At least the grim poverty of Old France was familiar; an encounter with the *Gougou* was not. Even the Council of the Marine at Versailles in 1720 reported that in one area of New France there existed "another nation [of Indians] also very numerous whose men have but half a body, one eye, one arm, and one leg. . . ."[11] However, probably as a French reaction to these wondrous tales of His Majesty's newly discovered subjects, the Council hastened at add that the women of this tribe had very perfect bodies: perhaps this was some measure of comfort to the *coureurs de bois* of New France.

Missionaries went into New France to sacrifice themselves for the True Church and to bring the Gospel to these strange peoples, who, it was mused, could be the Ten Lost Tribes, representatives of man in a state of nature before the Fall. But even the church had its doubts about the savages and the land, a land which could not even produce the bread and wine necessary for the Holy Eucharist. By 1649 the initial Jesuit labors along the Huron ended with the destruction of Ste. Marie and the martyrdom of three Jesuit missionaries at the hands of the fierce Iroquois.[12] Was this the land of the New Jerusalem about which many clerics in France had waxed so eloquent? If Ste. Marie among the Hurons was any example, it probably was not. It was difficult enough to keep people in Montreal and Quebec, let alone have any increase in French families outside of those town areas in the so-called wild areas of New France. There were fears that once outside of the towns, Frenchmen became barbarians. Cornelius Jaenen observed:

Frenchmen who settled in New France, according to officialdom's interpretation of the process of colonization, were as apt to regress into a state of barbarism as to forge a good life in the New World.[13]

Carl Brasseaux cites the following passage about the potential for conversion of Indians of the Mississippi Valley, and one can only imagine what effect this must have had on the devout of Old France:

> The Illinois, as most of the Savages of America, being brutish, wild, and stupid and their Manners being so opposite to the Morals of the Gospel, their conversion is to be despair'd of, till time and commerce with the Europeans has removed their natural fierceness and ignorance, and thereby made them more apt to be sensible of the charms of Christianity.[14]

As Brasseaux has demonstrated, these visions of *l'homme sauvage* seriously tarnished the image of Louisiana as well as that of New France, a conclusion which is confirmed by the work of Jaenen, Boucher, Giraud, and others. In dealing with this subject, however, Jack D. L. Holmes warns us "that the total result of French attempts to populate Louisiana with hard working settlers was a failure does not detract from the superior efforts of France to fulfill the dreams of John Law."[15] Certainly there were great efforts made, but in Louisiana as in New France, the perception of the colony mitigated against cheerful migration to the unknown.

In comparing the contemporary French literature—travel accounts, metropolitan propaganda, etc.—the same themes that one finds in regard to New France are present in describing Louisiana. Those interested in this new colony, named for Louis XIV, saw it as the New Jerusalem, a land rich in minerals, a new world of exotic animals and *les hommes sauvages,* ready and eager to hear the Gospel of Christ, preached, of course, by missionaries sent by the True Church. Marcel Giraud tells us that Louisiana was founded as a buffer zone against the British Protestants, eternally opposed to the obvious Glory of France and her Sun King.[16]

Why then did the king and his advisors at Versailles have to resort to forced emigration to this rich, grand land? Again, as in the case of New France, the literature, while extolling the virtues of this country, painted dim views of the Indians, the terrible monsters, and the climate. In short, Louisiana land was portrayed as a swamp, filled with dangers to the body and to the soul. One early explorer stated that the smallest alligator he saw was at least eighteen feet long, giving the impression that some of these dragons were huge monsters, like *Monsieur le Gougou* of New France! In fact, the situation became so critical that several thousand Germans had to be recruited at one point to go to this French colony, an experiment that at first did not fare especially well.[17]

In a system where the state under Louis XIV and his ministers imposed censorship on the presses of France, it is surprising that more attention was not paid to the adverse effects of exciting and convincing reports of monsters, alligators, and wild Indians. Of course Pontchartrain was instrumental in imposing regulations on "the production side of the industry," and he was aware of the impact of the printing industry in France. Be that as it may, discouraging accounts continued to be printed in France, just as dismal, depressing reports continually arrived at Versailles. For example, in a note to Pontchartrain in 1713, a despairing Cadillac wrote that Louisiana was "an unhealthy country, without bread, without wine, without meat and without clothes." What Cadillac wanted for the Louisiana colony was more French women for the male colonists who, it seemed, had a disturbing tendency to cohabit with Indian women, thereby endangering the stability of the colony, which already had a bad reputation in France for its low moral tone.[18]

In a series of articles, Vaughn B. Baker, Amos Simpson, and Mathé Allain have suggested, as a result of preliminary research, that one must also see the great problems of populating the Louisiana colony in the light of the status of women, which, according to the authors, underwent a major alteration in the colony due to the sheer necessity of having them there. Baker has written:

Although emigration to Louisiana was predominantly male, the social disruptions of early death, the property laws which pro-

tected women's rights and the necessities of family survival in a
hostile environment created circumstances which profoundly altered sex-role definitions.[19]

In 1710 Iberville requested that France send to Louisiana "a few
girls, sensible, and well built." Canadians, now residing in
Louisiana, seemed to like Indian women, who were considered
easy, and this sort of alliance led to concubinage which the
Church decried as a threat to the True Faith.[20] When Bienville
refused to marry the ugly daughter of Cadillac it was counted as
a scandal, because she was Christian and French, and they could
have discussed the True Religion.

Reports of problems in climate, relations with the Indians,
and the difficulty of getting wives from France who did not
arrive with a terrible reputation or jail record plagued the Louisiana colony, and these reports had wide circulation in the metropole. Coupled with persistent stories of the terrible hardships
on the Louisiana frontier, these extra tales of difficulties made
Louisiana, despite the desires of Louis XIV and his councilors, a
place where few but the daring or the forced cared to go.

As with the popular views of New France, Louisiana's image
did not inspire confidence in a public already skeptical of the
colonial adventure. It was one thing to thrill to travel accounts;
it was indeed another to actually go to the French colonies in the
New World. As for Louisiana, Glenn Conrad tells us that after
1719, "overnight Louisiana became a term of terror, not only
for illicit salt dealers but for vagabonds, beggars, even the tem-
porarily unemployed."[21] It eventually became a near impossibility to erase the image of Louisiana, in spite of the Indians be-
decked with feathers and gaudy ornamentation who were
paraded about in Paris. There was a sincere effort at this time to
encourage migration to the colony, but it appears that the damage had already been done, since the popular image of Louisiana
in the metropole had been formed.

It would be quite wrong to eliminate from the list of French
North America's ills such problems as economics, the colonial
rivalry between England and France, and the cycle of wars upon
which both states had embarked in the 1690s. But as Philip

Boucher has written, there is a correlation between the views held in the metropole about New France and the desire to migrate. Carl Brasseaux stresses this same theme in regard to Louisiana. The simple question was, would anyone leave a familiar France, even if one faced grim poverty, unreasonable taxes, and a rigid social system rent with discord and bias, for a new land filled with horrible monsters, wild savages, strange half-developed, half-human Indians? The Church certainly painted a terrible picture of spending Hell in eternity; why go there before one's time was up? To say that the French were reluctant imperialists is to present a theme which runs through the whole of French colonial history for over three hundred years. In an article on French views of West Africa in the late nineteenth century, Richard Smith sees much of the same propaganda.[22] In dealing with colonial Algeria in the nineteenth and twentieth century, this writer has seen the same contradictory concept of a land of milk and honey, or should we say bread and wine, which held many grave dangers. This time it was not *le gougou,* a frightening monster, that threatened the *colon,* it was the "Islamic fanatic," veiled, sword-wielding, bent on anti-Christian (anti-French—it was the same thing) atrocities.

The French as colonialists present some disturbing paradoxes to historians. First there was a tendency to talk to Versailles and Paris about the economic value of the empire, from furs of New France to tobacco from Louisiana to grains from Algeria to rubber from Indochina; yet, on the other hand, economic exploitation faced an official contempt for profit. The minds and souls of Indians, Muslims, Annamites, Dahomeans meant more to France, so they said. But could one really bring the benefits of such civilization to those areas which were inhabited by *les hommes sauvages?* Of course they were savages: they spoke no French. Hear the words of the Great French socialist Jean Jaurès in defending expansion into Africa and southeastern Asia in the 1880s: "[our subjects will be upraised] when by intelligence and heart they have learned a little French."[23]

It appears now that the French colonialists, spanning over three hundred years of imperial expansion, played old tunes of glory on broken fifes and drums, tunes that no one, or possibly everyone, heard. The images of the empire, from travel accounts to novels and films in a more modern period, were formed to excite, to interest, to frighten, to sell. The popular image of the empire—be it New France, Louisiana, Algeria, Dahomey, or wherever—was one which in the long run backfired. New France had furs and souls to save, but there was also *le gougou* and the savage with one leg, one eye, and one arm. Louisiana had mounds of emeralds, but also dragons. One could go on. In dealing with reactions of the imperialists of France to the New World, we are also dealing with the whole tapestry of French expansionism, and we can see that their concepts, their fears, and their doubts about these new lands made them reluctant imperialists indeed.

Notes

[1]France under the reign of Louis XIV has been the subject of many scholarly investigations. I have relied heavily on John B. Wolf's *Louis XIV* (New York, 1968); Pierre Golibert, *Louis XIV and Twenty Million Frenchmen* (New York, 1966), especially Chapters 1, 2, and 5; W. H. Lewis, *The Splendid Century: Life in the France of Louis XIV* (New York, 1953), Chapters 3, 6, 7, and 13; Maurice Ashley, *Louis XIV and the Greatness of France* (New York, 1965), Chapters 2, 4, 5, 10–12; Hubert Deschamps, *Méthodes et doctrines coloniales de la France* (Paris, 1953), 1–72; Robert Delavignette and Ch-André Julien, *Les Constructeurs de la France d'outremer* (Paris, 1946), 1–159. One cannot work in French expansionism in America without paying special attention to William J. Eccles, *France in America*, and of course, Marcel Giraud, *Histoire de la Louisiane française*. Gabriel Louis Jaray, *L'Empire française d'Amérique, 1534–1803*, is and remains a classic source for the French in America.

[2]Cited in Glenn R. Conrad, "Emigration Forcée: A French Attempt to Populate Louisiana," 64.

[3]Philip Boucher, "French Images of America and the Evolution of Colonial Theories, 1650–1700," 221.

[4]Martine Astier Loutfi, "The Political Significance of the Exotic Novel," in Alf Heggoy (ed.), *The French Colonial Historical Society Proceedings* Vol. 1 (Athens, Ga., 1976), 15. Also see idem, "North Africa in French Movies, 1895–1921," in Alf Heggoy and James J. Cooke (eds.), *Proceedings of the Fourth Annual Meeting of the French Colonial Historical Society* (Washington, 1979), 132–36. Also: Loutfi, *Littérature et colonialisme, l'expansion coloniale vue dans la littérature romanesque française, 1870–1914* (Paris, 1971).

[5]Carl A. Brasseaux, "The Image of Louisiana and the Failure of Voluntary French Emigration, 1683–1731," 52–53. Also see idem, *A Comparative View of Louisiana, 1699 and 1762: The Journals of Pierre Le Moyne d'Iberville and Jean-Jacques-Blaise d'Abbadie*. These two journals, translated and edited by Brasseaux, give an early and a late view of Louisiana—the animals, Indians, conditions, etc. Throughout one is struck by certain consistencies in respect to Louisiana over many decades.

⁶Cornelius J. Jaenen, "Conceptual Frameworks for French Views of America and Amerindians," 1–22.

⁷Olive Dickason, "The Concept of *l'homme sauvage* and Early French Colonialism in the Americas," 5. For an interesting new work on the concept of *l'homme sauvage* and its effects on Enlightenment France see: Carminella Biondi, *Ces esclaves sont des hommes: Lotta abolizionista e letteratura negrofila nella Francia del settecento* (Pisa, 1979).

⁸Conrad, "Emigration Forcée," 57. Marcel Giraud, *A History of French Louisiana,* 262–63.

⁹Jaenen, "Conceptual Frameworks," 13–14.

¹⁰Ibid.

¹¹Ibid., 14. Also see idem, "The Images of New France in the History of Lescarbot," 209–19.

¹²Eccles, *France in America,* 45–7.

¹³Jaenen, "French Views of New France and Canadians," 1.

¹⁴Brasseaux, "The Image of Louisiana," 47.

¹⁵Jack D. L. Holmes, "The Failure of French Immigration, 1700–1765: A Comment," 67–9.

¹⁶Giraud, *History of French Louisiana,* 91–140.

¹⁷Reinhard Kondert, "German Immigration to French Colonial Louisiana: A Reevaluation," 70–81.

¹⁸Vaughn B. Baker, "Les Louisianaises: A Reconnaissance," 8–9.

¹⁹Ibid., 12.

²⁰Cited in Mathé Allain, "Manon Lescaut et ses consoeurs: Women in the Early French period, 1700–1731," in James J. Cooke, (ed.), *Proceedings of the Fifth Meeting of the French Colonial Historical Society,* 18.

²¹Conrad, "Emigration Forcée," 62.

²²Richard L. Smith, "A Popular View of Imperialism: The French Mass Press and the Conquest of West Africa." in Cooke (ed.), *Fifth Meeting, FCHS,* 51–7.

²³*Jean Jaurès, textes choisis I, contre la guerre et la politique coloniale* (Paris, 1959), 75. This is not to imply that Jaurès was an admirer of colonialism, but he did see a definite value in the *mission civilisatrice.* What disgusted Jaurès was the tendency to see concepts such as the *mise en valeur* eclipse the civilizing mission of France.

Reluctant Imperialist:
France in North America

GLENN R. CONRAD

•

The story of France's participation in the Great-Power struggle for control of large portions of the Western Hemisphere can best be described as a century and a half of hesitancy and half-heartedness. There is little substantive evidence to indicate that the French nation between 1600 and 1762 possessed a zeal for colonial endeavors comparable to that found among other European nations, particularly the Spaniards, Portuguese, British, and Dutch. Indeed, as France entered the modern age, Frenchmen remained ideologically divided on the subject of empire, with the balance weighted heavily in favor of the internalists. They were, however, periodically faced with active, vocal opposition from the expansionist minority.

Careful investigation reveals that three elements within the national power structure had it within their means to formulate long-range colonial programs. These were the crown, the corporate sector, and the church. Throughout the seventeenth century, these elements repeatedly failed to assume this responsibility and by doing so doomed France's initial imperial effort. Governments from Henry IV to Louis XV repeatedly neglected the creation of an ideological framework for empire, in general, and a program for North American colonialism, in particular. The crown's neglect in this regard was seconded and compounded by that of the corporate sector and the church. Thus, when a handful of French imperialists succeeded in establishing the foundations of a Gallic empire in North America, their work was soon eroded by a national elite unwilling to commit themselves fully to this extension of the motherland. Once international rivals recognized this tendency, France's days of empire were numbered.

As the religious wars of the sixteenth century ended and the

Bourbon dynasty entered upon the throne of France, the French elites were far more concerned with reestablishing order and rebuilding the nation's economy than they were with pouring treasures into a wilderness half a world away. As a consequence, the new king, Henry IV, when formulating policies for the reign, *could* elicit ministerial consensus for moves designed to enhance France's prestige in Europe. When, however, he attempted for the same reason a colonial intrusion into the Americas, ministerial opposition coalesced. Henry therefore discovered that for France to enter the international game of imperialism, her colonial probes had to appear as a cooperative venture of the crown and French corporate interest, with the latter assuming the major financial burden. For the next century or so, Henry's successors would indulge in the same subterfuge.[1]

The French anti-expansionist element was always well represented at court during the seventeenth and eighteenth centuries. Early in the era their voice was none other than that of Baron Rosny, the future Duke of Sully, the finance minister. Rosny set the pattern for many of his successors when he argued that a sound national economy was far more important to France than were colonies. When, in 1603, Henry ignored Rosny's advice and sanctioned the first company under Champlain to trade with Canada, the minister declared that "there is no kind of riches to be expected from all those countries of the New World which are beyond the fortieth degree of latitude."[2]

Rosny's statement was quite in tune with the pre-industrial economic thinking of the times, but certainly did not reflect the thinking of the Commercial Revolution. The commodities which European metropoles could not supply for national markets were primarily the plantation crops: tea, coffee, tobacco, sugar, cocoa, and some naval stores. Colonies, therefore, were desirable only when there was sufficient national demand for these products, for it was inconceivable at the time to produce for export to other countries. Because these commodities were largely limited to the tropical and subtropical zones, between the fortieth degrees of north and south latitude, Rosny's appraisal was seen as having merit. Moreover, given France's previous experiences in Brazil and Florida, there was little available to them in the tropical or subtropical regions of the Americas.[3]

Generally speaking, funding for expansionism in seventeenth-century France had to come from the three major vested interests: the crown, the commercial sector, and the church. Since colonialism was expensive, indeed a national luxury, only these three centers of wealth were capable of the necessary expenditure. Expansionists, in and out of the ranks of these vested interests, therefore maintained a constant pressure on king, cleric, and merchant for investment funding, while dangling before each one visions of rewards such as aggrandizement, religious mission, or unparalleled profits. The agents of expansionism, those who actually went out to the colonies, were usually young and ambitious, possessing the youthful dream of power and riches before attaining the age of thirty. They were usually minor military officers, minor clergymen, and the younger sons of the French bourgeoisie.

Whenever the power brokers of France remained unconvinced of the merits of a colonial venture, an agent seeking funding would spend a season, often at his own expense, in the colonial wilds, followed by a glowing report (usually in person) to king, cardinal, or corporate executive. This ploy would generally elicit a degree of financial assistance for the desired colonial scheme. The enterprising expansionist might even succeed in securing support from two or more vested interests. In most cases, however, financial assistance was far below what was requested or what was required to undertake a basic colonial endeavor. This, indeed, was to be the story of French colonialism in North America.

Economic motivation for the exploitation of Canada was sufficient to warrant a limited capital investment to produce dried fish and beaver pelts for the French market. The overall financial risk was so great, however, that merchants sought a monopolistic trade with North America to insure a profitable return on their investment. Moreover, investors and traders were quick to discover that the indigenous American population would supply the desired colonial products far more cheaply than Europeans. A European settlement always had the potential of becoming a financial drain as soon as it began to demand the services of civilization: schools, hospitals, law and order.

Thus, the usual commercial response to colonial proposals was to recruit and fund a few stalwart individuals willing to chance the perils of the Atlantic crossing, the dangers of the seemingly endless wilderness, and the primitive culture of the indigenous population. Such individuals could be maintained abroad for a fraction of the cost of an emigrant family. Because the colonial exploitation of North America remained a basically short-run and marginal activity of French corporate interests, the systematic development of a New France was virtually impossible.

One last word about corporate investment in North America. Like good businessmen everywhere, French merchants sought ways to underwrite or insure their American investment as best they could. What better way to accomplish this (in the days before Lloyds of London) than to enlist church support for a colonial intrusion into the primitive cultures of America. In the face of such commercial-clerical cooperation, the mercantile exploitation of the natives, together with all of the resulting ramifications, could be morally justified.[4] Such justification was becoming necessary in some European quarters following Spain's century-long abuse of Mexican and Peruvian natives.

French colonization of the St. Lawrence and Mississippi watersheds can be seen falling into eight epochs: four periods of short-lived vitality and expansion interspersed with four longer eras of stagnation and decline. The eras of growth correspond roughly to the years from 1603 to 1627, 1662 to 1682, 1698 to 1702, and an artificial period of growth between 1718 and 1721. The periods of vitality more or less correspond to years of peace for France, further evidence that French North American colonialism was fundamentally weak and erratically structured, usually depending on a meager cooperative enterprise between crown and corporate entity.

The initial era of expansion came when Henry IV commissioned Pierre du Gua, Sieur de Monts, lieutenant over the vast region of Acadia and the St. Lawrence valley. This title would have been meaningless, of course, had not Henry also granted de Monts a ten-year monopoly over the fur trade of these regions. A further term of the commission was to the effect that sixty persons be settled in the new territory. Already recognizing the disinclination of French farmers to quit their homesteads for foreign adventures without the proper economic incentive, the commission allowed for the transportation of vagabonds, if other colonists could not be found. Thus was generated a French colonial policy that would be pursued for the next century and which would prove to be one of the weakest elements in the French penetration of North America. Vagabonds, prostitutes, smugglers, and criminals, particularly the urban variety skimmed from the whey of Parisian society, did not in any sense of the term constitute the character of true colonists. As was typical of these cooperative ventures, it was short-lived. De Monts and his lieutenant, Samuel de Champlain, maintained their base in Acadia for only three years. By 1607 the merchants of northern France, who were bitterly opposed to the monopoly trading rights granted de Monts, succeeded in having the fur trade opened to all the king's subjects.

Even though the attempt at monopolistic exploitation failed, there would be numerous subsequent attempts, demonstrating repeatedly the short-range view of French colonialism. Perhaps two of the more celebrated attempts should be mentioned before analyzing this approach to colonization. In 1627, Cardinal Richelieu, chief minister to Louis XIII, cancelled all previous grants (which were defunct in any case) and set up a comprehensive Company of New France (known also as the Company of the Hundred Associates) with a perpetual monopoly on the fur trade, full sovereignty over the territory, and a monopoly on all trade except fishing for the next fifteen years, with the duty of organizing settlements so long as only French Roman Catholics were admitted as settlers.[5]

After a difficult beginning, born of troubles with rival English fur traders, the Company of New France soon discovered that it could not defend its territory, it could not reestablish a profitable fur trade, and it could not induce adequate emigration. A few sturdy peasants were recruited for settlement in Canada, but twenty years after the monopoly had been granted, there were no more than 300 European settlers, all of whom were dependent on the fur trade and on European food and supplies.

Nearly a century later, the French government was still attempting to establish colonies through the aegis of monopolistic companies. To paraphrase Marcel Giraud, it is difficult to determine under exactly what circumstances Louis XIV decided to revive the idea of the proprietary company as a colonizing agent; suffice it to say that he did, and that this approach to colonization was next applied to Louisiana, that is, the Mississippi Valley from Illinois to the Gulf.[6]

Louis XIV's decision was to cede a monopoly of Louisiana's commerce to Antoine Crozat, the king's counsellor and a wealthy merchant. Reluctantly, Crozat entered into the agreement. He was to have a monopoly on the commerce of the colony for fifteen years. In return, his only obligation was to send two ships each year to Louisiana, transporting ten young men or women and twenty-five tons of goods and munitions for the service of the king.

Even such a modest arrangement as this proved to be a failure. Within five years of obtaining the monopoly, Crozat was happily surrendering it. Giraud concludes that he failed because "he confined himself to a narrow commercial policy supported by insufficient capital, with no other aim than his quest for immediate profit." Crozat, a successful businessman, could not see how it was possible to breathe new economic life into a colony so sparsely populated. Moreover, neither he nor the government was prepared to underwrite the cost of establishing a viable agricultural colony in the Mississippi Valley.[7]

The first grantees of royal monopoly, de Monts and Champlain, and every proprietor or company thereafter, learned a lesson that apparently could never be fully understood by French policymakers at Versailles: interlopers—French, Indian, or European—could easily make a mockery of any monopoly in such a vast, underpopulated land where law and order was an ideal, never a fact. But Crozat was not the last to experience the failure of this approach. As late as 1731, when the Company of the Indies relinquished its patent on Louisiana, there were loud complaints from company officials that the monopoly was not only leaking, it was occasionally hemorrhaging.

The problem with the monopolistic approach to colonization was that the method was fundamentally flawed. It was not because there were no families in France ready to emigrate to a new life in Canada and Louisiana; there were plenty of these, particularly in the eastern provinces. The problem was that the government failed for over one hundred years to recognize that the colonial program to which it adhered was incapable of giving the emigrant what he sought most: a better way of life than he knew in France. Privileged corporations held a monopoly on the only trades in which there was a chance of acquiring wealth. The government and/or its corporate partners thereby kept the monopoly on all rewarding opportunities. By doing so, French governments from Henry IV to Louis XV, and ministers from Sully to Richelieu to Colbert to John Law, effectively used the power of the state to thwart emigration, colonization, and the creation of a genuine New France.

Only during the thirty short years that Louisiana was a royal colony, and then only in the brief interlude of truce between the War of the Austrian Succession and the outbreak of the Seven Years' War, did the French government actively sponsor the emigration of French peasants, mainly Alsatians, as yeoman farmers in the New World. The response to this novel policy was so overwhelming that officials became alarmed, and had not war broken out with England in 1756, the government would probably have taken steps to halt the peasant exodus.[8] Even in peacetime the warnings of the anti-expansionists were heeded: France needs her manpower at home, for world hegemony will be determined in Europe, not in far-flung empire. Frenchmen continued to subscribe to that concept at least through the Napoleonic era—a theory which the British proved fallacious as early as 1759 on the Plains of Abraham.

The fact remains, however, that reluctantly or not France did create a major sphere of colonial influence in North America in what would be termed New France and Louisiana. It is equally factual to say that neither of these two entities was the result of well-formulated, comprehensive policies which evolved with or complemented national economic or foreign policies.

What, then, was the catalyst of France's North American empire? A studied examination of France's role in the St. Lawrence and Mississippi valleys will demonstrate that empire was the result of a few colonial agents—a handful of imaginative, ambitious, perhaps ingenious men. They were the individuals who possessed a vision of French empire in North America—a vision, however, that was only partially shared from time to time by some of their countrymen in the metropole.

Seen from this vantage point, it would be a simple matter to adopt, as some nineteenth-century historians did, the "Great Man" theory for the colonization of French North America. For the modern historian, however, it is also easy to recall that "great men are only celebrated puppets, pushed ahead on the moving front of history." Great men do not make or determine history; their greatness stems from their ability to sense the next phase of the historical process. They identify themselves with the wave of the future, conform their purposes to the march of events, and thereby become inexorably identified with a chapter of history. Great men, moreover, do not stand alone; they simply march in the vanguard of history.[9] Whenever, and for whatever reason, they deviate from the course of the mass, their label quickly changes and the hero of today becomes the fool of tomorrow.

There are a handful of men who must be recognized for their exceptional vision and energy in laying the foundations of a French empire in North America. Among these I would include Samuel de Champlain; Jean Talon; Louis de Buade, comte de Frontenac; René-Robert Cavelier de La Salle; and the Le Moyne brothers, Pierre and Jean-Baptiste, better known to history as Iberville and Bienville. Each man provided depth and meaning to the conceptualization of a French North American empire. Each, in his own way, contributed far more to French imperialism than has been generally recorded in monographs and biographies. If the French imperial dream in North America was ultimately shattered on the Plains of Abraham, that was in no way owing to a lack of mental acumen and tireless energy on the part of these truly brilliant strategists.

The pioneering work of Champlain is well recorded and needs no elaboration here. Let me simply recall, however, that it was he who kept the flame of the imperial idea flickering during the first three decades of France's hesitant penetration of North America. It was he, also, who recognized what is considered to be the most militarily strategic site on the continent and there founded what would become the core of French culture in the Americas, the city of Quebec.

Jean Talon ranks as one of the greatest of France's empire builders. Treading in Champlain's footsteps barely 30 years after Champlain's death, Talon, in many ways, projected Champlain's imperial vision into the late seventeenth century and complemented it with his own theories. He was Intendant of New France from 1665 to 1672, but his thinking affected the continent long after his name was associated with its administration. We must attribute to Talon's imagination a new direction for France's penetration of North America. The natural inclination of a young administrator might have been to achieve short-run success by urging more rapid exploitation of the fur trade. Talon, however, rejected this approach for two reasons: furs were a highly speculative economic resource that would be quickly expended; secondly, and more importantly, the fur trade would direct French exploration and colonization toward the north and west, an area that Talon astutely perceived to be a dead end for French imperialism.

He therefore not only altered the direction of the French thrust from the northwest to the south and west but he also laid the groundwork for a viable colonial economy. His genius was responsible for propelling his country's interests into the Mississippi Valley and across Sully's demarcation line into the promised land south of the fortieth parallel. The new policy was quickly implemented and realized startling results with the celebrated exploration of Marquette and Jolliet.

Louis de Buade, comte de Frontenac, would guide the destiny

of New France as governor from 1672 to 1682 and from 1689 to 1701. Unfortunately for Canada, Frontenac and Talon were intellectual and political rivals, and, in the end, Talon was recalled to France. Fortunately for the French imperial dream, Talon's vision was shared by Frontenac and Frontenac's close associate, René-Robert Cavelier de La Salle.

The results of the Marquette-Jolliet expedition were not known until after Talon had sailed for France. The explorers' conclusion that the Mississippi flowed into the Gulf of Mexico, however, set the Canadian frontier afire. Their journey confirmed that there was a practicable waterway from Canada to the south. It also gave promise that a French North American empire was not only possible, but could be strategically designed to confine the English imperialists east of the Allegheny Mountains.

With that in mind, Frontenac undertook a series of tactical moves designed to encircle the English and thereby halt, perhaps reverse, their colonial advance into North America. Toward this end, he thwarted the move of the Iroquois, Indian allies of the English, into the Ohio and Illinois country with the construction of Fort Frontenac on Lake Ontario. The fort was well sited for the purpose, impressed the Iroquois, and prevented a threatened desertion of France's Indian allies to the English.

Frontenac's next move was taken in cooperation with La Salle. René-Robert Cavelier de La Salle has been portrayed by historians from Parkman to Osler as a many-faceted individual displaying the characteristics of the adventurer, the speculator, the explorer. Seldom, however, are his exploits as an imperialist emphasized. As such, La Salle, first working with Talon and then with Frontenac, sought to develop an economic base which would tie together the commerce of the St. Lawrence, the Great Lakes, and the Mississippi. Acting upon and projecting the thinking of Talon and Frontenac, La Salle understood that to establish a continent-wide economic base, the French would have to establish their presence, for "a series of posts would give to France the right to the heart of the continent; having made such a claim and substantiated it with forts, France would then colonize and rule."[10] By 1682 La Salle undertook his most celebrated mission and, as every schoolchild knows, swept down the Mississippi to its mouth, claiming the watershed for France and calling it Louisiana. From the strategic point of view, the first step had been taken toward enclosing and restricting the English colonies. If the French now went on to establish a defensible colony at the great river's mouth and to develop in the valley a viable colony, England's position on the continent was surely threatened.[11]

Understanding this strategy probably better than any of their contemporaries in France or in the New World were the brothers Le Moyne. Iberville and Bienville were to be the last in this series of remarkable French empire builders. They were Franco-Americans, more precisely Canadians, and as such they had not only the benefit of prior theoretical considerations but also their experience on the American frontier.

For Iberville, sensing the dangers of France's weak colonial position in the late seventeenth century, the conclusion of peace in Europe in 1698 was the signal that France must consolidate her hold on the Mississippi Valley and establish her presence in the Gulf-Caribbean region. To this end, he persuaded the crown to launch a series of expeditions designed to stabilize the French position in Louisiana. Stabilization could come only after a suitable location had been found for a southern counterweight to Quebec—thus forming a geopolitical axis sweeping southwestward from the St. Lawrence to the Gulf of Mexico.[12]

Iberville did not live to see his plan implemented, but his brother Bienville, imbued with comparable appreciation for imperial strategy, pushed forward the idea of a French presence in the Mississippi Valley. In 1718, in the face of seemingly insurmountable odds, Bienville selected a site on the Mississippi that not only supervised traffic on the river but was also in a position to repulse foreign probes into the continent's soft underbelly. That site and the ensuing colonial settlement was, of course, New Orleans.

Bienville would spend the next quarter century struggling to establish the French presence along the northern Gulf Coast and its outposts along the Mississippi and its tributaries. When he left the colony in 1742, he must have harbored mixed emotions for the future of France in North America. He saw weak and vacillating colonial policy continuing to emanate from Versailles at a time when the situation in America had reached the point where the slightest encouragement from the metropole could have made the difference between success and failure. Bienville, the last of the great French imperialists in America, would unfortunately live to see all of his work and that of his predecessors discarded by a careless monarchy. He did not live to know that twenty-odd years later this indecisive monarchy would itself be swept aside by the rush of history.

Thus, between Talon's arrival in New France and Bienville's founding of New Orleans, a total of fifty-three years had elapsed. In that time several men of extraordinary imagination and vigor had laid the groundwork for a French North American empire that could have been the Gallic counterpart of Hispanic South America or of British India. Within less than fifty years after the founding of New Orleans, however, France had dispossessed herself of this immense territory.

The question arises, why? For an answer I must return to my premise that France did not possess, throughout the seventeenth century and into the eighteenth, the political and economic framework for empire. This shortcoming was largely owing to the ideological split in the metropole between internalists and expansionists—a situation which had the effect of producing at best a hesitant, half-hearted approach to colonialism. This, in turn, meant that any colonial activity would have to be short-range in scope and generally insufficiently funded. Thus, although the genius for empire building was present in seventeenth-century France, as we have seen, the seed of empire that was planted in North America was never allowed to bloom and come to fruition. French governments from Henry IV to Louis XV were never more than reluctant imperialists.

Notes

[1] A treatment of France's colonial policy toward North America can be found in A. J. Grant, *The French Monarchy (1483–1789)*.

[2] Hesketh Pearson, *Henry of Navarre, The King Who Dared* (New York, 1963), 181.

[3] For an account of the French attempts to settle in Florida and Brazil, see Charles W. Baird, *History of the Huguenot Emigration to America*, 2 vols. (New York, 1885), 1, 21–77; also see William J. Eccles, *France in America*, 1–28.

[4] For a brief treatment of the merchants and missionaries in French North America, see Eccles, *France in America*, Chapter 2, 19–59.

[5] James Breck Perkins, *Richelieu and the Growth of French Power* (London, 1926), 227. Perkins remarks (225) that "France had already begun a career of colonial development which, if it had been pursued with intelligence, might have made her one of the greatest colonial powers of the world."

[6] Marcel Giraud, *A History of French Louisiana*, 249.

[7] Ibid., 253.

[8] For a discussion of French emigration to Louisiana in the 1750s, see Glenn R. Conrad, "L'Immigration alsacienne en Louisiane, 1753-1759," 565-77.

[9] *The Great Ideas: A Syntopicon of Great Books of the Western World* 1, 717.

[10] E. E. Rich, "Europe and North America," in *The New Cambridge Modern History*, vol. V, *The Ascendancy of France, 1648–88*, ed. F. L. Carsten (Cambridge, 1961), 362.

[11] E. E. Rich expresses this view in ibid.

[12] For a detailed discussion of French strategy for the Gulf-Caribbean area following the Peace of Ryswick, see William Edward Dunn, *Spanish and French Rivalry in the Gulf Region of the United States, 1678–1702*.

Andrés de Pez and Spanish Reaction to French Expansion into the Gulf of Mexico

JACK D. L. HOLMES

•

WHETHER GREAT MEN influence the times in which they live or whether momentous events produce outstanding men, Admiral Andrés de Pez was an outstanding Spanish naval hero whose life was spent protecting the Spanish Empire and opposing Spain's enemies, particularly the French. Like his contemporary, Sieur de La Salle, Pez was at the heart of the international struggle for control over the Mississippi Valley and the Gulf of Mexico. Except to a few specialists, however, Pez is relatively unknown: no American automobile was ever named for him. As Douglas Southall Freeman wrote, "A man's place in history depends, in large part, on care and fortune—care in preserving essential records, and good fortune in having a biographer who uses those records sympathetically."

Spain's insistence on full reports and correspondence and archival preservation of those primary sources has saved these essential records. Until now, however, Pez has received less-than-sympathetic treatment by historians. One of the earliest treatments of his life and career, the 1917 work of William Edward Dunn, gave the following appraisal of Pez:

> In spite of his steady rise to prominence, Pez does not seem to have been a man of brilliant attainments. He was intensely egotistical, often unpopular with his associates and subordinates, especially during his younger years, and guilty of serious mistakes, which came near interrupting permanently his upward career. He seems to have been born under a lucky star, however, and succeeded in retaining the royal favor in spite of his indiscretions.[1]

Yet, upon examining the same sources, it is possible for an

observer to reach a different value judgment on Pez and his contributions, at least a more kindly evaluation.

He was a product of his times, bridging the closing years of the Austrian or Hapsburg dynasty in Spain and the opening stages of the Bourbon dynasty of the eighteenth century. These were years during which the Spanish preeminence in North America was challenged by England and France. This was particularly true in the lower Mississippi Valley, the Caribbean Sea, and Spain's proud *mare nostrum,* the Gulf of Mexico. Much has been made of La Salle's April 9, 1682, formal act of possession of the entire Mississippi Valley, but he was hardly the first explorer to reach "the great and mysterious river of the west."[2] Objective writers agree, "there is no doubt that the Spaniards discovered and possessed the delta long before the English or French occupied it. The records of their discoveries bear date of the sixteenth century."[3] And a century ago Congressman Randall L. Gibson from Louisiana gave his equally memorable "March 7 speech" in which he averred "The Spaniards discovered the Mississippi River."[4] By prior exploration and actual settlement dating to the early sixteenth century, Spain's claim to the valley was incontrovertible, and it is difficult to understand just what Chesnel had in mind when he noted that La Salle had taken possession of that same country and, "in conformance with international law, had made of it a French colony."[5]

Still, French aggression against Spanish property was nothing new. French pirates had ravaged the Caribbean during the sixteenth and seventeenth centuries, and it was no secret to Spain that Louis XIV and his minister Colbert desired a French foothold in the Gulf of Mexico. As usual, Spanish foreign policy and defense served as a reaction to the chess-like moves of another power, either the Dutch or the English, and now the French. The Spanish council recognized French aims in the Gulf of Mexico and Caribbean Sea and directed all their resources in an effort to prevent such an imminent danger to Spanish shipping and the rich mines of New Spain.[6]

Two outstanding Mexican viceroys tried to carry out Spanish policy in stopping the French. The twenty-ninth of New Spain's colonial rulers was Don Melchor Porto-Carrero Laso de la Vega, better known as the Conde de Monclova, who took office on November 16, 1686. On November 20, 1688, he turned over the reins of office to the thirtieth viceroy, Don Gaspar de la Cerda Sandoval Silva y Mendoza, more familiarly known as the Conde de Galve, who was replaced on February 27, 1696.[7] Together these two brilliant administrators faced the challenges of French pirates and the La Salle expedition, reorganized the naval defenses of New Spain, and set into motion initial steps which led to the successful establishment of a Spanish presidio at Pensacola in 1698.

In all these exciting movements and naval combat, Andrés de Pez had a key role. If, as his critics have charged, he was less than the man for all seasons, he must be considered as the right man for the right job in the aftermath of La Salle's 1682 voyage. Spanish mariners from the valleys and slopes of the Bay of Biscay have earned a well-deserved reputation for courage and persistence. From a traditional naval family of Vizcaya came Andrés de Pez, although he was born in Cádiz, where his father, Captain Andrés de Pez y Capetillo, was stationed as commander of the warship San Antonio, the flagship of the Armada de Andalucía. Our protagonist's mother, María de Malzárraga, came from the Valley of Orozco, not too far from the Sopuerto Valley town of Valmaseda, the ancestral home of Pez. The infant was baptized in the Cádiz cathedral by Father Joan Gonzáles on July 10, 1657, with the name of Andrés Matías de Pez y Malzárraga.[8]

At the age of sixteen the younger Andrés entered the naval guard as an ordinary soldier and rose through the ranks to become Admiral in the famed Barlovento Squadron. In his early career, however, he served on convoy ships from Spain to the Americas and back, and it was at this time that he became a skilled draftsman, cartographer, and naval cosmographer. He came by his life-long distrust of the French quite naturally: he fought at the Battle of Palermo (June 2, 1676), where he saw his brother and father, both naval captains, die in mortal combat with the French.[9]

Pez served in the ranks of ensign and captain before becoming commander of a Spanish company with the Armada de Barlovento—the famed Windward Squadron organized by Mexican viceroy Don Lope Diez de Armendaris, Marqués de Cadereyta, in 1638–1639. This naval guard had as its primary purpose the mounting of search-and-destroy missions to wipe out piracy in the New World. In one sense, the squadron represented the sheriff's deputy riding shotgun on the stagecoach to prevent bandits from robbing it on the highway. The Armada represented law and order trying to protect legitimate Spanish commerce against the Dutch, English, and French bandits, the so-called privateersmen who were eagerly sanctioned and rewarded by their home governments, as Sir Francis Drake was by Queen Elizabeth I when he succeeded in raiding Spanish ports and bringing home the booty to share with his joyful merchant backers. Once again, Spanish policy was a reaction to another nation's threats.

During the viceregal term of Antonio de la Cerda y Aragón, Marqués de Laguna (1680–1686), the pirate attacks against New Spain caused considerable trouble. They struck at Veracruz in 1683, where a pirate named "Lorenzillo" held the townspeople hostage in the church and threatened to burn them alive if a huge ransom was not paid. Two years later, the pirates ravaged the coast of Campeche, and the Barlovento Squadron was charged with their extermination.[10] In one of the battles in which he was engaged against these pirates, Pez was wounded five times and saw sixty-five of his men killed. Pez quickly won a reputation for courage and recklessness in his daring.[11] An alliterative epitaph on Pez's tomb recalls these exploits: "The bravest of men and deserving of fame, fulfilled his measure and the worth of his name. He led a fleet against gold-thirsty pirates, another Tiphys, tamer of the sea . . . before whose sight the surge of Tethys lay subsided while the hard-pressed pirate panted."[12]

On June 18, 1686, Captain Pez was named infantry commander for the presidio at Veracruz.[13] Since the fortress of San Juan de Ulúa was barely a mile from the town, this "strongest fort in the New World" became Pez's headquarters, and he held the title of *Castellano,* roughly equivalent to a castle-warden or military governor.[14]

Perhaps the Spaniards did not totally defeat the French pirates in the Gulf, as has been suggested,[15] but during the time Pez was around, they were definitely controlled. But, as in physics, "to every action there is an opposite and equal *reaction,*" so the 1682 and 1684 expeditions of La Salle stirred Spanish administrators, captains of the sea and land, and our hero, Andrés de Pez, to undertake vigorous defense of Spanish hegemony in the Gulf of Mexico.

It is an almost-Biblical recital: Peñalosa begat La Salle and La Salle begat Pez! Diego de Peñalosa was the mendacious Spanish turncoat who proposed to Louis XIV an expedition to drive the Spaniards from their fabulous mines in northern New Spain,[16] and this supposedly led to the La Salle expedition. A host of campaigns, expeditions, and search-and-destroy missions were sent by Viceroy Conde de Monclova, and Pez had an important role in several of the naval expeditions which resulted in the discovery of the battered remains of the French settlement near Matagorda Bay (called San Bernardo then) and led inexorably to the strong Spanish defense post of Pensacola in 1698.[17]

Colbert and Louis XIV justified this aggression against Spain and usurpation of Spanish territorial claims on the flimsy grounds that Spanish weakness was "an invitation to the French to force their old colonial rival to relinquish another share of Adam's inheritance. . . . Irresistibly, the warmer regions of the south, more like the climate and vegetation at home, exercised their appeal on many Frenchmen acquainted with conditions in North America."[18] Folmer denies Spain had any "moral recognition" for her prior claims in America because those claims were not based on recognized moral principles but on "arbitrary, scholastic theories, easily questioned by other nations." Then Folmer revives the old *leyenda negra* by concluding that "this very lack of justice of the Spanish claims [!] and her cruel dealings with the Indians constituted a future menace to Spanish empire."[19]

Spain was not an idle spectator to these French machinations, however, and despite William Robertson's assertion that Spain did not maintain "a regular communication of either public or private intelligence, between the mother country and its American settlements,"[20] the truth is that Spain learned quickly of what France was doing and why. The first major expedition, the "Spanish Re-Exploration of the Gulf Coast in 1686," as Irving Leonard described it, was entrusted to two experienced Barlovento Squadron officers, Juan Enríquez Barroto and Antonio Romero, both captains and pilots. As Juan Jordán de Reina recorded the cruise in his diary, the *Nuestra Señora de la Concepción y San José* sailed from Veracruz on November 21, 1685, and from Havana on January 3, 1686. By February 6 they were at Pensacola Bay, which they recognized as the best harbor on the northern shores of the Gulf. They returned to Veracruz and were anchored March 13, 1686, and Jordán de Reina completed his diary on March 16.[21] "If this expedition resulted in failure as far as discovering La Salle's colony, or any other French settlement, or even the Bay of Espiritu Santo," writes one authority, "it did succeed as far as Pensacola Bay's having been brought to life after having been forgotten for over a century."[22] Likewise, "a large portion of the Gulf coast had been re-discovered," says Dunn.[23]

Viceroy Conde de Monclova ordered two "pirogues" built for a new expedition, but these were hardly the cajun pirogue common to the bayous of south Louisiana! Equipped with sails and forty oars each, they carried six cannon and a crew of sixty-five men per craft. They were christened *Nuestra Señora del Rosario* and *Nuestra Señora de la Esperanza*. Captain Martín de Rivas commanded the first with Juan Enríquez Barroto as his pilot. Captain Antonio de Iriarte and his pilot Antonio Romero were aboard the other pirogue. On Christmas Day of 1686 they sailed, and reached Tampico on the eastern shores of Mexico three days later. The expedition proceeded carefully northward along the Gulf Coast and then followed the shoreline eastward until they reached Mobile Bay (they called it Espíritu Santo!) on May 22, 1687. Without stopping at Pensacola, the party continued to Havana and from thence returned to Veracruz, where they anchored on July 3, 1687.[24]

Before the two pirogues returned, however, the Spanish

officials became so worried and impatient that Viceroy Conde de Monclova ordered Captains Andrés de Pez and Francisco de Gamarra of the Armada de Barlovento to take advantage of the remaining few weeks of good weather in the Gulf to search for the missing expedition and to keep an eye peeled for possible French settlements. Ironically, three days after Pez and Gamarra sailed from Veracruz, the delayed pirogues finally arrived, but attempts to recall the Pez-Gamarra expediton were unsuccessful.[25]

Captain Pez sailed aboard the frigate *Santo Cristo de San Román,* which left the island-fortress of San Juan de Ulúa guarding the Veracruz harbor on June 30, 1687, and by 4 p.m. on July 3 they were at Tampico (see Fig. 1). Pez's pilot, Captain Luis Gómez Raposo, recorded in his diary the prominent landmarks and soundings of the coast and checked locations of promontories and inlets. On Saturday, August 2, 1687, the expedition had reached the southwest pass of the Mississippi River, which they called the Rio de la Porciúncula.[26] Although previous expeditions had not distinguished among the various mouths of the Mississippi, Pez and Gamarra defied the elements to check each of the four channels through which the Father of Waters spilled the rich accretions of a thousand miles into the delta.

The expedition continued on its easterly course, reaching Mobile Bay after having skirted the Chandeleur Islands in a smaller launch under Captain Pedro de Quintanilla, another pilot aboard the *Santo Cristo de San Román.* It was Monday, August 11, 1687, and the difference in depth as recorded by Julio Enríquez Barroto's expedition was attributed to the difference in seasons; Barroto had been there in winter. The distance between Mobile and Pensacola Bays, however, was closer to eighteen leagues than the thirty usually given in nautical charts.[27]

High seas and contrary winds caused a slight delay, and the expedition did not reach Pensacola Bay until a contrary current reached such force that it was impossible for Pez to enter it. Accordingly, they sailed to the east along Santa Rosa Island and

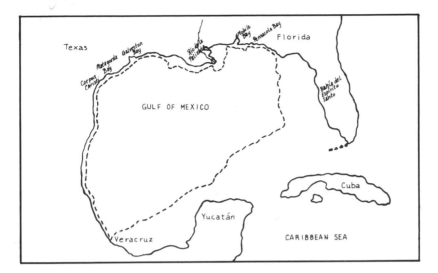

Figure 1. Route of Captain Andrés de Pez, 1687. After Plate VIII, Luis Cebreiro Blanco (ed.), *Colección de diarios y relaciones para la historia de los viajes y descubrimientos*, Vol. IV, following text of voyage.

discovered Choctawhatchee Bay, which was explored with the frigate's launch. By August 18 they were at the fishhook-shaped Cabo de San Blas, which Pez's diarist recorded as "cabo de Apalache." He was apparently confused over the two distinct spots.[28]

It was time to return to Veracruz, but stormy "nor'westers" dashed the frigate up and down the savage waves until the 24th of August, when calm returned for several hours as the wind changed direction. After sixty-seven days of navigation, the ships returned to the fortress of San Juan de Ulúa, anchoring there the afternoon of September 4, 1687.[29] In an excellent summary of this expedition and its importance, Weddle states:

Although Pez and Gamarra had contributed little toward finding La Salle's colony, they did much to advance geographical knowledge of the gulf coast. Not only had they established the true nature of the Mississippi Delta, of which their examination probably was the most thorough that had been made up to that time, but they also had made observations against which to check those of other expeditions.[30]

There was no time for the Spaniards to rest, however, for a new teller of tales arrived at Veracruz, destined to spark yet another expedition. Among the pirates captured and sent to Cuba was an Englishman named Ralph Wilkinson. Since he had nothing to lose, facing the gallows, he invented the story of a strongly-fortified French settlement named St. Jean, located near the ubiquitous "Bahía del Espíritu Santo." Wilkinson claimed he had dwelled among the settlers—1,000 strong!—for six months. He spun yarns worthy of the 1,001 nights of Scheherazade's Arabian tales, but as the voyage grew longer and his reliability grew shorter, the game was soon up. Reluctantly, he admitted he had based his accounts on hearsay evidence, rather than actual observance. When this expedition returned to Veracruz on April 24, 1688, Wilkinson was condemned to hard labor in the galleys.[31]

But still the rumors survived. The latest were spread by a captured Frenchman named Jean Géry brought to Mexico City by Governor Alonso de León. A native of St. Jean de Orléans in France, "Yan Jarri" claimed he had lived among the Indians for three years. He described a fabulous town built fifteen years earlier by the French with fancy castles for protection. The more he told the story the more ridiculous and contradictory it became, but the nagging suspicion remained: he *was* a Frenchman, and he was found in Spanish territory. This prompted the fifth maritime expedition searching for La Salle under the direction of Martín de Rivas, Antonio de Ibarra, and Andrés de Pez. Using the same pirogues as had been tried on the second expedition, they left San Juan de Ulúa on August 8, 1688. They discovered the spot where Enríquez Barroto had discovered the hulk of a wrecked French ship and on August 14 sailed around Bahía San Bernardo (Matagorda Bay), but found no French settlement.[32]

On June 2, 1689, Andrés de Pez wrote an important memorial which incorporated the findings of several navigators and the work of Dr. Carlos de Sigüenza y Góngora. Pez has been criticized for putting his name on the report, but this is hardly worth the discussion given it by Professor Leonard.[33] As Count Galeazzo Ciano remarked in 1942, "As always, victory finds a hundred fathers but defeat is an orphan."[34] As Dunn has astutely observed, "One of the most notable results of the series of maritime expeditions sent out in search of La Salle's colony had been the rediscovery of and revival of interest in Pensacola Bay."[35] Official reports, like the speeches of famous men, often hide the true authors, just as the hard work done by George Gauld in mapping the Gulf of Mexico before the American Revolution was incorporated into the writings of Bernard Romans without benefit of a footnote acknowledging such authorship. Since Pez had important friends in Spain and was the person sent to carry out the "sell-Pensacola" advertising campaign, it is hardly likely he would put the name of a colonial college professor on the report, as honest as that sounds by twentieth-century measures.

The report is called the "Pez Report," and it contained information of the rich natural resources of Pensacola, particularly the timber most useful for shipbuilding. Its harbor was unexcelled along the entire northern shore of the Gulf of Mexico. By constructing a fort or battery at the tip of Santa Rosa Island—named Punta de Sigüenza in 1693—cannon could cross fire with another battery constructed on the mainland so as to block any attempt to storm into the bay.[36] Time was of the essence, claimed Pez, for if Spain failed to act immediately and fortify Pensacola Bay, "the French would soon follow up La Salle's expedition by a more formidable one." If the French had made one such effort at San Bernardo Bay (Matagorda Bay) at the western end of the Gulf, surely they would repeat the attempt at such a desirable port as Pensacola. Once France had a base there, she could bring in her pirates and threaten Spanish shipping through the Gulf, the channel of Florida, and the Caribbean. The cost might be great, he averred, but the risk was even greater. Moreover, by abandoning the fort at Saint Augustine, he claimed he would save almost 100,000 pesos yearly for the crown.[37] Here Pez had made a serious tactical error, one which would haunt him in 1691.

In 1689 Alonso de León discovered the ruins of La Salle's

abandoned Fort St. Louis. He returned to Mexico City with two of the five survivors, Frenchmen named Santiago Groslet and Jean Larchevêque, self-styled "archbishop," a play on his name! Interrogated by Viceroy Conde de Galve and Andrés de Pez, the witnesses gave testimony as to what happened to La Salle and the French plans for settlement. Armed with his own memorial and a letter of support from the viceroy to the Marqués de los Veles, the president of the Council of the Indies, Pez sailed in the summer of 1689 with his two French prisoners for Cádiz.[38] He arrived probably before the December date given by Alessio Robles.[39]

While in Spain Pez had fourteen months' leave to accomplish various tasks, including the honor of being knighted in the prestigious order of Santiago on August 29, 1690.[40] The personal accolade, a recognition of his heroic contributions in fighting the pirates of the Gulf and Caribbean, took second place to his primary selling program for Pensacola. It was hardly an easy task! Faced with a chronic shortage of funds with which to wage war against Spain's enemies—English, French, and Dutch— Carlos II could ill afford the expenditure on creating a solid defensive bastion in the Gulf at Pensacola. Not even the support of the Conde de Galve seemed to help.[41]

The Marqués de la Granja, barely cognizant of the geography of America, accused Pez of trying to win favor by claiming to be the "first" to discover Pensacola Bay and claimed if Spain's enemies had not settled that "strategic" spot by now, it wasn't worth settling! Better to spend what little money Spain had in beefing up the Armada de Barlovento, he argued, since Pensacola would prove nothing more than a convenient "backdoor for contraband trade."[42]

Another foe of the project was the Marqués de los Vélez, who gave his ideas on March 22, 1691. Surely, he claimed, the great distance of 180 leagues by sea from Veracruz to San Bernardo Bay, and another 200 leagues from San Bernardo to Pensacola, would make Pensacola impractical for Spain to supply and make a part of the Gulf coast defenses. Spain's enemies—France, England, and Holland—had other bases from which to attack

Spanish shipping, so they would not require Pensacola. Moreover, Pez had not actually sailed into Pensacola Bay, so his observations were based on hearsay, not personal inspection. Still, he concluded, perhaps Viceroy Conde de Galve should do what he deemed most expedient for the defense of his realm.[43]

When the *Junta de Guerra* met to consider these various pro-and-con arguments in 1691, their final decision was hardly decisive. "Myopic in view of the serious consequences which might have occurred, they could find no better argument than to cite the great distance, as they perceived it, from Pensacola to Mexico, and claimed this lessened the possible menace."[44] The report of September 27, 1691 concluded that La Salle had been lost in San Bernardo lagoon, 184 miles from Espíritu Santo Bay, and that his intention was to establish a foothold for France along the Gulf coast.[45]

Carlos II issued his royal decree embodying the recommendations of his council on June 26, 1692. To the Conde de Galve he wrote, "send the person in whom you have the greatest confidence, and the most competent and experienced engineer and pilots of their respective professions, with proper orders and instructions to reconnoitre Pensacola Bay, take soundings of it, and obtain precise knowledge of the nature of its entrance. . . ." After doing Pensacola, the expedition should repeat the inspection of the "whole country surrounding the two bays of Pensacola and Espíritu Santo, or Mobile, and the rest of the coast, a careful and rigorously accurate report shall be written." Accurate maps of the area should also be made so that the king would have an understanding of Pensacola Bay and its relative importance to the Gulf of Mexico.[46]

Pez returned with the documents and orders and promotion to Admiral of the Armada de Barlovento. Sir Andrew now, he met with the ever-supportive Conde de Galve and decided to select the outstanding mind of colonial Mexico to conduct the expedition. Dr. Carlos de Sigüenza y Góngora, retired mathematics professor of the University of Mexico and Royal Cosmographer (Geographer), would have been a wise selection for any scientific undertaking. A humanist with the broadest training and felicity of expression, he had earned a niche among Clio's favorites by preserving the records of the Mexican *ayuntamiento* (municipal council) during a wild mob riot in 1692.[47]

The expedition included a frigate, the *Nuestra Señora de Guadalupe*, and a war-sloop, the *San Joseph*. The Conde de Galve drew up the goals of the expedition on January 12, 1693. They were to sail directly from Veracruz to Pensacola with a crew of one hundred sailors and twenty soldiers. Enough provisions for an eighty-day round trip were loaded on the two craft. In addition to taking soundings and exploring the entire bay, they were to analyze its importance as a roadstead for large-draught ships, possible places for battery placement, flora and fauna, and those materials available locally for building the presidio. Dr. Sigüenza was to draw up the map of Pensacola Bay. Following the work at that place, the expedition was to sail west to Mobile and repeat the same tasks. Skirting the coast as far as the Mississippi River, the expedition was to repeat the soundings and search for suitable roadsteads. Finally, the admiral was to "exercise the same care in observing and noting the character of the Indians on its shores," paying particular attention to treating "very kindly all natives that he meets on this expedition and try to win their friendship." Still fearful of French expansion from Canada to the Gulf, the viceroy ordered Pez to quiz the Indians as to what French forts or settlements were in the hinterland.[48]

Sails were raised and the ships left San Juan de Ulúa on March 25, 1693. Seven days later the Río Palizada (Mississippi) was spied, and the ships continued toward "La Bahía de Santa María de Galve." Although first visited in 1559 by Tristán de Luna y Arrellano, the date of August 14 by which it was named for the Virgin Mary is in error. The Saint's Day for the Virgin is August *15!* Still, the name continued in force until the heroic capture by Bernardo de Gálvez in 1781, at which time it was renamed "Santa María de Gálvez."[49]

After planting a large cross at Sigüenza Point on the western terminus of Santa Rosa Island, the explorers sailed to Mobile Bay and continued their journey to the west. On May 2, sixteen men used a smaller coasting shallop to explore the Mississippi and Louisiana coast as far as North Pass of the Mississippi River, but the omnipresent "mud-lumps," driftwood, and sand bars once again prevented an internal analysis. The small boat returned to the larger ships, and the expedition returned to Veracruz after a five-day sail on May 13, 1693.[50]

In his excellent report, Dr. Sigüenza wrote a glowing account of Pensacola Bay: "I hereby assert that that bay is the finest jewel possessed by His Majesty—May God Protect Him!—not only here in America but in all his kingdom, because it combines in itself the separate virtues which make other bays great."[51] Sigüenza was honored by having the tip of Santa Rosa Island named after him, and Pez had the Almirante River named after him, but ironically, it is known as Blackwater River today. "Laguna de Pez" likewise did not survive. It is shown on the charts in the vicinity of Chandeleur Sound or Lake Borgne.[52]

Only a quirk of fate, Pez wrote, had prevented La Salle from accomplishing his ambition of settling Frenchmen near the mouth of the Mississippi. Would France, once the European wars were concluded, return to her original ambitions in the Gulf? Pez was convinced they would, and the Viceroy Conde de Galve joined him with new material penned by Dr. Sigüenza which urged the prompt establishment of Pensacola by Spain.[53]

By December, 1693, Pez was again in Spain arguing his case, and on June 13, 1694, a royal order urged the occupation of Pensacola.[54] But the Conde de Galve, that long-time proponent of the Pensacola presidio, turned his office over to the bishop of Puebla because of ill health, and he died in 1697.[55] Once again, the Pensacola project slowed to a bare walk.

With the death of the Conde de Galve and the change in command, Pez found his detractors had mustered their offense against him. Accused of "cowardice and neglect of duty" in an engagement with pirates off the coast of Cuba in 1697, Andrés de Pez, now General of the Armada, was court-martialed along with Admiral Guillermo Molfi of the Barlovento Squadron. He was cleared of all charges by 1701, but in the interim, Pensacola had been established by Andrés de Arriola and Dr. Sigüenza in 1698.[56]

Events in Europe stimulated Spain to take the final step and found Pensacola in 1698. Spain's effective spy network learned that Louis XIV was preparing four ships filled with Caribbean settlers and destined for a new French settlement on the northern shore of the Gulf of Mexico. Again, French movement galvanized Spanish reaction. Charles II on April 19, 1698, issued a royal decree ordering Don José Sarmiento Valladares, Conde de Moctezuma, the new viceroy of New Spain, to occupy Pensacola Bay and build a presidio fortress. This task was to be the Spanish Empire's number-one priority for 1698![57]

Although the 1697 Treaty of Ryswick ended King William's War, it did not end Franco-Spanish rivalry in the New World. More than ever the Sun King was determined to plant a French colony in the Gulf. When Carlos II died on November 1, 1700, the Austrian House of Hapsburg died with him, and his selected heir, Philip of Anjou, turned out to be Louis XIV's grandson. The War of the Spanish Succession plunged Europe into another of the dynastic wars, but one in which the outcome at the Treaty of Utrecht would be far reaching, particularly for Spain. In America, the French continued their advance into the heart of the Gulf with settlements at Mobile and Biloxi and exciting voyages by Pierre Le Moyne, Sieur d'Iberville.[58]

Admiral Andrés de Pez fought valiantly during the War of the Spanish Succession, especially against the Catalán rebels of Barcelona who refused to accept Philip V as their legitimate king. Pez served under the Third Conde de Fernán Núñez, who had embraced the Bourbon cause with such fervor the Cataláns called him "el gran butifler de España."[59] Fernán Núñez and Pez worked well together, but in the spring of 1708, Pez was off to America again with the command of a squadron. So valiantly did he fight against pirates near Veracruz that he earned special commendation. He returned to Spain by way of Cádiz as commander of a ten-ship merchant fleet laden with needed supplies for the Bourbon war effort in 1710.[60]

Even as diplomats discussed peace terms at Utrecht, Andrés de Pez commanded the fleet of Philip V against the more-numerous small-boat fleet of the revolted Cataláns off the Costa Brava. An incident shows the intense *pundonor* of Pez, that superb Spanish sense of honor, patriotism, and personal pride. Philip V had requested aid from the French, and three warships under Lieutenant-general Ducassé arrived at Barcelona. Pez was ordered to lower the Spanish colors from his warship, *Nuestra Señora de Borgoña*. At first he refused, but realizing the end might justify such insulting means, he acquiesced but immediately requested his relief from command.[61]

Pez left the Catalán campaign, where he had commanded all the ships and galleys outfitted at Barcelona, and by August of 1715 a grateful monarch had rewarded him with membership on the Supreme Council of War. He retained this post when in January of 1717 he was named governor of the Council of the Indies. One of his notable contributions, in cooperation with Intendant José Patiño, a favorite of Philip V, was the transfer of the judicial bodies of the *Casa de Contratación* ("House of Trade") and the *Consulado* (Merchant Association) from Sevilla to Cádiz. Henceforth, Cádiz would be the sole port through which American commerce might enter Spain.[62]

The Bourbon alliance between Spain's Philip V and his grandfather, Louis XIV of France, necessarily changed the foreign policy of both powers. England was the common enemy, and it was to France's advantage to support Spanish hegemony in the Gulf. No longer an enemy, France's nascent settlements at Mobile and Biloxi had to be aided by Spain from Pensacola. It was a story astonishing enough to delight the George Orwell of *1984:* yesterday's enemy is today's friend and vice versa! For several years the "honeymoon" between France and Spain continued.[63]

Andrés de Pez was not lulled into a false sense of security, however. His distrust of the French was deep and life-long. On March 5, 1718, as he watched the French expand to Natchez up the Mississippi and to Natchitoches in northwestern Louisiana on the edge of Spanish Texas, Pez revived Spanish fears of French aggression in the Gulf area. His "paper" is a classic summary of French activities and Spanish reaction thereto dating back to La Salle's 1684 expedition.[64]

Pez noted the various expeditions which finally resulted in the successful founding of Pensacola in 1698, just months before the French expedition to the Gulf arrived. As a result of Pez's work for decades, Pensacola was Spanish, not French. The harmony between France and Spain was disrupted, according to Pez, when the French stockpiled arms and provided guns and ammunition for the hostile Indians in the Southeast. John Law's mercantile dream, the Company of the West, threatened Spanish commerce according to Pez. He had specific measures to counter this new danger to Spain.

The Mexican viceroy and the governor of Campeche must close their ports to all French ships, thus preventing them from securing refuge even if they were crippled. The missions of Texas should be reinforced and expanded along a line to check the French who had expanded to Natchitoches on the frontier of the *Provincias Internas.* Presidios should be built to protect the advanced missions. All trade in horses should be stopped. Any Frenchman found in the Gulf in Spanish territory would be arrested and either imprisoned at the Acapulco dungeon or put on hard labor at Mexico City's public works. A fort should be established at San Bernardo Bay (Matagorda Bay), supplied by Veracruz just five or six days away, thus saving a costly overland trip of 500 leagues.[65]

On May 20, 1718, the Council of the Indies gave full approval to Pez's suggestions. They cited Don Andrés's long experiences acquired in his naval duty in the Gulf. A royal decree of June 11, 1718 further directed "that the ports of New Spain and Cuba be closed to all French ships," and that vigorous steps be taken in the region between Florida and Texas to block further French expansion.[66]

A contemporary French document proves Pez's arguments concerning French ambitions. "It would be very agreeable during time of peace," it said, to occupy Mobile Bay and fortify it to use as a base of attack against Pensacola and Havana and for cutting off communications between Mexico City and her northern Texas *Provincias Internas.* The *flota* returning from Peru to Spain could be attacked by French ships in a Gulf squadron to be stationed at Mobile. The founding of New Orleans in 1718, however, obviated the need for such a plan, but the project should be filed in Paris for "future reference" should the need arise.[67]

Pez must have experienced a wry sense of *déjà vû* during the Franco-Spanish War of 1719–1722, during which Pensacola fell to invading armies not once, but on three different occasions![68] In the meantime, Pez had been governor of the Council of the Indies when he was named Secretary of State and Navy in January, 1721. While sources disagree, apparently he died in Madrid "on May 7, 1723, at half past four in the afternoon."[69] Ironically, the epitaph printed opposite that factual information gives his death as on "the nones of March in the Year M.DCC.XXIII [March 9, 1723]."[70]

In 1723 Captains Wauchop and Primo de Rivera of the squadron returned to Pensacola from Veracruz to discover in what condition the departing French had left it. A few dismantled cannon barrels covered by sand, an old bake oven, and a cistern with lid covered with rotten cross beams—these were the remains of Pensacola's village and fort.[71] Yet Pensacola would rise, phoenix-like, from its ashes and become the capital of British West Florida, 1763–1781. Captured by Bernardo de Gálvez in 1781, it would become the capital of Spanish West Florida until Governor Andrew Jackson raised the Stars-and-Stripes forty years later. Pez's prediction for Pensacola would prove true. "Let the earth to thee never a burden be," reads his epitaph, "But on thee buried may she lightly rest."[72] Pensacola lives on, a fitting monument to the seventeenth-century Spanish naval hero who saw what it could become fully a century earlier.

Pez's work, combined with the reports of Dr. Carlos de Sigüenza y Góngora, should have ended misinformation such as that recorded on an 1822 Florida map: "In 1682, M. de la Salle visited West Florida or Louisiana, and proceeded as far as the Illinois country. Pensacola was settled about 1696, by the French [!], who met with so many discouraging adventures, that, according to M. de Raynal, they would have abandoned it but for the sassafras tree, the fragrance and medicinal virtues of which animated them to continue their exertions."[73]

Among those making use of Pez's reports were Andrés Gonzáles de Barcia Carballido y Zúñiga (1673–1743) in his *Ensayo cronológico, para la historia de la Florida . . . desde el año de 1512 que descubrió la Florida, Juan Ponce de León, hasta el de 1722,* first published in Madrid just after Pez's death in 1723.[74] Fray Juan Augustín Morfi used Pez in his *History of Texas, 1673–1779,*[75] as did Fray José Antonio Pichardo, whose monumental 3,000-page study of the historical boundary of Louisiana and Texas was completed in 1812.[76]

The last of the great Spanish chroniclers, Juan Bautista Muñoz, collected the reports of Pez and Sigüenza to use in his projected history of America and placed in the margin of the dossier, "of important information."[77] About the same time, Minister of the Indies Joseph de Gálvez asked his brother, Matías, then viceroy of New Spain, for all information concerning the Pez-Sigüenza expedition of 1693 so that the crown would have important sources on the early history of Pensacola.[78] As a result of exaggerated claims by the United States to Spanish Texas in the west and to Spanish West Florida in the east, as belonging to Louisiana and therefore after 1803 to the United States, Manuel de Godoy ordered his Lieutenant-colonel of Engineers, Joseph de Gabriel y Estenoz, to examine the Archives of the Indies in Sevilla and compile historical data which would substantiate Spanish claims. The resulting 1806 "Historical Description of Louisiana" made good use of the early work of Pez, as well as his 1718 "paper" on how to block French expansion in the Gulf.[79]

Although virtually ignored by Mexican historians such as Lucas Alamán,[80] and relegated to a brief comment, with his name given as "Andrés Pérez" by Hubert Howe Bancroft,[81] present-day historians from Dunn to Gil Munilla and Weddle fully appreciate who Pez was and what he tried to do.[82] He is deserving of a lasting place in the roster of naval heroes and great Spanish statesmen.

Notes

[1] William Edward Dunn, *Spanish and French Rivalry in the Gulf Region of the United States*, 147.

[2] Paul Chesnel, *History of Cavelier de La Salle, 1643–1687*, 147–49.

[3] E. L. Corthell, *A History of the Jetties at the Mouth of the Mississippi River* (New York, 1880), 9.

[4] Randall L. Gibson, "Discovery of the Mississippi Valley," in *The Louisiana Book: Selections from the Literature of the State* (New Orleans, 1894), 169.

[5] Chesnel, ibid., 150.

[6] Roberto Gil Munilla, "Política española en el golfo mexicano, expediciones motivados por la entrada del Caballero La Salle," 510–11.

[7] Baronesa de Wilson, *México y sus gobernantes de 1519 a 1910*, 1, 211–22; Jorge Ignacio Rubio Mañé, *Introducción al estudio de los virreyes de Nueva España*, 1, 258–60, 295.

[8] "Pez" in García Carrafa, *Diccionario heráldico*, vol. 71; copy of baptism, enclosed in "Pez y Malzárraga," *Expediente* (dossier) for entering order of Santiago. I wish to thank Dr. Eric Beerman of Madrid for supplying me with copies of these essential sources. "Pez," in *Enciclopedia universal*, vol. 44, gives his birth as "about 1653," but is correct in identifying 1723 as the year of his death.

[9] Relación de servicios for Pez, 28 April 1689, in Gil Munilla, "Política española," 560; "Pez," in *Enciclopedia universal*, vol. 44.

[10] Rubio Mañé, *Los virreyes*, 1, 295; 2, 118–29; Wilson, *Gobernantes de México*, 1, 205–10.

[11] Dunn, ibid., 146.

[12] Epitaph of Pez, in Andrés Gonzáles de Barcia Carballido y Zúñiga, *Barcia's Chronological History of the Continent of Florida*, 399. Tiphys was the mythological pilot of the Argonauts. Tethys was the wife of Oceanus and mother of the sea nymphs in Greek mythology.

[13] Title of Pez cited in Irving A. Leonard, *The Spanish Approach to Pensacola, 1689–1693*, 71, note 42.

[14] "Pez," in *Enciclopedia universal*, vol. 44. On the fortifications at Veracruz and San Juan de Ulúa, see Hubert H. Bancroft, *History of Mexico*, vol. 11, 210–15; and José Antonio Calderón Quijano, *Fortificaciones en Nueva España*, 64–76, 259.

[15] F. González Ruiz, *De la Florida a San Francisco: los exploradores españoles en los Estados Unidos* (Buenos Aires, 1949), 445–46.

[16] Henry Folmer, *Franco-Spanish Rivalry in North America, 1524–1763*, 137–66; Charles W. Hackett, "New Light on Don Diego de Peñalosa: Proof that He Never Made an Expedition from Santa Fé to Quivira and the Mississippi River in 1662," *Mississippi Valley Historical Review* 6: 313–35.

[17] Robert S. Weddle, *Wilderness Manhunt: The Spanish Search for La Salle*.

[18] Folmer, ibid., 137.

[19] Ibid., 28–29.

[20] William Robertson, *The History of America* (Paris, 1828), 441.

[21] Leonard, *Spanish Approach*, 11–16; and idem, "The Spanish Re-Exploration of the Gulf Coast in 1686," 547–57.

[22] Gil Munilla, ibid., 551.

[23] Dunn, ibid., 59–63.

[24] Ibid., 75–80.

[25] Ibid., 80. Dunn did not locate the diary of this expedition. There is a certified copy of the diary in the Museo Naval, Madrid.

[26] Luis Gómez Raposo, "Diario del descubrimiento que hizo el Capitán Don Andrés del Pez," 114–30; Weddle, ibid., 108–13.

[27] Gómez Raposo, ibid., 134–36.

[28] Ibid., 136–39.

[29] Ibid., 143–49.

[30] Weddle, ibid., 117.

[31] Dunn, ibid., 81–93.

[32] Ibid., 88–95; Gil Munilla, ibid., 563–64.

[33] Leonard, *Spanish Approach*, 92–96.

[34] John F. Kennedy paraphrased this after the Bay of Pigs disaster: "There's an old saying that victory has a hundred fathers and defeat is an orphan." Bartlett's *Quotations*, 1053.

[35] Dunn, ibid., 146.

[36] That Pensacola was *not* easily defended is shown by its conquest three times in the Franco-Spanish War, 1719–1722, and by Bernardo de Gálvez's conquest of 1781: Jack D. L. Holmes, "Dauphin Island in the Franco-Spanish War, 1719–22," in *Frenchmen and French Ways in the Mississippi Valley*, ed. John Francis McDermott (Urbana, 1969), 103-25; and idem, "Bernardo de Gálvez: Spain's 'Man of the Hour' During the American Revolution," in *Cardinales de dos independencias (Noreste de México-Sureste de los Estados Unidos)*, ed. Beatriz Ruiz Gaytán, Samuel Proctor, *et al.* (México, 1978), 161–74.

[37] Although Dunn, *Spanish and French Rivalry*, 147–49, had not used the memorial, he did have supplementary data to give an idea of its content. Leonard, *Spanish Approach*, 77–98, translates the memorial and discusses its authorship.

[38] José Antonio Pichardo, *Pichardo's Treatise on the Limits of Louisiana and Texas*, I, 178–79.

[39] Vito Alessio Robles, *Coahuila y Texas en la época colonial*, 359–60.

[40] "Pez," in García Carraffa, *Diccionario*; "Pez y Malzárraga," *Expediente* for Order of Santiago (1690), both sources provided through the kindness of Dr. Eric Beerman of Madrid, for which I am grateful. Leonard, *Spanish Approach*, 27–28, erroneously reproaches Pez for his pursuit of the honor at the king's expense, and on page 71, note 40, gives the wrong source of the Santiago documents as Biblioteca Nacional instead of the correct Archivo Histórico Nacional.

[41] Ibid., 99–102.

[42] Opinion of the Marqués de la Granja, October, 1690, in ibid., 103–11.

[43] Opinion of Marqués de los Vélez, March 22, 1691, in ibid., 103-22.

[44] Gil Munilla, "Política española," 590.

[45] Report of the War Committee, Madrid, September 27, 1691, in Leonard, *Spanish Approach*, 132–37.

[46] Royal Decree of Carlos II, Madrid, June 26, 1692, in ibid., 138–41.

[47] Weddle, ibid., 237. Among the best studies of Sigüenza are Leonard, *Don Carlos de Sigüenza y Góngora, a Mexican Savant of the Seventeenth Century*, the appendix of which, 210-77, contains Sigüenza's valuable description of the Mexico City corn riot of June 8, 1692, in a letter to Admiral Andrés de Pez of August 30, 1692; Francisco Pérez Salazar, *Biografía de D. Carlos de Sigüenza y Góngora, sequido de varios documentos inéditos* (México, 1928); Edmundo O'Gorman, "Datos sobre D. Carlos de Sigüenza y Góngora, 1660–1677," *Boletín del Archivo General de la Nación* (México), 15 (1944), 593-621; and José Rojas Garcidueñas, *Don Carlos de Sigüenza y Góngora, erudito barroco (México, 1945)*.

[48] Conde de Galve, Instructions to Andrés de Pez, México, January 12, 1693, in Leonard, *Spanish Approach*, 145–48.

[49] Weddle, ibid., 237; Holmes, "Bernardo de Gálvez," 173.

[50] Report of Andrés de Pez, México, June 1, 1693, in Leonard, *Spanish Approach*, 149–51; Instructions to Sigüenza and log of his journey, in ibid., 152–92; Sigüenza's report, México, June 1, 1693, in ibid., 193–95.

[51] Report of Sigüenza, México, June 1, 1693, in ibid., 193.

[52] Dunn, *Spanish and French Rivalry*, 162–63.

[53] Ibid., 162–69; Leonard, *Spanish Approach*, 74, note 97.

[54] Weddle, ibid., 240.

[55] Leonard, *Spanish Approach*, 68, mistakenly says he died in 1695. Actually, he died at Puerto de Santa María (Cádiz province, Spain) on March 12, 1697, shortly after his return from Mexico. Rubio Mañé, *Los virreyes* 1, 260; Baronesa de Wilson, *Gobernantes de México* 1, 222.

[56] "Causa y prisión del General de la Armada de Barlovento D. Andrés de Pez y el Almirante D. Guillermo Molfi," is in Archivo General de Indias, Audiencia de Santo Domingo, old style legajo 55-6-2, as cited in Dunn, *Spanish and French Rivalry*, 175, note 46. On the founding of Pensacola, see also Albert Manucy, "The Founding of Pensacola—Reasons and Reality," 223–41; and Stanley Faye, "The Contest for Pensacola Bay and other Gulf Ports," 167–95.

[57] Weddle, ibid., 240–46. The Conde was named viceroy of New Spain on April 9, 1696, took office December 18, 1696, and left office November 4, 1701. Rubio Mañé, *Los virreyes* 1, 260–62, 296; Baronesa de Wilson, *Gobernantes de México* 1, 227–31.

[58] Richebourg G. McWilliams, *Iberville's Gulf Journals*.

[59] Marqués de Villa-Urrutia, *Fernán Núñez el embajador* (Madrid, 1931), 10.

[60] "Pez," in *Enciclopedia universal*.

[61] Ibid. Barcelona was not captured from the rebel Cataláns until September 12, 1714, but its fall marked a new birth of a united Spain, marked by a revival and expansion of trade under the Bourbon monarchs. John D. Bergamini, *The Spanish Bourbons, The History of a Tenacious Dynasty* (New York, 1974).

[62] "Pez," in *Enciclopedia universal*.

[63] J. H. Parry, *The Spanish Seaborne Empire* (New York, 1969), 267.

[64] Copy of a report ("*papel*") presented by Andrés de Pez to the Council of the Indies, Madrid, March 5, 1718, certified copy made by Lieutenant-colonel Joseph de Gabriel y Estenoz, Sevilla, January 7, 1806, in Archivo del Servicio Histórico Militar (Madrid), legajo 5-1-9-9.

[65] Ibid.

[66] Shelby, "International Rivalry in Northeastern New Spain, 1700–1725," 155-60.

[67] "Idée d'un mémoire en espagnol concernant la Mobile," Ministère des Colonies, série C13A, 5, transcript in Mississippi Department of Archives and History (Jackson), Mississippi Provincial Archives, French Dominion, Vol. VIII (1717–1720), 178–80.

[68] "Pez," in *Enciclopedia universal*.

[69] Barcia Carballido y Zúñiga, *Chronological History*, 398.

[70] Epitaph of Pez in ibid., 399.

[71] Faye, "Contest for Pensacola Bay," 327–28.

[72] Barcia Carballido y Zúñiga, ibid., 399.

[73] "Geographical, Statistical, and Historical Map of Florida," published at Philadelphia by Carey and Lea, 1822.

[74] Barcia Carballido y Zúñiga, ibid.

[75] Fray Juan Agustín Morfi, *History of Texas, 1673–1779*.

[76] Pichardo, *Treatise on Limits*. Pichardo (1748–1812), a native of Cuernavaca, Mexico, succeeded Fray Melchor de Talamantes in carrying out the Royal Order of May 20, 1805, for the "compilation of all pertinent data concerning the true boundary between Texas and Louisiana."

[77] Muñoz (1745–1799) published his *Historia del nuevo mundo* only as far as 1500 (Madrid, 1793), but his magnificent collection of manuscripts is catalogued by the Royal Spanish Academy of History: *Catálogo de la Colección de Don Juan Bautista Muñoz*, 3 vols. (Madrid, 1954). Material on the Pez-Sigüenza expedition is described in 1, 51–56.

[78] Joseph de Gálvez to Viceroy of México (Matías de Gálvez), San Lorenzo, Novem-

ber 16, 1783, Archivo General de la Nación (México), Reales Cédulas, CXXVI, fols. 199–200.

[79] Gabriel y Estenoz, "Descripción histórica de la Luisiana," Sevilla, March 29, 1806, in Archivo del Servicio Histórico Militar (Madrid), legajo 5-1-9-14. Sir Jack D. L. Holmes and Professor William S. Coker are preparing this valuable manuscript for publication.

[80] Lucas Alamán, *Disertaciones sobre la historia de la república megicana desde la época de la conquista que los españoles hicieron a fines del siglo xv y principios del xvi des las islas y continente americano hasta la independencia*, 3 vols., Vols. 5-8 of *Obras de D. Lucas Alamán*, 2nd ed. (México, 1969), 8, 315–17.

[81] Bancroft, *History of the North Mexican States and Texas* 1, 413; and *History of México, 1600–1803*, 3, 227.

[82] Dunn, *Spanish and French Rivalry*, 80; Weddle, ibid., 117; Gil Munilla, ibid., 561.

The English
Reaction to La Salle

WILLLIAM S. COKER

•

WHEN ASKED if I would prepare a short report on the English reaction to the La Salle expedition, 1684–1687, I agreed to do so because of the research which I had already completed on Dr. Daniel Coxe, the proprietor of Carolana. Inspired by the narratives of Father Louis Hennepin and Henri de Tonti, whose earlier connections with La Salle need no elaboration, Coxe planned to establish a colony of Englishmen and French Huguenots on the Gulf Coast in 1689–1699. In fact, Coxe's plans triggered the French and Spanish race for the Gulf Coast. The French mission of 1698/99 led by the Sieur d'Iberville was the long awaited follow-up to La Salle's ill-fated expedition. But Spain intended to thwart France by reaching the Gulf Coast first. Unfortunately for Spain, its occupation of Pensacola Bay in November of 1698 did not prevent Iberville, a few months later, from establishing a French colony, Fort Maurepas, at present-day Ocean Springs, Mississippi. When Coxe's expedition under the command of Captain William Bond sailed up the Mississippi River in September of 1699, it encountered the Sieur de Bienville, Iberville's brother, already on the river. Bond left but promised to return with a larger force and warned that he intended to lay claim to that country for England. Thus the French had not only successfully challenged Spain's exclusive claim to the Gulf coast, they had also discouraged England— Dr. Coxe—from establishing a settlement there.[1] This much is well known. What is not so well known is the English reaction between the time La Salle left France in 1684 and the expeditions of England, France, and Spain to the Gulf Coast in 1698–1699.

The Sieur de Beaujeu, who commanded the naval vessels on the ill-fated final La Salle expedition, returned to France on July 5, 1685, by way of Cuba, French Santo Domingo, and Virginia.

There is no record that Beaujeu, or any of those with him, confided any information about La Salle to the Englishmen they met on their return voyage. Shortly after they reached France, however, Beaujeu and several of his companions wrote a series of letters and reports and within a few weeks the details of the expedition were common knowledge among a number of top French officials.[2] But if they in turn divulged any information about La Salle, it has not come to light. It appears instead to have been a well-kept secret. In March of 1686, when Spain first learned about La Salle's settlement, the news came from Cuba and not from France.[3] Likewise there is no evidence that anyone in England knew anything about the La Salle expedition until the summer of 1686, unless the Marquis de Bonrepaus mentioned it during his diplomatic mission to England from January to April, 1686; but there is nothing to suggest that he did.[4] Although it is difficult to believe, James II, the recently (1685) crowned Catholic King of England, may not have known anything about La Salle until the Spanish Ambassador Pedro de Ronquillo informed him about La Salle on June 30, 1686.[5]

This lack of knowledge about what the English knew, or did not know, when and how they obtained their information, and precisely what they did once they knew about La Salle, are the major problems confronting the investigator. If any collection of English documents about La Salle between 1684 and 1689 exists, I have been unable to find any reference to it. My research has revealed only a very few English documents which even mentioned La Salle, and none written by James II or any of the English ambassadors to France or Spain.

There are a few references to La Salle before and after he left New France (Canada) in the *Documents relative to the Colonial History of the State of New-York*, and in the *Calendar of State Papers, Colonial Series, America and West Indies.*[6] In March of 1687, Governor Thomas Dongan of New York sent a map to London which showed the great river (the Mississippi) discovered by La Salle. Dongan had learned that La Salle planned to return from France with three ships to settle there. He wrote that if La Salle did so it would be inconvenient for the Spaniards as well as the English. He even offered to send a ship or two to discover the river.[7] It is not known where he obtained that information, but perhaps it was from the French in New France. Beyond that there is precious little said about La Salle in the English documents for those years. Almost exclusively historians have used only Spanish or French documents for information about the English reaction to La Salle. Perhaps the documents for which I have searched do exist and someone more knowledgeable than I might know where they are located. If so, I hope they will respond to this article with a learned treatise upon the subject.

The La Salle expedition which created near panic in Spain hardly produced a ripple on the English pond. Diplomats and politicians seemed to have ignored it. Only the business community or the merchants appear to have been upset by the news, but more about that later. The London *Gazette*, which devoted about one-half of its two pages to events abroad, did not even mention La Salle, at least I did not find any such references, in any of its issues between 1685 and 1689. But this should not be considered unusual, because the *Gazette* reported very little news about the Americas at all. Here and there you will find a note about a new viceroy for Peru or New Spain, or a comment about the departure or arrival of the *flota* at Cádiz, but little more than that.

On the other hand, news of La Salle's settlement on the Gulf Coast, this French invasion of territory claimed exclusively by Spain, shocked Spanish officials.[8] Ronquillo received instructions in early June, 1686, to cultivate James II and to enlist his support against France. After all, Spain hoped that James, as a Catholic, might help keep the French King, Louis XIV, in check. Even before news about La Salle arrived, however, Ronquillo had endeavored to alert the English to the French threat.[9] During Bonrepaus' visit he attempted to play down the fears excited by Ronquillo and to reassure the English that they had nothing to fear from France.[10] Spain had also instructed Ronquillo to exert all of his influence to prevent the conclusion of a neutrality treaty between England and France that was then under consideration. The treaty called for neutrality between English and French colonies in the Americas even if the mother countries were at war in Europe. If he could not prevent the successful negotiation of the treaty, then Ronquillo should try to insure that the treaty contained no provisions prejudicial to Spain.[11] Although he failed to prevent the enactment of the neutrality treaty, some historians have concluded that Ronquillo succeeded in securing James II's support against French expansion in America.[12]

During the summer of 1686, after the news of La Salle's settlement became known in London, the French Ambassador, the Marquis de Branges, wrote Louis XIV that while James II did not appear to be disturbed by the news, the English merchants were.[13] In response to this information the French Minister of Marine, the Marquis de Seignelay, wrote Branges that the English attitude toward La Salle had caused alarm in France.[14] Seignelay seemed surprised that the English merchants were upset by the news. He remarked that if anyone should take umbrage, it should be the Spaniards because of Mexico.[15] This is the only direct evidence which I discovered that England had assumed an unfriendly attitude toward France over La Salle. Those historians who have written about Ronquillo's successful diplomacy with James II have not cited these letters. Instead they have based their conclusions upon Ronquillo's correspondence and upon France's failure to send a relief ship or supply expedition to La Salle. While they may be correct in their conclusions, they have not offered any evidence from English or French sources to support them.

Quite the contrary, when France sent a 700 tun ship to French Santo Domingo in late 1686 or early 1687, it carried 130 women as wives for the buccaneers. Beaujeu, whose dislike for La Salle and his project are well known, had proposed that the ship also be used to carry supplies to La Salle. A financial pinch, however, was given as the reason for not doing so. There is no suggestion that the failure to send the ship on to La Salle was in any way connected with James II or his hostility toward France over the La Salle expedition.[16] Did the London merchants or

Ronquillo get James II to intercede with Louis XIV, thus causing him to abandon La Salle? Until further evidence is uncovered, I must conclude that we still do not know to what extent James II influenced Louis XIV not to support La Salle. In the case of the vessel sent to French Santo Domingo, the decision not to send it on to La Salle originated in France's financial dilemma and not because of any pressure from James II.

By the time of the outbreak of King William's War on May 12, 1689, the fate of La Salle's colony was already known in France.[17] The Spaniards finally discovered what was left of La Salle's settlement on Garcitas Creek on April 22, 1689, and before the year was out officials in Spain were apprised of the discovery.[18] For the next eight years, or until September 20, 1697, when the Treaty of Ryswick ended King William's War, England, Spain, and France were so absorbed by the war that not one of these powers attempted to establish a settlement on the northern Gulf rim. To be sure, Spain and France evinced a desire to do so.[19]

Spain directed the occupation of Pensacola Bay in 1694, after several expeditions to that location had rendered favorable reports on the bay, then known as the *Bahía Santa María de Galve*. But a lack of funds prevented the viceroy in Mexico City from carrying out those instructions.[20] In the same year, 1694, Henri de Tonti felt it imperative that France should complete the La Salle enterprise. By that date English traders were already advancing into the Mississippi Valley and Tonti foresaw the danger in this.[21] In January of 1698, just a few months after the end of the war, English newspapers were reporting French plans to erect a colony at the mouth of the Mississippi.[22] This was quite in contrast to the lack of information in England about La Salle's plans in 1684. Of course, by 1698, England and Spain had also made plans for expeditions to the Gulf Coast. As we know, Dr. Coxe's activities spurred France and Spain in their contest to see who would reach there first. Thereafter it was a combination of European politics and colonial rivalry motivated by commercial competition—the fur trade—which caused a renewal of the war for empire begun in 1689. It finally culminated with the French expulsion from North America in 1763.[23] Thus in the long run the English reaction to La Salle and those who followed him was the elimination of France as a colonial rival in the New World.

Notes

[1] Daniel Coxe, *A Description of the English Province of Carolana, By the Spaniards call'd Florida, And by the French La Louisiane*, xxi–xxix; William Edward Dunn, *Spanish and French Rivalry in the Gulf Region of the United States, 1678–1702*, 146–215.

[2] Pierre Margry, *Découvertes et établissements des Français dans l'ouest et dans le sud de L'Amérique Septentrionale* 2, 577–610. Beaujeu departed Virginia on May 26 and arrived at Rochefort on July 5, 1685, ibid., 2, 582–83.

[3] Dunn, ibid., 40–41.

[4] Ibid., 49; René Durand, "Louis XIV et Jacques II à la veille de la Révolution de 1688: Les Trois Missions de Bonrepaus en Angleterre." According to Durand, Bonrepaus devoted his activities in England to the commercial problems, the French Huguenots, and the neutrality treaty with England. There is no reference to La Salle until after Bonrepaus had departed England.

[5] Dunn, ibid., 53–54. Ronquillo already knew that La Salle had departed France in 1684, but it was thought that he had returned to New France and would reach the Gulf of Mexico from the north, ibid., 52.

[6] *Documents relative to the Colonial History of the State of New-York; Procured in Holland, England, and France* 3, 447–48, 452; J. W. Fortescue (ed.), *Calendar of State Papers, Colonial Series, America and West Indies* 11, 365.

[7] Fortescue, ibid., 12, 329.

[8] Dunn, ibid., 42.

[9] Ibid., 48–54.

[10] Durand, ibid., 39.

[11] Dunn, ibid., 49, 54–56; Frances Gardiner Davenport and Charles Oscar Paullin (eds.), *European Treaties bearing on the History of the United States and its Dependencies* 2, 309–23.

[12] Dunn, ibid., 56–57; Henry Folmer, *Franco-Spanish Rivalry in North America, 1524–1763*, 189–90.

[13] Davenport and Paullin, ibid., 313; Dunn, ibid., 56. *Rivalry*, 56.

[14] Seignelay to Barillon [Marquis de Branges], August 20, 1686, Archives de la Marine, série B², vol. 58, fol. 636.

[15] Durand, ibid., 43.

[16] Copia de relacion hecha al Rei Xmpo tocante a la vahia del Spiritu ss.ᵗᵒ que remitio el S.ᵒʳ Dⁿ Pedro Ronquillo Embax.ᵒʳ de su Mg.ᵈ en Inglaterra al Conde de la Monclova mi. S.ᵒʳ en carta fha en Londres a 7 de febr.º deste año de 1687, Archivo General de Indias, Mexico 61-6-20, copy in Dunn Transcripts, University of Texas Archives, Austin, pp. 139–45. My thanks to Ann R. Graybiel for securing a copy of this document for me. This document is translated in part in Robert S. Weddle, *Wilderness Manhunt: The Spanish Search for La Salle*, 103–106.

[17] *Documents relative to the Colonial History of the State of New-York* 9, 398.

[18] Dunn, ibid., 103.

[19] Marcel Giraud, *A History of French Louisiana* 1, 3–15, provides an excellent summary of English and French rivalry and the great need of the French to follow up on the La Salle adventure.

[20]Dunn, ibid., 171–73; see also Holmes, "Andrés de Pez and Spanish Reaction to French Expansion into the Gulf of Mexico," this volume.

[21]Verner W. Crane, "The Tennessee River as the Road to Carolina: The Beginnings of Exploration and Trade," 4–5.

[22]Verner W. Crane, *The Southern Frontier, 1670–1732,* 48, note 5.

[23]Ibid., 39–325; Folmer, *Franco-Spanish Rivalry,* 189–310.

Part III

French Settlement and Indian Neighbors

Mobilian: The Indian *Lingua Franca* of Colonial Louisiana

KENNITH H. YORK

•

THERE IS EVIDENCE that American Indians communicated and transacted with one another in a *lingua franca* in the southeastern United States. This common or commercial language was referred to by earlier writers as the trade language of the southeastern Indians. James Mooney gave a brief description and an estimate of the range of its use:

> This trade language, based upon Choctaw, but borrowing also from all the neighboring dialects and even from the more northern Algonquian languages, was spoken and understood among all the tribes of the Gulf states, probably as far west as Matagorda Bay and northward along both banks of the Mississippi to the Algonquian frontier about the entrance of the Ohio. It was called Mobilienne by the French, from Mobile, the great trading center of the Gulf region. Along the Mississippi it was sometimes known also as the Chickasaw trade language.[1]

There have been other earlier references in the literature to a trade language or jargon used by Indians of the southeastern part of North America. John Sibley reported that Mobilian "was spoken in addition to their native languages by all the Indians who had come from the east side of the Mississippi. Among those using it are the Alabama, Apalachi, Biloxi, Choctoo, Pacana, Pascagula, Taensas, and Tunica."[2] Thomas S. Woodward also commented on the jargon, stating that "there is yet a language the Texas Indians call the Mobilian tongue, that has been the trading language of almost all the tribes that have inhabited the country. . . . It is a mixture of Creek, Choctaw, Chickasay, Netches, and Apelash."[3]

Several Indian languages also served as media of communication among tribes who spoke their own native languages in the Southeast. James Adair noted that the "seven nations living near the late Alebahma garrison [Fort Toulouse at the junction of the Coosa and Tallapoosa rivers] understood Creek, in addition to their own language."[4] Robert Beverley also wrote that "the tribes of Virginia had a general language which they used for purposes of intercommunication" and that "this general language was that of the Occaneeches, who lived in central Virginia near the North Carolina line."[5] According to John Lawson, "the most powerful Nation of these Savages scorns to treat or trade with any others in any other Tongue but their own, which serves for the *Lingua* of the Country."[6]

The *lingua franca* which developed in the lower Mississippi Valley region was based on the Western division of the Muskogean language. Mary Haas reported that "there is evidence that Choctaw or Choctaw-like languages, including Chickasaw, were prestigious and widespread in the region."[7] According to James Crawford, the Mobilian trade language may have had its origin in the numerous Choctaw dialects spoken south of the Chickasaw.[8] The French called the common language Mobilian indicating that the language was similar to, although not necessarily identical to, the language of the Mobile tribe which lived on Mobile Bay.

In his book entitled *The Mobilian Trade Language*, Crawford argues that the *lingua franca* used for trading in the 1700s was the result of the French influence in the lower Mississippi.[9] Although Crawford does not rule out a native origin for the trade language, he does indicate that the needs of European traders and diplomats may have spread the usage of the common language now referred to as Mobilian.[10] In any case, Crawford also reported that "the language was used by whites, as well as by Indians."[11]

Why would a trade language, such as Mobilian, have its beginning in the first place? Some of the answers may be found by looking at the stage of development of Indians at the time of European contact. As an example, a *lingua franca* was important and beneficial to the Choctaw Indians because of their advanced economic and political position. Angie Debo wrote that "they [the Choctaws] surpassed all their neighbors at the time of the first coming of the white man."[12] At this time the Choctaws were primarily interested in agribusiness, raising corn, beans, pumpkins, melons and other items in their fields and garden plots. For instance, John R. Swanton wrote that "although they [the Choctaws] owned less land than any of the surrounding tribes, they raised more corn and beans than they needed for their own use and sold the surplus to their neighbors."[13] So it seems that the stage of development of these tribes created a need for intercommunication and that a *lingua franca* may thus have evolved.

Another reason that a trade language may have been needed was an increase in travel. When one studies the development of roads and highways of this country, he will find that most roads and highways were built on Indian trails, as was the famous Natchez Trace. Swanton reported an extensive Indian trail system offering numerous occasions for intertribal communication and trade.[14] There were Indian trails connecting Canada with Mexico and running from the east to west coasts of the continent.

But perhaps the most important issue about Mobilian has been its origin. This writer feels that the common language now known as Mobilian had its origin from the Choctaw language. A few lexical data were collected by James Crawford and the data were analyzed by Crawford and Mary Haas. The rest of this paper will attempt to show why it is believed that Mobilian originated from Choctaw.

Mary Haas reported, after examining some data recorded by Crawford:

> In the material that has been examined so far I have not found any traces of the Algonquian ingredients mentioned by Mooney, but as more material becomes available, some may still turn up. On the other hand, Woodward's description of Mobilian can be seen to fit very well.[15]

As mentioned earlier, Woodward reported that Mobilian was a mixture of Creek, Choctaw, Chickasaw, Natchez, and Apalachi. Haas concluded that Mobilian appears to be a mixture of Choctaw and Alabama.[16] The kind of vocabulary mixture which was reported can be found in the following list.

	Alabama	*Choctaw*	*Mobilian*
fish	łało	nani	šlašu
squirrel	ipło	fani	fani
horse	čičoba	(is)suba	suba
dog	ifa	ofi	ofi
eat	ipa	apa	apa
fire	tikba	lowak	lowak
water	oki	oka	oki
rain	oyba	omba	hoyba
friend	am-okla	ankana	mog(u)la fina

First of all, a native speaker of Choctaw can comprehend all of the Mobilian words except *šlašu*. Secondly, a native speaker of Choctaw should comprehend most of the Alabama words except *łało* and *ipło*. However, the word *am-okla* in Choctaw literally means "my people."

Haas also reported that Mobilian has a simpler morphology than Alabama and Choctaw.[17] She gave an example by providing the independent personal pronouns of Mobilian as follows:

	Alabama	*Choctaw*	*Mobilian*
I	inu	ano	inu
You	išno	čišno	išnu
We	pošno	pišno, hapišno	pošnu

The Mobilian examples seem to be a corruption of both Alabama and Choctaw, although some dialects of Choctaw do include some of these words, such as *išno* and *pošno*. Some Chickasaw words do include Choctaw influences, such as *čišno* and *pošno*, but Chickasaw speakers drop the initial consonant and substitute other vowels when pronouncing the words, as the Mobilian speakers apparently did, also.

Haas also reported on the negative construction in Choctaw and Alabama in comparison with Mobilian. The Choctaw and Alabama negative construction is more complex, as given in the following example:

Choctaw Positive		Choctaw Negative	
falaya	'long, tall'	ikfalayo	'not long, tall'
lawa	'many'	iklawo	'not many'

The negative construction of Koasati, another Western Muskogean language, also indicates a complex structure. The following was reported by Haas:[18]

Koasati Positive		Koasati Negative	
alokpa	'sharp'	alokikpo	'not sharp', 'dull'

However, all of the negative constructions in Mobilian have been more simplified, such as the following reported by Haas:

Mobilian Positive		Mobilian Negative	
falaya	'tall'	falayakšu	'not tall', 'short'
		(or falaya ekšu)	
alokpa	'sharp'	alokpakšu	'not sharp', 'dull'
lawa	'many'	lawakšu	'not many'
čito	'big'	čitokšu	'not big', 'small'

In Haas' analysis, she reported that a vowel-deletion rule is present, but is the reverse of the usual Muskogean rules in that it deletes the first vowel of *ekšo* and the final vowel of the preceding word is retained.[19] This form of construction is found in present-day Choctaw, although limited to only a few dialects. In Chocktaw words such as *falayakšu* are considered contractions of two distinct words, eg. *falaya* 'long' and *ikšo* 'not any'. Thus far, most of the Mobilian vocabulary items reported by Haas and Crawford are used by Choctaw speakers.

James Crawford later reported on one hundred and fifty words and phrases in Mobilian:

The greatest portion of them are Western Muskogean and closely resemble Choctaw and Chickasaw. Some of them, about twenty items, resemble Alabama and Koasati as closely as they resemble Choctaw and Chickasaw. About fourteen items are closer to Alabama and Koasati than to Choctaw and Chickasaw. Two words which resemble Choctaw are ultimately from Spanish. One word which resembles Choctaw and Alabama is ultimately from French. Three words, one by way of Alabama, came in from English. One word apparently entered directly from French and another directly from Algonquian.[20]

After examining additional data, Crawford reported that the independent personal pronouns analyzed by Mary Haas are "equally similar to the personal pronouns of Chickasaw;" thus the references to this common language as the Chickasaw trade language.[21] But Crawford concludes that "the source language need not have been Chickasaw, but it was a language closer to Chickasaw than to Choctaw and was also one with a close connection to Alabama, a connection which was certainly closer than that between Alabama and Choctaw."[22] A look at the entire vocabulary recorded in Mobilian by Crawford, however, indicates that the trade language is much closer to Choctaw than he wishes to credit.[23]

Finally, John R. Swanton recorded some words from a Pascagoula descendant whose mother was a Pascagoula and whose father was Biloxi. Swanton wrote that "the words were not Biloxi, but may be the words belonging to the Mobilian trade language."[24] Swanton also collected words from an old Houma woman. He reported that "all the words look like Choctaw and could be taken as proof that Houma is a dialect of Choctaw. But it is equally possible that the words are from the Mobilian trade language and are not at all representative of the language of the Houma."[25]

In conclusion, the description given by James Mooney seems to be closer to the true origin of Mobilian than all the others; that is:

This trade language, based upon Choctaw, but borrowing also from all the neighboring dialects and even from the more northern algonquian languages, was spoken and understood among all the tribes of the Gulf states.[26]

If the above assumption and description proves to be true, the Mobilian trade language may be alive and well in present-day Mississippi. It certainly needs further inquiry and investigation.[27]

Notes

[1] James Mooney, "Myths of the Cherokee," 187.

[2] John Sibley, "Historical sketches of the several Indian tribes in Louisiana;" Mooney, ibid., 187.

[3] Thomas S. Woodward, *Woodward's Reminiscences of the Creek, or Muscogee Indians,* 79.

[4] James Adair, *The History of the American Indians,* 267.

[5] Robert Beverley, *The History of the Present State of Virginia,* 24.

[6] John Lawson, *A New Voyage to Caroline,* 225.

[7] Mary H. Haas, "The Classification of the Muskogean Languages."

[8] James M. Crawford, ed., *Studies in Southeastern Indian Languages,* 46.

[9] Idem, *The Mobilian Trade Language,* 21.

[10] Ibid., 27.

[11] Crawford, *Studies,* 46.

[12] Angie Debo, *The Rise and Fall of the Choctaw Republic,* 10.

[13] John R. Swanton, *Source Material for the Social and Ceremonial Life of the Choctaw Indians,* 2.

[14] Idem, "List of Trails," 746.

[15] Mary R. Haas, "What is Mobilian?" 261.

[16] Ibid., 258.

[17] Ibid., 259.

[18] Ibid., 260.

[19] Ibid., 260.

[20] Crawford, *Mobilian Trade Language,* 76.

[21] Ibid., 79.

[22] Ibid., 80.

[23] Ibid., 81–97.

[24] John R. Swanton, *Indian Tribes of the Lower Mississippi Valley and Adjacent Coast of the Gulf of Mexico,* 32.

[25] Ibid., 28.

[26] Mooney, "Myths of the Cherokee," 187.

[27] A recent doctoral dissertation on Mobilian by Emanuel J. Drechsel ("Mobilian Jargon: Linguistic, Sociocultural, and Historical Aspects of an American lingua franca," Ph.D. dissertation, University of Wisconsin, 1979) explores many of these problems in greater detail.

Henri de Tonti
du village des Chacta, 1702:
The Beginning of the French Alliance

PATRICIA GALLOWAY

•

IN THE WRITING of ethnohistory, the importance of documents describing the first European contacts with Native
American peoples cannot be overstated. For the interior tribes
of the southeast first contact is generally reported from the
"false dawn" of 1540–43, but since it is still not clear what route
the Soto expedition took through the Alabama and Mississippi
areas,[1] nor precisely what forerunners of the later historic tribes
they met, it is hard to make maximum use of the expedition
accounts as first contact documents; they are more useful, and
have been so used, for documenting the sociopolitical structure
of the late Mississippian societies that preceded the development
of the historic tribes.[2]

In the hundred and sixty years that intervened between the
passage of the Soto expedition and the arrival of the French to
found the Louisiana colony, great changes seem to have taken
place. It is still argued whether the so-called "Mississippian decline" was caused or merely hastened by the Spanish passage,
with its probable introduction of disease into the Mississippian
heartland and its possible effects upon the balance of power
between various Mississippian chiefdoms,[3] but what is certain is
that profound changes did occur. Although such changes were
not everywhere uniform, and for example the Natchez, Koroa,
and Taensa groups of the Mississippian heartland seem to have
brought a "Mississippian"-style sociopolitical structure essen-
tially intact into the French period,[4] it seems to be the case that
most of the numerically predominant historic tribes—
specifically here the Chickasaw and Choctaw are cases in
point—were organized as egalitarian societies with autonomous

village groups rather than centrally organized chiefdoms, and achieved rather than ascribed status for their leaders.[5] Because this change had taken place, and because its dynamics are still not clear, the documents reporting the first French contact with these tribes have special importance because they report the new situation before the effects of continuous contact and acculturation began to be felt. In other words, the societies they document had changed since contact with the first Europeans to penetrate the area, but they had changed within an environment still dominated by the aboriginal societies themselves.

More evidence is needed to determine just how sweeping this societal revolution had been. There are, for example, scattered references in the very early European documents that suggest that certain features of earlier ceremonial practices survived among even such a reduced remnant tribe as the Mobilian is assumed to be.[6] And Adair reported that the Mississippian Nanih Waiya mound had been built against other tribes,[7] implying that some such tradition may have attached to it in his time. The full story, in short, is not yet in, and there is still much to be learned from the maximum exploitation of the earliest of the French documents.

The documents which are to be the subject of this study, Henri de Tonti's two letters sent to Iberville from his tour among the Choctaw and Chickasaw in the late winter of 1702,[8] have not lain in complete obscurity since they were first written, but they have never been exploited in this manner. Instead, they have served the purpose of amplifying the history of the French colony and the biography of Henri de Tonti,[9] and indeed Higginbotham's use of the documents, which almost amounts to complete paraphrase and partial translation, obscures their importance by misapprehension and downright mistranslation. In this study I will attempt to extract from these documents the specifically ethnohistorical information that they contain. This evidence is indeed ample: it includes locational information for Choctaw, Chickasaw, and Chakchiuma alike; valuable information about the political relationships among the Mobilian, Tohome, Choctaw, Chickasaw, Chakchiuma, Alabama, and Conchak (Abihka) tribes of the Mississippi/Alabama area; much hard evidence for Choctaw subsistence patterns before the skin trade had distorted them substantially; and finally very crucial information about the effects upon the tribes of the English-backed slave trade that had already been going on for some years. In addition, the documents also offer support for inferences regarding Choctaw and Chickasaw sociopolitical organization and perhaps even myth. I hope that this exercise in ethnohistorical *explication de texte* will demonstrate just how much there is still to be learned from these documents and make a beginning at disproving Swanton's contention that the student's perception of the Choctaw through the early documents is one of "a powerful indefiniteness."[10] It will become obvious that this indefiniteness is due more to our failure to use these documents than to a lack of evidence in them.

My representation of the Tonti letters as first contact documents should not mislead the reader into thinking that they represent the reporting of the very first post-Soto recontact, since, as has been hinted above, English trading and slave-raiding activities had already established contact of a sort. There was earlier, if indirect, French contact, too; although La Salle's expedition of 1682 did not directly encounter any tribes from the eastern hinterland of the Mississippi River area except the Chickasaw, two of whose warriors joined it for a time, during that expedition Henri de Tonti himself scouted out a location for the placement of a fur trading house among the Quapaw on the Arkansas River, and in 1686 he established that trade house. It is likely that even before the renegade *coureur de bois* Jean Couture began to establish a sideline in trade with the English colonies to the east via the Tennessee River,[11] the interior tribes or their intermediaries had begun to bring furs and skins to the Arkansas post. Nor were the English laggard once they began to understand the vastness and richness of the interior. They certainly used Couture's route to the Mississippi River,[12] but they also forged what was later to become famous as the overland Upper Path from Savannah through the Upper Creek towns on to the Chickasaw and thence to the Mississippi, reaching the latter goal as early as 1698.[13] This path then became useful for convoying the skins and increasingly the more profitable slaves that were the products of the interior.[14]

The French had contacted the Choctaw previous to 1702 as well; in fact, the Choctaw must certainly have been aware of the new French initiative from very shortly after the landing of Iberville's first expedition in late January of 1699, and must additionally have been aware of the intentions of this and the succeeding expeditions and the value that such a new group might have to them in balancing the English-inspired threat to the north and east. Possibly Choctaw observers had blended in among the Mobilians who early observed the doings of the French; certainly the Choctaw had already sent observers to the coast to begin making contact.[15] Hence although Tonti's was the first penetration into the interior carried out officially by the French, and certainly the first one reported in some detail, there was already a situation obtaining there that was, if not European-dominated, at least European-influenced to some extent.

Before I begin to examine the two Tonti letters, a word on method. I shall not proceed sequentially through the documents, but shall rather discuss their contents under the various headings suggested above. The translation of the documents is included as an appendix to this paper, so that the interested reader can check my conclusions and perhaps find even more in the documents than I have space to explore here. The chronological spine of the documents is briefly related: Tonti and his party, which included two Mobilians, two Tohomes, one "chief" of the Choctaw, and ten Frenchmen, left a Tohome village on February 14 and arrived at the main Choctaw village they visited on the 22nd. They remained there one day, during which Tonti wrote the first of the letters and sent it to Iberville. Leaving the Choctaw village on the 24th, the party arrived among the Chickasaw on March 3 and remained for two days to convince the Chickasaw to come and negotiate a peace with the Choctaw and the French in Mobile. On the 6th the party, now augmented by ten Chickasaws (including three women) began the return journey, arriving back at the Choctaw village on the

13th. From this village Tonti wrote the second letter, which he sent on ahead with a Frenchman to advise Iberville to prepare to receive the Indian embassy. Tonti's party passed through only two Choctaw villages and one of the Chickasaw, and he names none of them nor any of the people he met. He was neither concerned to make a complete record of the journey nor to describe everything he saw, but just because his primary intentions were not involved with most of the descriptions he does give, they may be that much less tinged by built-in bias.

The originals of these letters are not extant. The reason we have copies of them at all is that the copies were made by the geographer Claude Delisle for use in the new maps he was making;[16] information from these letters first appears incorporated into Delisle's map of 1703. The copies are characterized as *extraits* (extracts or abstracts—the French term is ambivalent), and this characterization has been questioned,[17] but Delisle's commentary on the documents, which accompanies them, together with the marginal notes he made and with information occurring in other documents which incorporate Tonti's new knowledge, suggest that in fact the letters originally were longer and perhaps contained more in the way of description of the events of the journey. But even as they are—or rather especially as they are—they provide most directly what Delisle copied them for: locational data on the tribes encountered by Tonti.

This data is often quite difficult to evaluate. Late February and early March are now a season of heavy rains in the Southeast, and the same was true in 1702. Tonti actually reported rain on only one of the twenty-nine days of the journey, but we know from Iberville's diary that there was heavy rain at the time in the area,[18] and these weather conditions made passing through the terrain the party encountered very difficult and subject to delay because of flooded streams. The path they took seems at least in its lower part from the Tohome to the Choctaw to have passed between the Tombigbee and the Chickasawhay, retracing an established Indian route to the salt springs in the vicinity of the Tohomes.[19] Tonti notes only one river emptying into the Pascagoula; this must have been the Chickasawhay, since the Pascagoula was understood to have two main branches at this date. But in spite of the paucity of westward-tending streams there was no lack of tributaries of the Tombigbee, some of them large and in flood, and Tonti crossed some seven to nine of them from the Tohome to the Chickasaw. All of this adds up to a laborious, uncomfortable, and difficult trip (Tonti complained of the cold and bad food), so that the distances recorded had to have been greatly exaggerated—a fact that Tonti seems to have realized and that Delisle suspected in his commentary.

Be all that as it may, the fact is that even without a clear interpretation of the distances and compass points that Tonti records, the information on the relative locations of the three tribes, given with reference to landmarks and to each other, is quite informative (see the reconstruction in Fig. 1). We must first realize as Tonti did that he was passing along only the eastern margin of the Choctaw lands, and this in itself is significant because it indicates that already by 1702 the Choctaw had been driven by Chickasaw/Creek/English pressure to the west of the Tombigbee, although they continued to claim land to the east of the river into the nineteenth century.[20] We cannot estimate how many Choctaw villages may have lain to the west of Tonti's route, although the report of a Pascagoula Indian in 1699 enumerated forty-five,[21] but the first village he encountered is clearly situated with reference to landmarks that are still identifiable: it was found three leagues (7.5 miles) northwest and then eighteen leagues (forty-five miles) north of the point where the party crossed the only river observed to empty into the Pascagoula: probably the Chickasawhay, since Tonti mentions no more river crossing until he enters Chickasaw country. Additionally, we have the information that there were hills from the Tohome village, known to have been located in the Mobile/Tensaw delta near the Alabama River confluence with the Tombigbee, as far as the Choctaw, and we know that except for the last eighteen leagues northward, the whole of the journey had tended northwest. It seems then that Tonti may have passed through the northwestward-tending Central Hills physiographic region of the state of Mississippi, and that his

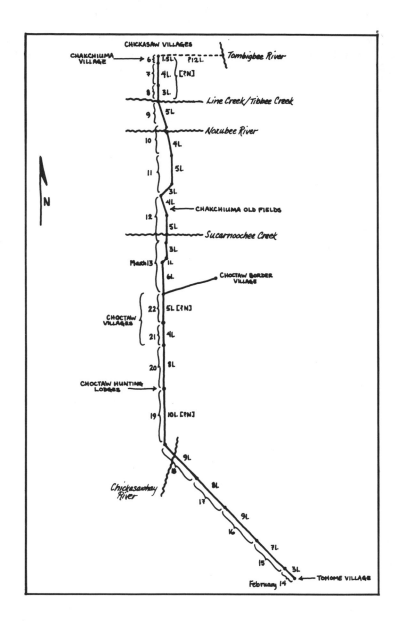

Figure 1. Diagrammatic presentation of route taken by Henri de Tonti in 1702, according to distances and directions indicated in the Tonti letters.

152

route took him to the western part of Kemper County (see Fig. 2). It would not be too risky given this information to assert that the village he cites as located ten leagues (twenty-five miles) to the east-northeast, which was fortified against enemy incursions, could well have been located on the Tombigbee, not far from a very late Mississippian site where distinctively Choctaw-like burial practices have been defined archaeologically.[22] Tonti did not visit that frontier village, but continued on after a rest on a more northerly route toward the Chickasaw lands.

For the northward part of the journey we cannot trust the distances or compass headings—as Tonti himself states—because the presence of slave-raiding parties in the field caused Tonti's Indian guides to take roundabout routes. The clue to the location of the Chickasaw comes when on the return journey Tonti observes that the Chickasaw village he visited was situated on a soil characterized by the inclusion of large fossil shells. In addition, he estimates that the location of the Chickasaw is at the distance of a journey of a day and a half from the main stream of the Tombigbee. We know that this fossil shell occurs in the Prairie Bluff and Selma formations underlying the soils of the Pontotoc Ridge and Black Prairie physiographic zones, which form the watershed boundary and part of the drainage area respectfully for the Tombigbee in Mississippi (see Fig. 2).[23] If we gauge the length of a journey of a day and a half by Tonti's experience, we would place it at about twelve leagues, or thirty miles.[24] Yet at no point is any location on these fossil-shell soils as far as thirty miles due west of the Tombigbee, so it seems that either the distance is very distorted or it refers to a distance east and south to some undefined head of navigation or ford. A more certain indication comes from the number of major Tombigbee tributaries that Tonti crossed on his southward journey. Beginning at the Chickasaws, there were three of them; they are drawn in on Fig. 1 and conjecturally labelled Line Creek / Tibbee Creek, Noxubee River, and Sucarnoochee Creek, which fit the rest of the specifications fairly well (see Fig. 2). If these identifications are correct, then the Chickasaw that Tonti visited were located north of Line Creek / Tibbee Creek, probably in

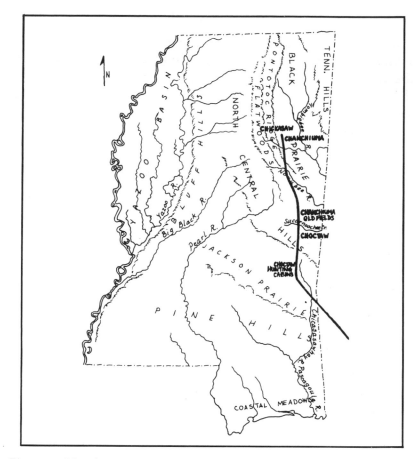

Figure 2. Tonti's 1702 route superimposed on physiographic map of Mississippi (after Erwin Raisz).

present-day Clay County, from which several large ridge-top Chickasaw sites are known from surface survey.[25] It will be noted that Tonti thus records the Chickasaw much further south than their later well-known location in Lee County;[26] only additional archaeological investigation can show whether there is any temporal distinction between the occupation of these two areas.

Perhaps more importantly, since we did already have some notion of the areas occupied by the Choctaw and Chickasaw, Tonti locates the Chakchiuma quite clearly at a distance of "three *arpents*" (two to five kilometers?) south of the Chickasaw village he visited. If we are right in assuming that the Chickasaw are in Clay County, then this location would tend to substantiate the tentative identification of a site near Starkville as Chakchiuma.[27] Even more interestingly, Tonti observes cleared lands explained to him as Chakchiuma old fields some twenty-two leagues generally southeast of the Chickasaw, only four leagues south of the end of the fossil shell. This would indicate that the southward journey had in fact tended southeast as Tonti notes, roughly paralleling the Tombigbee. It would also place these old fields in the northern part of Kemper County, the later Choctaw heartland. These two locations reflect the intermediate position—both politically and physically—seen to be occupied by the Chakchiuma throughout the French period.[28]

If we examine the Delisle maps of 1701, 1703, and 1718 (Fig. 3), we can see the substantial effect of Tonti's information on the European conception of the location of these tribal groups. Iberville's reports had been enough to change what may have been an old tradition that the Choctaw resided on the Black Warrior, as portrayed on the 1701 map. By 1703 better information from Iberville and Tonti has moved the Choctaw to the west of the Tombigbee and put the Chakchiuma on the map below the Chickasaw. By 1718, however, although Tonti's route now appears on the map, the influential information from missionaries and military men on the Yazoo river has placed the Chakchiuma on that river and removed them entirely from Tonti's route, in spite of continuing hints of their remaining located further east as well.[29] No version of the Southeast as rendered by Delisle captures all of the data reported by these letters, hence the study of locations from the map is incomplete without the evidence of the documents. And this series of identifications suggested by the Tonti letters has the further advantage of being archaeologically verifiable.

Even more crucial evidence that the maps cannot give is the pattern of intertribal alliances witnessed by Tonti. The French at Mobile saw the close relations between the Mobilian, Tohome, and Choctaw,[30] which was later to eventuate in near absorption

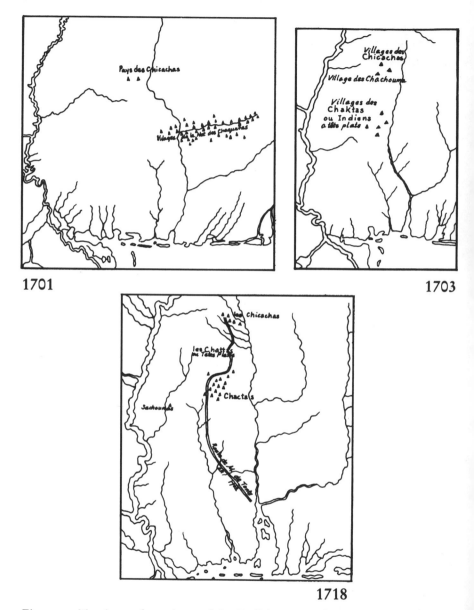

1701

1703

1718

Figure 3. Tracings of portions of the Delisle maps of 1701, 1703, and 1718, showing the evolution of knowledge of the placement of Choctaw and Chickasaw villages.

of the two smaller groups by the Choctaw.[31] More problematic is the political position of the Chakchiuma, who have such an intimate place in the Choctaw migration legend[32] and whose old fields were shown to Tonti at a location much closer to the Choctaw than the Chickasaw, for in these documents they are quite clearly both living in close proximity to the Chickasaw and joining them in the English-led slave raids on the Choctaw. Not seen by Tonti but mentioned as allied with the Chickasaw and Chakchiuma in this aggression against the Choctaw are the Alabama and the Conchak (Abihka). These groups taken together with those on the Mobile River nearly define the Western Muskogean linguistic group, yet here we see them split almost down the middle, and that before there were two European sides to create the kind of tension that should lead to such factionalism. This suggests that there may be some other factor at work here; that perhaps this slave-raiding disguises a struggle over which tribes are to succeed in becoming middlemen in the skin / European goods trade.[33]

We can investigate this question more thoroughly by looking at the evidence Tonti gives us about Indian subsistence patterns. Tonti, his French stomach rebelling against rations of unseasoned wheat gruel, remarks bitterly on the scarcity of game for the first hundred miles of his journey, during his passage through the mixed pine forests of the coastal plain. At the limit of this area he encounters Choctaw hunting lodges, apparently permanent, where both his experience of being offered deer meat supplies and the very presence of these lodges suggest that deer hunting was both profitable enough and important enough to justify the absence of warriors at the same time the Choctaw villages were being attacked to the north. Further, since Tonti complains no more of his fare and since once he reaches the Choctaw villages he finds an abundance of skins to trade for, we may infer that if hunting was important for food supply, it had also already become important as the source of a trade currency. That the Choctaw were aware of this is confirmed by their insistent request for a French trading post in the nation. Other sources suggest that there may already have been an English trade house previously established in the nation and subsequently withdrawn.[34]

The growing importance of hunting, however, had not substantially affected dependence upon the staple that had supported and influenced Mississippian societies: maize agriculture. Though there is no notice of agriculture among the Chickasaw and only the passing reference to old fields to identify it among the Chakchiuma, Tonti's party passed through enough of the Choctaw lands for him to observe that the Choctaw lived in dispersed hamlets and planted their fields in the river bottoms. One of his distance observations permits us to conclude that in at least one case the fields were as far as two leagues from the hamlet to which they belonged; this five-mile distance represents about an hour's walk, which has been shown to be the outside limit of the catchment area for non-mechanized agricultural communities.[35] Without a precise identification of the village in question, which would permit us to analyze the availability of suitable soils in the vicinity and thus evaluate the reasons for this exploitation of soils at the outside limit of efficiency, it is not possible to suggest why this boundary seems to have been strained at. Assuming that Tonti has indeed correctly identified the home village, this picture is not inconsistent with a pattern in which exhaustion of soils caused the catchment area of farming villages to be pushed out until the reaching of this limit forced relocation of the village nearer to productive areas. The result of this patterning was the strung-out "villages with dependent hamlets" (as they looked to European observers) which characterized the Choctaw settlement system as reported in later and more complete documents.[36]

The two Tonti letters provide us with the first clear glimpse of the effects that the English penetration from the east was having on this established aboriginal subsistence base. Although he did not visit it, Tonti explains that the Choctaw had one village nearest to the Chickasaw which was unable to engage in farming activities because it was too hard-pressed by Chickasaw, Alabama, and Conchak enemies. And as already observed, the ample supply of skins for trade in the Choctaw village where he rested for a day suggests that hunting for a surplus of skins beyond what would be needed for domestic use had begun, though to what extent we do not know. One implication of this pattern which should be borne in mind is a change in the balance of proteins and carbohydrates in the diet of a large segment of the population, since the meat yield of the game sought for skins would hardly be completely wasted.[37] Tonti's puzzling reference to the fact that the Choctaw "could be compared with the Natchez"—which may of course refer only to physical appearance and not to cultural similarities—is juxtaposed with the description of farming practices, and this may mean that in spite of this postulated new emphasis on the hunt, the strong involvement of males in agriculture which was characteristic of the Tunica[38] and possibly the Natchez[39] could also be observed in Tonti's time among the Choctaw.

These letters also offer direct evidence of the slave raids which is unique in that it is viewed from "inside." As a European moving under some kind of safe-conduct between both the slavers and the enslaved, Tonti had the opportunity to observe the effects of this practice on both parties and the way it was carried out. His observation of the method of making slave raids is most interesting for the continuity it shows with the "normal" mode of aboriginal intertribal warfare. Tonti was informed as he traveled from the Choctaw into the Chickasaw territory that there were two Chickasaw / Chakchiuma parties in the field, one of 10 and the other of 400 men, both of them led by Englishmen. It seems reasonable to conclude that the small party would constitute a scouting group, while the large one, in accordance with what Tonti was told, would be divided up into smaller groups to make brief surprise attacks for the capture of slaves. In the raids themselves the practice was to kill any men who were encountered and to carry off captive the women, children, and adolescents. The captives would be bound with the Indian slave cords described by Lamhatty[40] and then held by the English slavers in some sort of barracoon-like holding area until enough slaves had been accumulated to ship off to Carolina.

This last part of the pattern, and undoubtedly the intensity with which the raids were being prosecuted, represent the only substantial departures from the established patterns of aboriginal warfare in the protohistoric period. European descriptions of this warfare from as early as the Soto expedition have been widely quoted[41] and compared with archaeological evidence of Mississippian sites and later ethnohistorical evidence to show that this pattern of guerilla raids and capture of women and children, with some men where possible for ritual torture by the victors, was a continuous one from at least the sixteenth through the early nineteenth centuries in the Southeast.[42] In the instance of these slave raids, the primary change that can be observed is that the proceeds—the captive women and children—were sold into slavery in the English seaboard colonies or overseas instead of being integrated into the capturing tribe. We have no evidence from Tonti to explain whether the motivation for these raids (in the aboriginal case, blood revenge, status enhancement, possible territorial encroachment[43]) had indeed changed into simply a commercial enterprise or had been overlaid on the earlier motivations in some complex way, which the English slave-buyer claims and which is what the later evidence suggests, since once the slave-raiding period had passed these established motivations did still clearly dominate.

We are given a close look through Tonti's eyes at this Englishman who was behind the activity, and Tonti's view of him is pretty jaundiced; it should be remembered that the defection of Jean Couture and the subsequent English penetration to the Mississippi had caused the downfall of Tonti's trade house at the Arkansas. The Englishman's adoption of native dress is complete, and Tonti has trouble at first in recognizing him for an Englishman in his breechcloth, beads, blanket, and none-too-clean shirt. There are related documents which detail Iberville's efforts to have arrested the English mastermind of slave raids and the threatened assassination of the missionary Davion on the Yazoo river.[44] Tonti identifies this man as the culprit, though the Englishman denies it. One feels in the presence of this circumstantial evidence that one is very close to finding an identity for this man among the ranks of the Carolina traders who had been making their way along the Upper Path all the way to the Mississippi since at least 1698 and probably before.[45] But documents for this early period are few and far between from the English side, and most of the men who made up this group whom we know by name were only the most important of them, the men who established the routes and then settled in Carolina to profit from them. Adair's involvement in the area was just too late for him to have been well-acquainted with these early backwoodsmen, and the near-illegal character of their activities precluded their recording their activities in any effective manner. Thus, though Tonti refers to the man he met as "ce coquin d'anglois dit a jean," and Higginbotham has attempted to render this as a name, possibly Johnson,[46] it seems far more likely that "a jean" renders the English word "agent," which Tonti would not have understood, certainly not as he heard it pronounced by the Indians who knew the man. The further clues we have to his identity include the possible involvement with events on the Yazoo of which Tonti accuses him and the fact that he asks Tonti if he can speak Shawnee. The latter acquaintance with Shawnee would imply some prior close association with that tribe, perhaps involvement with them as allies is the Westo war of the early 1680s, which so much favored the designs of the private traders or "Goose Creek Men" of Carolina.[47] As for trading and slaving activities on the Yazoo, this would connect our "a jean" with the traders Welch and Dodsworth who had established the overland route to the Mississippi just a few years before.[48]

But this Englishman's name is far less important than the information about his methods that Tonti does give us. He participates in slave raids, afterwards takes custody of the slaves for future transport, and controls the distribution of English trade goods in return for these slaves. Furthermore, Tonti's observation that he must have great influence in the nation because he is allotted the lion's share of the French presents that the Chickasaw chiefs receive must only be Tonti's misunderstanding of an arrangement probably reflecting the fact that in a few short years of trading the English had already managed to get the Chickasaw involved in the debt and credit pattern typical of the frontier Indian trade.[49] His other activities certainly do not imply such influence as Tonti assumes, since one of the Chickasaw chiefs is able to demand the return of a Choctaw captive to be traded to the French instead; the Englishman's reply is merely a threat to transfer his attentions to other tribes. Indeed when we sum up the effects of the English influence among the Chickasaw as seen by Tonti at this date, they do not seem to be very thoroughgoing, at least as far as slaving is concerned. Tonti had little trouble persuading the Chickasaw that it would be a good idea to come to Mobile and make peace with the Choctaw and the French, even if their understandable fear of Choctaw retaliation made persuading them to undertake the journey rather more difficult.

Up to this point the information taken from the two Tonti letters has been perfectly straightforward for the most part, though of course subject to interpretation. There is a great deal more that may be extracted in the way of inferences from the direct evidence, and I will present a few of these possibilities here to complete the discussion of the documents.

The bulk of these inferences comes under the heading of sociopolitical organization. Belaboring this evidence would be risky, but there are a few remarks that can be hazarded as suggestions. First we may say that the dignity and authority of those men identified as chiefs among the Chickasaw seems equivalent to that of the headman of a tribal group, since it does not seem to be coercive. The outward semblances of the chief's authority are the familiar ceremony of Tonti's reception on mats before the headman's house and the headman's ability to control the actions of the Englishman vis-a-vis his own people.

Perhaps the most interesting point about the Chickasaw social structure can be suggested from the composition of the negotiating team sent to Mobile. It consists of five *considerables*, two *louez*, and three women.[50] The term *louez* is ambiguous; if it means "hired" then we are dealing with burden-bearers, but if it means "praised," as may be the case, then these men may repre-

sent a rank distinct from the five *considerables;* Iberville's different perception of the ranks confuses the issue but argues for the
latter interpretation.[51] More interesting still is the presence of
the three women. Although Iberville's brief later account of the
treaty meeting does not mention them, there is the possibility
that in fact they were there as a functioning part of the embassy,
not simply as household drudges for the journey, since Tonti
makes no mention of their performing such duties. And if they
are part of the embassy, it may suggest that among the Chickasaw, as among tribes further east,[52] women sometimes played a
part in the tribe's political decisions.

There are equally interesting observations to be made regarding Choctaw sociopolitical organization, most specifically regarding the three divisions of which the tribe was composed.[53]
The Choctaw chief who accompanies Tonti on his journey from
Mobile to the Chickasaw seems to have been one of these division leaders, for it is he with two other chiefs who join the
expedition on its way back to Mobile who make up the Choctaw negotiating team. It is therefore significant that when he ha-
rangues the Chickasaw on the advisability of treating with the
Choctaw for peace and with the French for goods he states that
he speaks only for his own village (it is repeatedly obvious that
Tonti intends the word to have a more expanded meaning than
"hamlet"). It is thus possible to infer that the three divisions
were politically autonomous but that someone who could be
recognized as a headman over each of the divisions did exist. It
also seems clear that there was no single "great chief" of the
Choctaw at this date.

We have repeatedly remarked upon the frontier village of
which Tonti was told, which was unable to carry on agricultural
pursuits because of the depredations of the slave raiders. Yet this
village was persisting in its location, and though such is not
clearly stated, may have functioned precisely as a fortified outpost. But if such was the case, how did the inhabitants subsist?
There may be room here to infer that in some way this frontier
outpost was subsidized by the other towns that would benefit
by its protection and warning, and this inference would lead to

the necessity for demonstrating that some political authority existed to cause the subsidy to be gathered together. For comparison we may recall Adair's erroneous statement that the Nanih Waiya mound and earthwork had probably been built by the ancient Choctaw to serve as a border defense.[54] Swanton's "Anonymous Relation" names such a border fort, Ougoula tanap or "war people," located "near the Chickasaws on the road to the Alabamas."[55] In both cases there is the assumption that the inhabitants were subsidized by their society at large, but there is not enough evidence to suggest the kind of sociopolitical structure that made this possible.

Finally, there are a few little tidbits of information about the several tribes that do not fit under any of the topics so far discussed. The Choctaw treatment of guests is footnoted by the observation that Tonti's party was met by Choctaw people bearing food for the party's refreshment at several leagues' distance from the first Choctaw town on the return journey. The Chickasaw were known and notorious throughout the colonial period for their wide-ranging depredations on other tribes, and this is underlined by the fact that after some effort Tonti was able to locate in the Chickasaw village he visited a speaker of the Illinois language with which he was familiar; one of the promises made by the French in the treaty that followed was that they would announce to their Indian allies of the Illinois district that they were no longer at war with the Chickasaw.[56]

There is one item that may prove to be of great importance in the evaluation of the Chickasaw belief system. Tonti was very interested in the fossil shell beds which he encountered in the chalks and clays of the Pontotoc Ridge and Black Prairie, so much so that he asked a Chickasaw about their origin. He received the reply that the deposits dated from the time when the great chief was angered and caused all of the land to be flooded. Tonti remarks to Iberville, "notice that these people have a notion of the Flood." But the issue may be much larger than this. First, there is the fact that the Chickasaw had not yet attracted the sustained attention of the missionaries. Secondly, the fossil shell does exist in large quantity and is only too obvious to this day; the Chickasaw, who certainly knew that such shell must have something to do with a seacoast, would have needed an explanatory myth, which could easily have been prompted by the drastic floods of which the Tombigbee is capable. They used the shell constantly in the production of their pottery,[57] and the work of collecting it and crushing it for use as pottery temper must have been within the awareness of all. As a functional resource in the society it would be likely to receive explanation, but it is quite possible that the explanation preceded and motivated the use, since previous cultures in the same region did not use this fossil shell in pottery making. In a different vein, a similar myth reported from the Bayougoula by Father du Ru at the same period explained thunder as the firing of a great cannon by an angered Supreme Chief.[58] In both cases the connection between the anger of a supreme chief and storm or flood suggests that the chief himself was connected with the sun, as was so clearly the case with the Natchez.

The reader will have noticed that the pages of this commentary far outnumber the pages of the letters themselves, so that on the face of it such a lengthy commentary is guilty of the kind of overkill that footnoting of historical documentary publications has been accused of in recent years.[59] We are not, however, dealing with the doings of "Great White Men" when we write ethnohistory; the genre is different and its treatment of its primary sources must be different.[60] The example here has shown that narrative history is not the only thing that can be reconstructed from the use of such sources, and that even the most trivial of observations may gain significance when placed in a context of time, place, and other evidence from additional sources. The Choctaw did not have an Adair to record the traditions of their past, or if they did his work has not survived. And although Adair's work itself presents a truly exceptional body of ethnohistoric data, it does not date from as early as the period we are interested in. Here in Tonti's few pages we have seen a tantalizingly brief glimpse of Choctaw and Chickasaw life, whose modes were being changed by Tonti's very presence. However brief the glimpse or scanty the data, like the other early French documents these deserve full exploitation so that their evidence can take its place with all the other little scraps of data that can be gathered from this period. With the help of archaeology it may then be possible to reconstruct a picture of the lifeways of Mississippi Indians as they emerged into the destructive currents of European global politics.

[cover sheet]

No. 20.X, 20.

Extract from a letter from M. de Tonti
to M. d'Iberville, from the village of
the Chacta, February 23, 1702.

C3-19

[folio 1]

No.X,20   by Claude de l'Isle
Extract from a letter from M. de Tonty to
M. d'Iberville from the village of the
Chacta, February 23, 1702

I had the honor of writing to you from the Tome and I told you that I had taken 2 Mobiliens, 2 Tome, and a Chaqta chief to accompany me as far as the Chicacha and that I had promised each of them a gun and a little powder & balls; I have been obliged to take a guide here at the same price. The men that I am taking with me will bring the chief of the Chicacha to come and see you more easily, since he might find it difficult to pass through the villages of his enemies.

We did not arrive here without a lot of trouble; this is nothing but mountains & big hills, continuous pine forests mixed with oaks, walnut & chestnut trees. One sees quantities of limestone, quantities of streams, and a small river which empties into the one of the Pascogoula. All the streams are rivers that it is necessary to ford in water up to the armpits; no game at all except 2 deer; we have been reduced to wheat-meal gruel without seasoning. Here is the route that we have taken:

Departed from the Tome February 14; route to N.W.; slept 3 l. away; crossed 3 streams; beginning of hills as far as the Chacta.

The 15th 7 l. N.W.; crossed a stream. The 16th 9 l. N.W.; at 5 l. from camp found a small river & 1 l. from there the one which empties into the river of the Tome; mountains & large hills.

The 17th 8 l. N.W.; same kind of country; crossed a stream twice.

The 18th 9 l. N.W.; at 5 l. from camp found a small river and 1 l. from there, another which empties into that of the Pascogoula, overflowed for a quarter league from each bank.

The 19th slept 10 l. from there at the hunting cabins of the Chacta; they gave us a deer. Same kind of country.

The 20th slept 8 l. from there at the first settlements of the Chacta; our route to the N.; same kind of country.

The 21st slept 4 l. from there to the N. in the cabin of the chief of the free settlements. Same kind of country.

The 22nd slept 5 l. away at the house of the chief of the last settlements nearest to the Chicacha of the 2 villages. Gave [him] a gun.

[folio 2] The 23rd stayed over to obtain food supplies & skins. That, sir, in brief is our little itinerary which adds up to a good 63 leagues. This nation is numerous, which I judge by what I have been able to see of men & cabins, rather distant from one another, on mountains & hills. They sow in the bottoms; the men there are rather handsome and I can compare this nation with the Natche. They are very satisfied that you want to have peace made for them with the Chicacha; they have received us very well. I am leaving tomorrow on the 24th. You certainly see, sir, that the time that you have given me for my return on the 20th of March is short; that is why I am asking you for 5 more days' extension. It might be 50 l. from here to the Chicacha. We have only passed through 2 Chacta villages. There is one 10 l. away from here to the E.N.E. which does not sow, because their enemies, who are the Chicacha, the Conchaques, & the Alimamons do not give them any rest. We will not go that way. I gave a gun to the chief of this village before taking from here the things that we need.

I have promised each of the two Chaqta 6 knives, 2 hatchets,

& 2 fathoms of large *rassades* to carry you this letter. It has been so cold since our departure that I have not yet been able to get warm.

If the chief of the Chickasaw comes, the 3 chiefs of the Choctaw will accompany him to the settlement to learn your will.

Extract from another letter from the same to the same.

From the Chacta, March 14, 1702

I told you by my last that from the Tome to the Chacta I had gone 63 leagues to the N.N.W. That this nation, although mistreated by the Conchac, the Alimamon, and the Chicacha, would consent to peace with the Chicacha. If I had not perceived the usefulness that might come from peace between these two nations I would never have undertaken so hasty a journey.

I left the village of the Chacta the 24th of February to pursue my route to the Chicacha. At 34 l. from the village we found the tracks of some warriors who were going against the Chacta; that surprised my savages, who took various routes which lengthened our road and caused me to count 56 l. from one village to the other.

At 3 l. from the village of the Chicacha I heard a shot, [folio 3] I sent [someone] toward the shot & a Chicacha came to us who told us that there was a party of 10 men and another of 400 men against the Chacta, led by an Englishman. I believed my journey useless.

We arrived at the village on the 3rd of March having held our route to the N. quarter of N.E. We passed on a hill a village of Chachouma, and about 4 kilometers [3 *arpents*] from there we entered that of the Chicacha. They came before us and the savages took the packs of our Frenchmen and conducted us to the chief's cabin. They made us sit on some mats near the cabin. The chief was seated there & an Englishman that I had trouble recognizing for one. He was seated holding a gun in his hand and a saber at his side. He had on a rather dirty blue shirt, no pants, stockings, or shoes, a scarlet wool [*incarlatine*] blanket and some discs at his neck like a savage. Our Chacta notable [*considerable*] made his speech and then the Englishman whom I had regarded with nothing but anger came up to me & asked me if I knew how to speak Chouanon; I had him told no and that I had come to seek the chief on your behalf. That since I knew him by reputation for a wretch that he had better not make any speech against us, that if I noticed it he would be sorry. He had me asked why I believed he was so bad. I had him told that he had wanted to kill M. Davion when he was at the Chicacha (Which he denied) and then that he was having all these nations destroyed in order to obtain slaves and that he ought to be sated with human flesh, which he similarly denied, saying that it was the savages who had brought them to war, but when I asked him why his comrade was leading 400 warriors he had no answer to give me.

The 4th I presented the chief with a gun, some powder, some balls, and some knives in order to invite them to go to see you; the Chacta spoke, but he only spoke for his village.

The 5th I found a man who spoke Illinois, by whom I had the chief told what my interpreter had not understood; this caused 5 of the most notable [*considerables*] to decide to accompany me, apparently in the hope of receiving some presents.

The 6th we left: 5 of the notables [*considerables*], 2 hired bearers [*louez*], and three Chicacha women. The rain obliged us to camp [folio 4] 1½ l. from there. A warrior informed us that a young Chacta had been taken away. Straightaway I made the chief understand that it was necessary to have him back and that you would pay as much for him as the Englishman could.

The 7th the Englishman had the slave sent by another road, but the chief having gone to the village he brought him to us; he was about 15 or 16 years old. The chief told me that as he arrived at the village the Englishman was cutting the slave's cords & that he had snatched him from his hands; that the Englishman had threatened him with leaving & that he had answered get out; that the French had only one mouth & that he [the Englishman] had two; that he made them kill every day in order to get slaves, that the French only wanted skins & peace with all the nations and that the Englishman had put his head between his knees.

I assure you, sir, that this Englishman is a very bad character;

his cabin is full of slaves that he abuses. He has some influence, & I noticed that when the chiefs divided the presents I gave them on your behalf, he received the greatest share. The weather having cleared in the afternoon, we slept 4 l. from the village.

The 8th at 3 l. from camp we found an unfordable river. The savages told us that it was necessary to camp, that it would only take a night for the water to go down and that it would only be up to our ankles. We camped and at 2 o'clock in the afternoon a man came from the village who told us that the large party, being at the village of the Chachouma, sent some scouts to that of the Chacta, that they had killed 3 men & that they took the women & the children of one cabin, that this attack, having revealed them, had made the large party decide to go back. At this news the five Notables [*Considerables*] who were with me had me told that they were afraid that the Chacta would kill them, and there was one of them who wanted to return. I made the others understand that I was hired to come and seek them; that if they did not come with me to see the great Chief their wars would continue forever; that the French would not go any longer among them, whereas on the other hand there would always be many among the Chacta; that they [the Chacta] would have much powder & guns and that the 2 nations would destroy one another quickly; and that the English would come then to take the rest; [folio 5] That if they came with me you would give them some presents and some Frenchmen to escort them to their village; that you would send them boats loaded with merchandise by the Mobile river, which passes 1½ days' journey from their village; that they would have nothing to fear for themselves.

This speech reassured them; we left the 9th, we crossed the low lying lands of the river in water to just above the belt, and it took 1½ hours to reach dry land; our journey was only 5 l. Our route from the village to this camp was toward the S. quarter of S.E.

The 10th we sent 2 savages to sound the ford of a river; we took until half-past noon to cross it and made 5 l. Our route was

½ l. to the W. and as much to the E. and the four other l. to the S.S.E.

The 11th we left [behind] a thing rather ancient; from the village of the Chicacha as far as here there is a quantity of shells larger & thicker than oysters scattered in the prairies and hills. I asked them if it was men or the sea which had brought them there. The savages answered me that it was from the time when the great chief was angry & he flooded all the land; notice that these people have a notion of the Flood. Continuing the journey, at 1 l. we passed a river; at 2 l. from there we crossed another one; at ½ l. passed yet another. At ½ l. we found a prairie, old fields of the Chachouma which stretched for 2 l., and then slept 1½ l. further on; made 5 l. to the S. and then 3 l. to the S.W.

The 12th we took our route to the S.S.E. for 4 l. & crossed 2 little rivers. Then at 1 l. further on found a broad hunting path which led us to a river where there was a l. of country submerged and went to sleep 3 l. on, making southward for 5 l. There you have all the rivers that there are from the Chicacha to the Chacta which empty into the Mobile, and the country that we have passed through thus far is low country & a few hills & prairies. From the Chacta to the Tome there is only one river that empties into the one of Pascogoula, at 32 l. from the Tome; all the others empty into the Mobile, and the country consists only of hills & mountains, pine forests mixed with some oaks. [folio 6] At noon I will send the Chacta chief with Dubournai in order to persuade the savages to receive well the Chicacha who are with us.

The 13th, after having marched 3 l. to the S., we left the road to take up another at 1 l. to the S.W. which took us to the S. for 4 l. to the first cornfield where the men came to meet us with some food, and after having made 2 l. more on the same route we arrived at the first village where the Chiefs were all well received; they all appeared happy with the peace & to go and meet you to confirm it, and since I am well aware that you might have left for France before my return I am sending you

Denboursier to carry you this so that you might be informed of everything that has happened in my journey and that you might have the generosity to give orders for the reception of the savages whom I am bringing you, and for the presents that you wish to give them. There are 5 Chicacha, 2 hired men [*louez*], and 3 women, and 3 chiefs of the Chacta. I cannot write to you of what will follow. There being rather a crowd, I have told Denboursier to have made up at the Tome 5 sacks of wheat-meal gruel & a sack of oats and as much again at Mobile so that these people will not draw upon your food supplies and that they may be paid at the settlement.

Permit me to tell you, sir, that these two nations wish to be won over by considerable presents and that in making allies for ourselves of these people none of the other nations will dare to stir, and if they are not satisfied with the French one must not doubt that the English will do all they can to attract them and cause all your neighboring savages to be destroyed, and that they will strike the iron while it is hot.

The Chicacha want a trade among them, which is very easy by the Mobile [River], which lies one and a half days from their village. The Chactas, being more nearby, can bring their things to the fort, and if we trade with the Chickachas, very soon one will see the Conchacs and the Alimamons who are their friends and neighbors. This rascal of an Englishman called "a jean" complained that he was going to leave the Chicacha to go to the Conchaques & that he would invite them to destroy the Chicacha. You understand the manners of the savages better than anyone, which is why I hope that you will give your orders. When a journey like this one with presents for the savages totals up to 100 pistoles it is not a matter for the king; I will leave tomorrow & I will depart day after tomorrow [folio 7] from the settlements, and I hope to arrive the 25th. In case you leave, I beg you, sir to have the enclosed memorandum carried out. If the explorations to the West of which I have spoken to you do not please you & if you judge me to be useful elsewhere you know what my brother told you in France, and what I have told you also: use me however you will & be assured that I will always take pleasure in doing what you would wish.

Notes

[1] John R. Swanton, *Final Report of the United States De Soto Expedition Commission;* more recently: Jeffrey P. Brain, Alan Toth, and Antonio Rodriguez-Buckingham, "Ethnohistoric Archaeology and the De Soto Entrada into the Lower Mississippi Valley," *Conference on Historic Site Archaeology Papers* 7 (1974), 232–89; George E. Lankford, "A New Look at De Soto's Route through Alabama," *Journal of Alabama Archaeology* 23 (1977), 10–16.

[2] Brain, Jeffrey P., *On the Tunica Trail,* Louisiana Archaeological Survey and Antiquities Commission Anthropological Study 1 (1977); Christopher S. Peebles, "Moundville: Late Prehistoric Sociopolitical Organization in the Southeastern United States," paper presented at the American Ethnological Society Annual Meeting, 1979; Philip Phillips, James A. Ford, and James B. Griffin, *Archaeological Survey in the Lower Mississippi Alluvial Valley, 1940–1947,* Peabody Museum of Archaeology and Ethnology Papers 15 (1951).

[3] Edward G. Bourne (ed.), *Narratives of the Career of Hernando De Soto,* 3 vols. (New York, 1922), 2, 132–33.

[4] George I. Quimby, "The Natchezan Culture Type;" Jeffrey P. Brain, "Late Prehistoric Settlement Patterning in the Yazoo Basin and Natchez Bluff Regions of the Lower Mississippi Valley."

[5] Fred Gearing, "Priests and Warriors: Social Structures for Cherokee Politics in the Eighteenth Century;" Fred Eggan, *The American Indian: Perspectives for the Study of Social Change,* 15–44; John R. Swanton, *Early History of the Creek Indians and their Neighbors,* "Social and Religious Beliefs and Usages of the Chickasaw Indians," and *Source Material for the Social and Ceremonial Life of the Choctaw Indians.*

[6] The Bottle Creek site in the Mobile-Tensaw delta was identified as a widely-recognized ceremonial center by the Indians. See Pierre Margry, *Découvertes et établissements des français dans l'ouest et dans le sud de l'Amérique septentrionale* 1, 513; Pierre François Xavier de Charlevoix, *Histoire et description générale de la Nouvelle France avec le Journal Historique d'un Voyage* 6, 191; Cailup B. Curren, "Prehistoric and Early Historic Occupation of the Mobile Bay and Mobile Delta area of Alabama with Emphasis on Subsistence," 78–9.

[7] James Adair, *The History of the American Indians,* 376–7.

[8] Tonti to Iberville, February 23 and March 14, 1702; Archives du Service Hydrographique 115, 10: No. 20.

[9] Marcel Giraud, *A History of French Louisiana* 1, 76–8; Jay Higginbotham, *Old Mobile: Fort Louis de la Louisiane, 1702–1711,* 53–68.

[10] Swanton, *Source Material,* 1.

[11] Verner W. Crane, "The Tennessee River as the Road to Carolina: The Beginnings of Exploration and Trade."

[12] Ibid.; Margry, ibid. 1, 430.

[13] Verner W. Crane, "The Southern Frontier in Queen Anne's War."

[14] J. Leitch Wright, Jr., *The Only Land They Knew,* 102–150; Verner W. Crane, *The Southern Frontier, 1670–1732,* 134–6.

[15] Margry, ibid. 1, 460.

[16] Jean Delanglez, "The Sources of the Delisle Map of America, 1703."

[17] Higginbotham, *Old Mobile,* 63.

[18] Margry, ibid. 1, 515.

[19] Ian W. Brown, *Salt and the Eastern North American Indian: An Archaeological Study,* 18; Vernon J. Knight and Sherée Adams, "A Voyage to the Mobile and Tomeh in 1700, with Notes on the Interior of Alabama," 47.

[20] Angie Debo, *The Rise and Fall of the Choctaw Republic,* 34.

[21] Jay Higginbotham, *The Journal of Sauvole,* 35.

[22] Mary Lucas Powell, "Biocultural Analysis of Human Skeletal Remains from the Lubbub Creek Archaeological Locality."

[23] Lloyd William Stephenson and Watson Hiner Monroe, *The Upper Cretaceous Deposits,* Mississippi State Geological Survey Bulletin 40 (1940).

[24] Margry, ibid. 1, 520.

[25] Samuel O. Brookes and John Connaway, "Archaeological Survey of Clay County, Mississippi."

[26] Jesse D. Jennings, "Chickasaw and Earlier Indian Cultures of Northeast Mississippi."

[27] James R. Atkinson, "A Historic Contact Indian Settlement in Oktibbeha County, Mississippi."

[28] Régis du Roullet, "Journal," Jan. 12–March 23, 1730, Archives des Colonies, série C13A, 12, 117v–118; Bienville to Maurepas, Feb. 10, 1736, AC, C13A, 21, 130v–137; Bienville to Maurepas, Dec. 20, 1737, AC, C13A, 22, 115v; Vaudreuil to Maurepas, Nov. 4, 1748, AC, C13A, 32, 123–125.

[29] AC, série B, 57, 804.

[30] Margry, ibid. 1, 531.

[31] Régis du Roullet, "Noms des villages Chactas," 1730, AC, C13A, 12, 134v.

[32] Adair, ibid., 65; Swanton, *Source Material,* 30.

[33] George T. Hunt, in his *The Wars of the Iroquois: A Study in Intertribal Trade Relations* (Madison, 1940) argues that this motive could play a large role in intertribal relations.

[34] Higginbotham, *Sauvole,* 35.

[35] M. Chisholm, *Rural Settlement and Land Use* (London, 1968), 66, quoted in Christopher S. Peebles, "Determinants of Settlement Size and Land Use in the Moundville Phase," 404.

[36] Compare descriptions in Régis du Roullet, "Itinerary," April–August 1732, Archives du Service Hydrographique, V. LXVII², No. 14-1, Portfolio 135, document 21.

[37] Margry, ibid. 1, 517–18.

[38] John R. Swanton, *Indian Tribes of the Lower Mississippi Valley and Adjacent Coast of the Gulf of Mexico,* 317.

[39] Compare Quimby, "Natchezan Culture Type," 270.

[40] David I. Bushnell, "The Account of Lamhatty;" Wright, ibid., 146.

[41] See Jon L. Gibson, "Aboriginal Warfare in the Protohistoric Southeast: An Alternative Perspective," *American Antiquity* 39 (1974), 130–33.

[42] John R. Swanton, "Aboriginal Culture of the Southeast," 705.

[43] For a summary see Charles Hudson, *The Southeastern Indians,* 239–57; compare what John P. Reid says for the Cherokee in *A Law of Blood* (New York, 1970), 153–61.

[44] Margry, ibid. 1, 352.

[45] Compare Crane, "Tennessee River" and "Queen Anne's War;" Philip M. Brown, "Early Indian Trade in the Development of South Carolina," offers more detailed discussion of the traders themselves.

[46] Higginbotham, *Old Mobile,* 64.

[47] Wright, ibid., 111.

[48] Crane, *Southern Frontier,* 45–6; Brown, "Early Indian Trade."

[49] Daniel H. Usner, Jr., "Frontier Exchange in the Lower Mississippi Valley," 2; Wright, ibid., 172–4.

[50] See Crane, *Southern Frontier*, 69; figures from Margry, ibid. 1, 516.

[51] Margry, ibid.

[52] Hudson, ibid., 186–7; Gearing, "Priests and Warriors," 4.

[53] Swanton, *Source Material*, 55–6.

[54] Adair, ibid., 377.

[55] Swanton, ibid., 258.

[56] Margry, ibid. 1, 520.

[57] Jennings, ibid.

[58] Ruth Lapham Butler, *Journal of Paul du Ru*, 5.

[59] Frederika J. Teute, "Views in Review: A Historiographical Perspective on Historical Editing," *American Archivist* 43 (1980), 43–56.

[60] Patricia Galloway, "Dearth and Bias: Issues in the Editing of Ethnohistorical Materials."

An Archaeological Study of Culture Contact and Change in the Natchez Bluffs Region

IAN W. BROWN

•

Introduction

WHEN LA SALLE traveled down the Mississippi River in 1682, he had grand hopes for expanding French control over a major portion of North America. Four score years later, had he lived, he would have seen his dreams go up in smoke. Although Louisiana played a minor role in the Seven Years' War, its fate did rest on the outcome of this contest. Louisiana was divided between Spain and England in 1763, but the recipients did not receive the prize they had perhaps expected.

Some thirty-odd years earlier France was in the process of building a strong colony. Mobile was already well-established and New Orleans was progressing admirably, but the pride of Louisiana was the settlement at Natchez. This community, nestled on the bluffs overlooking the eastern bank of the Mississippi River, was located midway between New Orleans and the Arkansas Post. It had already proven itself to be an economic asset to the rapidly growing French empire. However, in the fall of 1729 Louisiana was crippled by a blow for which it was totally unprepared. The Natchez Indians, in a concerted attack, effectively massacred their French neighbors and put the torch to their homes. French settlement in the Natchez area was never able to recover fully from this devastating event.

The nature of French-Indian culture contact in the Natchez Bluffs region is the subject of a current project being conducted by the Lower Mississippi Survey (LMS) of Peabody Museum, Harvard University.[1] The Natchez Indians were, in historic times, the largest aboriginal group in the lower Mississippi Valley. They occupied a narrow stretch of land in southwestern

176

Figure 1. Natchez Project Area.

Mississippi between the Big Black River in the north and the Homochitto River in the south (Fig. 1). Heaviest settlement occurred in the vicinity of the present-day city of Natchez. Most French travelers in Louisiana were captivated by the unusual customs of the Natchez.[2] Because of their complex sociopolitical organization and unique religious practices, the Natchez Indians have played an important role in North American Indian anthropological literature.[3] Archaeologists working in the Southeast have also commonly made use of Natchez ethnography, especially in regard to discussions concerning prehistoric chiefdoms and states.[4]

The LMS has had an archaeological interest in the Natchez for quite some time. The steep loess bluff hills towering above the eastern banks of the Mississippi provide a marked contrast with the broad flat floodplain below. Reaching heights of over thirty meters along the edge of the valley, these wind-blown hills gently taper off to the east.[5] Human occupation in this ecologically rich and diverse region has been traced to the Paleo-Indian

Era, but most research on the Natchez Bluffs has focused on late prehistoric and historic times.[6]

Significant demographic changes occurred among the Natchez in the late sixteenth and seventeenth centuries, long before direct contact with Europeans. In order to comprehend what was happening to the Natchez at this time, it is first necessary to understand the nature of eighteenth-century Natchez society. The direct historical approach, a method of working from the known to the unknown, is an important methodological technique in our work. In this paper we will discuss the application of this method to the Natchez in light of some topics of anthropological concern. The major focus of the current LMS project revolves around the study of culture change as manifested in material remains. We are primarily interested in what ways Natchez Indian society and culture changed as a result of European influences. On a theoretical level, we are concerned with whether or not such historically recorded changes can be reflected in material culture studies. Although investigations are still in the beginning stages, the time seems ripe to present some of our research objectives.

Historical Background

The Natchez Indians first appeared in the historical record in the 1540s as the Quigualtam (or Quigualtanqui) of the De Soto Entrada. The haughty chief of the Quigualtam refused to make the pilgrimage to De Soto. He declared himself to be the descendant of the sun; one who was accustomed to having people come to him, not he to others. De Soto did not survive to meet the people of Quigualtam, but his men unfortunately did.[7] The domination of the Natchez in the mid-sixteenth century covered an extensive area along the eastern bank of the Mississippi. Their southern limit was basically the same as recorded in the eighteenth century, but their northern border extended virtually to the present-day city of Vicksburg.[8] According to the Elvas narrative, in descending the river from their point of departure at Aminoya (in northeast Louisiana), the Spaniards first encountered the natives of Quigualtam when the river's bluffs appeared in sight.[9] In the sixteenth century, as now, the river first met the bluffs at Vicksburg. The Indians of Quigualtam were probably from the Glass site and its surrounds. This major protohistoric mound center is located approximately ten kilometers south of Vicksburg.[10] Another protohistoric Natchez center, of equal or greater importance, was the Emerald site, located about seventy kilometers south-southwest of Glass (Fig. 2)[11] It is, therefore, interesting that the Conquistadors were attacked by a second group of Quigualtam some distance below their initial confrontation.[12] The latter warriors probably were under the control of the Emerald site center.

La Salle was the first known Frenchman to contact the Natchez. From the various accounts of his 1682 expedition, it is clear that the prestige and power of this tribe had diminished significantly since the mid-sixteenth century. Severe demographic changes had occurred in the intervening years. The actual mechanics of the changes are not known, but there can be little doubt that they were somehow associated with European contact. Diseases and increased warfare are the standard causes given, and, most probably, they are the correct ones.[13] Whatever the reasons, we do know, from both historical and archaeological data, that Natchez territory shrank in historic times.[14] The Natchez maintained their position as a formidable power by concentrating people in a more confined area and by adopting small foreign tribes from the north. The Tioux and Grigra, both Mississippian groups of the Tunican linguistic family, were two Yazoo Valley tribes that were incorporated into Natchez society.[15]

The French had relatively few relations with the Natchez between 1682 and 1700. In the latter year a mission was set up among the Natchez, but it was terminated in 1706. Because of the debilitating effects of her war with England, France was not able to give much attention to the Natchez Indians.[16] This oversight was to prove foolish, as the English were quite active in courting the affections of these Indians in the early years of the eighteenth century.[17] By the time the French finally established a trading post among the Natchez in 1712,[18] factions were al-

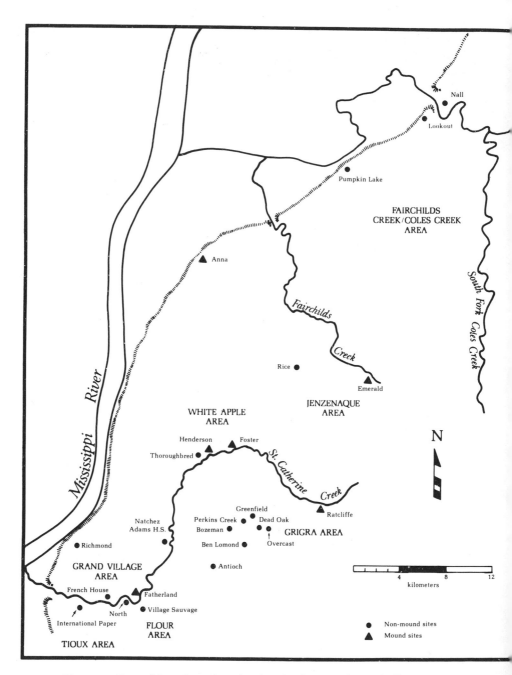

Labels within the figure:

Nall

Lookout

Pumpkin Lake

FAIRCHILDS
CREEK/COLES CREEK
AREA

South Fork Coles Creek

▲ Anna

Fairchilds

Creek

Rice ●

▲ Emerald

JENZENAQUE
AREA

WHITE APPLE
AREA

Mississippi River

Henderson ▲   ▲ Foster

Thoroughbred ●

St. Catherine Creek

N

Greenfield ●

Perkins Creek ●   ● Dead Oak

Bozeman ●

Ratcliffe ▲

GRIGRA AREA

Natchez
Adams H.S. ●

Ben Lomond ●   Overcast ↑

● Richmond

● Antioch

GRAND VILLAGE
AREA

French House ●

▲ Fatherland

● Village Sauvage

North ●

International Paper ↗

FLOUR
AREA

TIOUX AREA

4   8   12
kilometers

● Non-mound sites

▲ Mound sites

Figure 2. Protohistoric/Historic Sites in the Natchez Bluffs Region.

180

ready established. The pro-English faction, composed of the White Apple, Jenzenaque, and Grigra villages, as well as an unnamed group living along the banks of the Mississippi River (the Fairchilds Creek/Coles Creek group), were responsible for a number of minor atrocities in the early years of the French settlement. France generally over-reacted to these offenses, initiating major expeditions against the Natchez to maintain order. A total of four "wars" were waged between 1716 and 1729, and, in the aftermath of each confrontation, the Natchez were the ultimate losers. A number of lesser chiefs (Suns) were executed, and the offending Natchez often had to make further amends to the French by performing labor and/or providing food.[19]

After the establishment in 1717 of John Law's Company of the West, an organization set up to expand and develop the Louisiana colony, the French settlement among the Natchez began to grow dramatically.[20] Competition for land and resources eventually even served to alienate the pro-French faction, which consisted of the Grand Village, the Tioux village, and the Flour village. The end result was the Natchez Massacre. In 1729 the Natchez rose against the French colony, killing or enslaving most of the population.[21] This event did not go unpunished, as a major force of French and Indians were sent to Natchez in retaliation.[22] The French in Louisiana, however, were never able to recuperate from this devastating event. A small number of Natchez Indians continued to reside in the Natchez region following their last major confrontation with the French, but most of the survivors joined with the Chickasaw Indians in northeastern Mississippi. In later years small remnants of the once powerful Natchez tribe were scattered throughout the Southeast, finally ending up in Oklahoma in the nineteenth century.[23]

Archaeology in the Natchez Bluffs Region

Individuals interested in the origin of the Moundbuilders have often focused their attention on the Natchez Bluffs. The many mound sites in the region, such as Anna and Emerald, drew the interest of numerous nineteenth and twentieth century scholars.[24] Montroville W. Dickeson's discovery, in 1846, of a human pelvis in association with extinct Pleistocene mammals brought international attention to the Natchez Bluffs.[25] The importance of the region to the application of the direct historical approach has been apparent to Southeastern archaeologists for quite some time. James A. Ford and Moreau B. Chambers were the first individuals to prove that the location of the Grand Village of the Natchez was the Fatherland site. Their excavations at the site in the 1930s laid the foundations for historical archaeology in the lower Mississippi Valley.[26] A number of articles by George I. Quimby resulted from his reanalysis of the Fatherland excavations and this site continued to loom in importance in the 1960s and 1970s with the work of Robert S. Neitzel.[27] It is rather curious, however, when one considers all the archaeological and ethnological interest in the Natchez, that prior to 1971 the Fatherland site was the only known historic site in the region. Andrew C. Albrecht, possessing only historical documents and one site to work with, understandably offered a very simplistic interpretation of the location of the other Natchez villages.[28] With but one site recorded, the potential of using the direct historical approach for improving our knowledge of Natchez society and culture was severely limited.

In order to address such problems as the effects of European influence on the various sociocultural institutions of the Natchez, to determine the nature of the changing demographic situation between late prehistoric and historic times, and to investigate the question of the practice of adopting peoples of diverse cultural groups, additional historic Indian sites relating to specific known Natchez villages had to be found and excavated. Such a task was undertaken by the Lower Mississippi Survey in 1971 and 1972. In the years prior to and after 1971/1972 the LMS conducted extensive investigations in regions to the west (Tensas Basin) and north (Yazoo Basin),[29] thus providing context for the Natchez work. A number of articles and volumes dealing with material culture, culture history, and prehistoric/historic settlement patterns emerged from the Natchez research.[30] After the initial 1971 survey, it was found that several sites in the area had very late aboriginal materials.

With the hope of expanding our knowledge of historic Natchez Indian settlement patterns, excavations were performed at a number of these sites. Excepting Fatherland, all of the late prehistoric mound sites, including Emerald, Foster, Henderson, and Ratcliffe, were tested. International Paper and Village Sauvage, both located in the vicinity of the Grand Village, were also examined. When excavations were completed in 1972, the only definite aboriginal sites we could add to the list of Natchez settlements were International Paper, Village Sauvage, Bozeman, North, Thoroughbred, Pumpkin Lake, and Nall.

In the last decade ten additional sites were found to have protohistoric/historic Natchez components (Fig. 2). Two others, Natchez Adams H.S. and French House, have French components. These sites came to light as a result of an increase in agricultural activity in the area. The rather rapid expansion of the city of Natchez has also contributed to our growing data bank. Most importantly, the new information came to us through the medium of a number of local amateurs.[31] With a total of twenty-four protohistoric/historic Natchez sites known, we now have a unique opportunity to examine a number of anthropological issues by applying the direct historical approach to the Natchez.

Direct Historical Approach and the Natchez

The first explicit treatise on the use of the direct historical approach was by Julian Steward in 1942,[32] but the method itself was practiced long before Steward's article.[33] Steward argued that one must first find sites of the historic period, preferably, but not necessarily, of identifiable tribes. Secondly, the cultural complexes of the sites are determined; and thirdly, the sequences are projected backward in time to protohistoric and prehistoric periods or cultures.[34] David Baerreis took exception to Steward's statement that the historic sites were "preferably, but not necessarily," of known Indian groups. He argued that in order to take full advantage of ethnology and documentary history, it is essential that identifiable sites be used as a point of departure.[35] When one considers the vast population movements and demographic changes that occurred in the historic period, the difficulty of identifying sites with specific tribal groups becomes rapidly apparent. Detailed historical research has clearly revealed the problems involved in correlating specific sites with known historical groups.[36] But the purpose of the direct historical approach is not (or should not be) simply to determine which Indians lived at a particular site at what time. Archaeology, in combination with history and ethnology, provides a tool for understanding change and stability in the various Indian populations during the historic contact period. Knowing which aboriginal tribe occupied a specific site is of initial importance, but if archaeologists are to focus on problems of anthropological significance, it is imperative that they go beyond simple site-tribe correlations.

To address such concerns as the nature of aboriginal socioreligious organization, changing economic patterns, or the development of political factions resulting from cultural contact, specific sites must be identified with particular villages within a tribal group. Some years ago David Hally called for the excavation of such sites, rather than continuing the then-prevalent practice of reconstructing complexes based on vague political or linguistic groupings like Creek, Cherokee, and Timucuan.[37] Few investigators, however, have followed up on his suggestions. Part of the problem has been the lack of necessary controls over the cultural affinity and period of site occupation, so fundamental for addressing problems of sociocultural relevance. Notable exceptions are a number of recent works tracing the De Soto Entrada throughout the Southeast,[38] and Jeffrey P. Brain's research on the Tunica Indians.[39]

We are fortunate in the Natchez Bluffs region to have a large number of protohistoric/historic aboriginal sites that can be definitely associated with the Natchez Indians as a sociopolitical entity. Moreover, these sites all have components dating to the late seventeenth/early eighteenth centuries. Historical documents have revealed the existence of at least nine Natchez villages during the period of French involvement, but we have adequate information on only seven of them.[40] Through historical and archaeological research, we now have a good idea of the historic Natchez Indian settlement pattern.[41] The sites depicted in Fig. 2 are arranged according to village areas.

The French were confused by the aboriginal use of the landscape. Instead of conforming to the European model of nucleation, the Natchez settlement pattern was one of dispersal. The Grand Village, home of the Great Sun, served as sociopolitical nucleus for the Natchez as a whole. The rest of the society was divided into districts which fell under the domination of secondary members of the Sun class. White Apple was one district; Jenzenaque another; and Grigra still another. Each district had a minor ceremonial center that was surrounded by a number of hamlets, and each hamlet consisted of several houses. Therefore, a particular Natchez village may have extended over a number of kilometers and included a considerable number of sites. It is for this reason that each "village" is called an "area" in Fig. 2.

The villages listed above were divided into political factions during the historic period. The Grand Village, the Tioux, and the Flour villages are reported by historians to have been generally friendly with the French, whereas the White Apple, Jenzenaque, and Grigra villages were seemingly always pro-English. Also allied with English interests was an unnamed village complex located near the mouths of Fairchilds Creek and Coles Creek.

Assuming we are correct in our correlation of specific sites with certain village areas, it is possible to investigate the presence of political factions among the Natchez. Theoretically, opposing alliances should be reflected in the archaeology. One would expect that the French allies would have had more materials of French manufacture, and that the English allies would have had more materials of English manufacture. Moreover, it is reasonable to assume that individuals belonging to villages of the same faction had greater contact than did members of opposing factions. Intensive social interaction between members of the same faction may possibly have resulted in a higher frequency of marriage between members of the same faction than between individuals of opposing factions. As the political factions were in existence for over two decades, the emphasis on marriage preferences within the same faction may be reflected archaeologically. We therefore might expect closer correlations in the aboriginal material culture between groups of the same faction, than between groups of opposing factions.

Another topic of historical and anthropological concern that is being addressed in this project is the practice of adopting other aboriginal groups into the Natchez sociopolitical system. As discussed earlier, a number of small groups, remnants of once powerful tribes located to the north, were adopted by the Natchez in protohistoric times. The principal groups, situated in separate villages, were the Tioux and Grigra. Considerable archaeological work has been done on closely related historic Tunican sites in the Yazoo Basin to the north,[42] and the native material objects employed by these Indians are quite different from those that are typically found on Natchez sites; primarily as regards the heavy incidence of shell-tempered pottery among the former. Therefore, it is expected that sites identified as Grigra and Tioux in the Natchez Bluffs region will possess relatively distinct archaeological profiles when compared to sites of indigenous Natchez Indians.

The above topics are rephrased below in a series of hypotheses that are suitable for testing by archaeology. The cultural materials that are presently being compared and contrasted are from excavations, surface surveys, and private and public collections. Only the sites with unquestionable historic components are considered in the tests. A visual summary of the tests is presented in Fig. 3.

Hypothesis 1

Significant variations are expected in European material culture between groups of villages belonging to the two political factions. The historic items of European origin should be different in the villages of each faction, because of varying European ties prolonged over several decades.

TEST:

To examine the validity of this hypothesis, materials from the

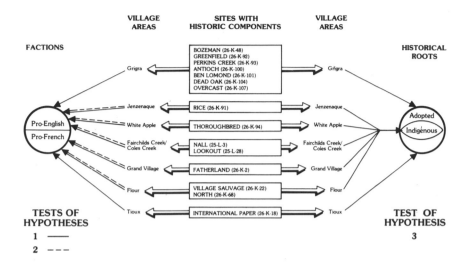

Figure 3. Tests of Hypotheses 1-3. Historic Sites to be Grouped Together for Material Comparison Studies.

various villages of the pro-English and pro-French factions
are being compared and contrasted. European materials from
pro-English sites are being grouped together and compared
with the same kinds of materials from pro-French sites. It is
expected that the pro-English group will have more items of
English derivation, while the pro-French group will have
more materials of French derivation.

Hypothesis 2

Historic materials of aboriginal origin are expected to be more
similar between villages of the same political faction, than
between villages of opposing factions, because of more intensive sociocultural interaction.

TEST:

Aboriginal materials from sites of the pro-English group are
being compared with materials from sites of the pro-French
group. The two adopted groups (Grigra and Tioux) are not
included in the test of Hypothesis 2, because it is believed a

187

different factor affected the aboriginal material culture of these two groups (see Hypothesis 3). It is expected that the native material culture of the pro-English group will be significantly different from that of the pro-French group.

Hypotheses 3

Variations in aboriginal material culture are expected between the indigenous Natchez villages, whose roots extend far into prehistory in the Natchez Bluffs region, and the recently adopted Mississippian groups (Grigra and Tioux) from the Yazoo Basin to the north.

TEST:

Disregarding political factions, the indigenous Natchez villages are being combined in this test. The aboriginal material remains are being compared with those recovered from the adopted Grigra and Tioux village sites. It is expected that the native materials of the adopted groups will have closer parallels with assemblages recovered in the Yazoo Basin to the north, where the Grigra and Tioux originated. The native materials of the indigenous village groups should bear closer parallels with the late prehistoric sites in the Natchez Bluffs region.

If all three hypotheses are validated in our research, we will be able to say with some confidence that historically recorded changes in the political structure and demography of a native group can be revealed by a comparative study of material culture. This research should therefore be of interest to all anthropologists concerned with culture contact situations.

Conclusions

This paper, which serves as on outline of the current LMS project in southwest Mississippi, shows how the direct historical approach is being employed in Natchez Indian archaeology. The method is an important, perhaps necessary, tool for understanding late prehistoric Natchez lifeways, but it is also being applied in our research to tackle problems of general anthropological concern.

In any archaeological study, there are many avenues of research that can be pursued. Settlement and subsistence patterns are two subjects which clearly are important aspects of historic Natchez lifeways, and information on these and related topics will be produced by our research. Our focus on material culture studies was chosen as the most expedient method of testing a series of hypotheses concerning culture processes. It is our expectation that comparative material studies will correlate with our model of regional Natchezan settlement patterns. Assuming our placement of the various Natchez village areas is correct, historically recorded differences between the villages should be apparent in the materials recovered from the various sites. The practice of adopting foreign aboriginal groups and the formation of political factions, as half the Natchez villages leaned toward the French and the other half toward the English, should be reflected in the archaeological record. If we do indeed detect the expected distinctions between the various site inventories, then our settlement model will have been strengthened and archaeology will have improved our understanding of Natchezan history. Moreover, we will have formed our conclusions by going through the scientific procedure of reviewing past data, generalizing from the data, and evaluating the generalizations by employing testable hypotheses. If the material distinctions do not turn out as expected, the settlement model will have to be modified and retested. Whatever the outcome, our knowledge of the lifeways and history of an important Indian group is advancing.

Notes

[1] This project, under the overall direction of Stephen Williams, is supported in part by Grant 2300-81, National Geographic Society, and in part by Grant RO-20184, National Endowment for the Humanities. A six week field season was conducted in the fall of 1981: Ian W. Brown and Stephen Williams, "Archaeological Investigations at Seven Historic Sites in the Natchez Bluffs Region, Mississippi: 1981 Season."

[2] Dumont de Montigny, *Mémoires Historiques sur la Louisiane;* Le Page du Pratz, *Histoire de la Louisiane;* Richebourg G. McWilliams, *Fleur de Lys and Calumet;* and John R. Swanton, *Indian Tribes of the Lower Mississippi Valley.*

[3] Swanton, *Indian Tribes,* 100–108; William C. MacLeod, "Natchez Political Evolution;" Charles W. M. Hart, "A Reconsideration of the Natchez Social Structure;" George I. Quimby, "Natchez Social Structure as an Instrument of Assimilation;" Elizabeth J. Tooker, "Natchez Social Organization: Fact or Anthropological Folk-

lore?"; John L. Fischer, "Solutions for the Natchez Paradox;" Carol I. Mason, "Natchez Class Structure;" Theodore C. Stern, "The Natchez;" Jeffrey P. Brain, "The Natchez 'Paradox';" and Douglas R. White, George P. Murdock, and Richard Scaglion, "Natchez Class and Rank Reconsidered."

⁴William H. Sears, "An Archaeological Manifestation of a Natchez-type Burial Ceremony," *Florida Anthropologist*, 5:1 and 2 (1952) 1–7; William H. Sears, "The State and Settlement Patterns in the New World," in *Settlement Archaeology*, ed. Kwang C. Chang (Palo Alto, California, 1968), 134–53; Jon L. Gibson, "Poverty Point: The First North American Chiefdom," *Archaeology*, 27:2 (1974), 96–105; John A. Olah, "An Investigation of Ethnographic and Archaeological Political Structure in Southeastern United States," *Journal of Alabama Archaeology*, 21:2 (1975), 145–69; and Vincas P. Steponaitis, "Location Theory and Complex Chiefdoms: A Mississippian Example," in *Mississippian Settlement Patterns*, ed. Bruce D. Smith (New York, 1978), 417–53.

⁵Harold N. Fisk, *Geological Investigation of the Alluvial Valley of the Lower Mississippi River*, War Department, Corps of Engineers, U.S. Army, Mississippi River Commission Publication, no. 52 (Vicksburg, Miss., 1944), 63; and Philip Phillips, James A. Ford, and James B. Griffin, *Archaeological Survey in the Lower Mississippi Alluvial Valley, 1940–1947*, 25.

⁶Jeffrey P. Brain, Ian W. Brown, and Vincas P. Steponaitis, *Archaeology of the Natchez Bluffs*.

⁷Edward G. Bourne, ed., *Narratives of the Career of Hernando de Soto*, 2 vols. (1904; reprint ed., New York, 1922), 1,153–55; Swanton, *Indian Tribes*, 186, 258; and Garcilaso de la Vega, *The Florida of the Inca*, ed. and trans. John G. Varner and Jeannette J. Varner (Austin, 1951), 574–89.

⁸Ian W. Brown and Jeffrey P. Brain, "Archaeology of the Natchez Bluffs Region, Mississippi: Hypothesized Cultural and Environmental Factors Influencing Local Population Movements."

⁹Bourne, *Narratives of de Soto* 1, 194–96.

¹⁰Clarence B. Moore, *Some Aboriginal Sites on Mississippi River*, 381–88; James A. Ford, *Analysis of Indian Village Site Collections from Louisiana and Mississippi*, 69–71; and Brain et al., *Archaeology of the Natchez Bluffs*.

¹¹Calvin Brown, *Archeology of Mississippi*, 256–64; Warren K. Moorehead, "Explorations near Natchez, Mississippi," 161–62; John L. Cotter, "Stratigraphic and Area Tests at the Emerald and Anna Mound Sites;" and Brain et al., *Archaeology of the Natchez Bluffs*.

¹²Bourne, *Narratives of de Soto* 1, 200–201.

¹³Phillips et al., *Archaeological Survey Lower Mississippi Alluvial Valley*, 419–21.

¹⁴Brown and Brain, "Archaeology of the Natchez Bluffs."

¹⁵Le Page du Pratz, *Histoire de la Louisiane* 2, 222–23; Swanton, *Indian Tribes*, 46–48, 334–36; and Newton D. Mereness, ed., *Travels in the American Colonies* (New York, 1916), 46.

¹⁶Swanton, *Indian Tribes*, 20–21, 188–92; and Jean Delanglez, *The French Jesuits in Lower Louisiana (1700–1763)*, 24.

¹⁷Benjamin F. French, *Historical Collections* 6, 124–27; Swanton, *Indian Tribes*, 193; Verner W. Crane, *The Southern Frontier, 1670–1732*, 89–92, 103–107; and Rowland and Sanders, *Mississippi Provincial Archives: French Dominion* 2, 39–41.

¹⁸Swanton, *Indian Tribes*, 192; and Marcel Giraud, *A History of French Louisiana* 1, 249–55.

¹⁹Swanton, *Indian Tribes*, 193–204, 207–17; Mereness, *Travels*, 33–7; Andrew C. Albrecht, "Indian-French Relations at Natchez;" and Jeffrey P. Brain, "French-Indian Interaction: Political Neutralization and the Destruction of the Natchez" (Paper delivered at the 5th French Regime Symposium, Fort de Chartres, Illinois, 1976).

²⁰French, *Historical Collections* 3, 159. N. M. Miller Surrey, *The Commerce of*

Louisiana during the French Regime, 1699–1763, 156–62; Rowland and Sanders, *MPA:FD* 1, 55; Delanglez, *French Jesuits,* 92; Marcel Giraud, *Histoire de la Louisiane française* 3; and Walter G. Howell, "The French Period, 1699–1763," in *A History of Mississippi,* 2 vols., ed. Richard A. McLemore (Hattiesburg, 1973), 1, 125–26.

[21] Swanton, *Indian Tribes,* 217–34; Delanglez, "A Louisiana Poet-historian: Dumont dit Montigny," *Mid-America* 19:1 (1937), 41–44; and Howell, "The French Period," 129–30.

[22] Swanton, *Indian Tribes,* 235–48.

[23] Swanton, ibid., 248–56; Jesse D. Jennings, "Chickasaw and Earlier Indian Cultures of Northeast Mississippi," 178–80; and Joseph V. Frank III, "In Defense of Hutchin's Natchez Indian."

[24] James Hall, *A Brief History of the Mississippi Territory* (Salisbury, 1801), 51–52; Henry M. Brackenridge, *Views of Louisiana; together with a Journal of a Voyage up the Missouri River, in 1811* (Pittsburgh, 1814), 278–81; Joseph H. Ingraham, *The Southwest. By a Yankee. . . .* (New York, 1835), 222–26; Ephraim G. Squier and Edwin H. Davis, *Ancient Monuments of the Mississippi Valley,* Smithsonian Institution, Contributions to Knowledge, no. 1 (Washington, D.C., 1848), 117–18; Cyrus Thomas, "Report on the Mound Explorations of the Bureau of Ethnology," *Bureau of American Ethnology, 12th Annual Report,* (Washington, D.C., 1894), 263–67; Moorehead, "Explorations to Knowledge, No. 1 (Washington, D.C., 1848), 117–18; Cyrus Thomas, "Report and "The Gordon Site in Southern Mississippi;" and Andrew Ellicott, *The Journal of Andrew Ellicott* (1803; reprint ed., Chicago, 1962), 134.

[25] Charles Lyell, *A Second Visit to the United States of North America,* 2 vols. (2nd ed., London, 1850), 2, 196–98; R. Stewart Culin, "The Dickeson Collection of American Antiquities," *Bulletin of the Free Museum of Science and Art,* vol. 2, no. 3 (1900); George I. Quimby, "The Locus of the Natchez Pelvis Find," *American Antiquity* 22 (1956), 77–79; and James B. Stoltman, "The Southeastern United States," in *The Development of North American Archaeology,* ed. James E. Fitting (Garden City, New York, 1973), 120–21.

[26] James A. Ford, "Outline of Louisiana and Mississippi Pottery Horizons;" idem, *Analysis of Indian Village Site Collections,* 59–64; Stephen Williams, "Historic Archaeology in the Lower Mississippi Valley;" and idem, "Historic Archaeology, Past and Present."

[27] George I. Quimby, "The Natchezan Culture Type," and "Natchez Archaeology: A Tribute to the Natchez for their Seeming Consistency in the Production of the Fictile Fabric;" Robert S. Neitzel, "The Natchez Grand Village," *Archeology of the Fatherland Site: The Grand Village of the Natchez,* "Excavations at the Fatherland Site," "A Double-barreled Detective Story," and *The Grand Village of the Natchez: Revisited.*

[28] Andrew C. Albrecht, "The Location of the Historic Natchez Villages."

[29] Philip Phillips, "Introduction to the Archaeology of the Mississippi Valley" (Ph.D. diss., Harvard University, 1939); idem, *Archaeological Survey in the Lower Yazoo Basin, Mississippi, 1949–1955;* Phillips et al., *Archaeological Survey Lower Mississippi Alluvial Valley;* Stephen Williams, "Settlement Patterns in the Lower Mississippi Valley;" idem, "On the Location of the Historic Taensa Villages;" Stephen Williams and Jeffrey P. Brain, "Archeological Surveys in Southwest Mississippi," *National Geographic Society Research Reports, 1970 Projects* (Washington, D.C., 1979), 581–90; Stephen Williams and Jeffrey P. Brain, *Excavations at Lake George, Yazoo County, Mississippi, 1958–1960;* Stephen Williams, William Kean, and Alan Toth, *The Archaeology of the Upper Tensas Basin;* James A. Ford, Philip Phillips, and William G. Haag, *The Jaketown Site in West-Central Mississippi,* American Museum of Natural History Anthropological Papers 45, pt. 1 (New York, 1955); John S. Belmont, "The Peabody Excavations, Coahoma County, Mississippi, 1901–1902" (Honors thesis, Harvard College, 1961); Robert E. Greengo, *Issaquena: An Archaeological Phase in the Yazoo Basin*

of the Lower Mississippi Valley, Society for American Archaeology Memoirs 18 (Salt Lake City, 1964); David J. Hally, "Post-Coles Creek Cultural Development in the Upper Tensas Basin of Louisiana," *Southeastern Archaeological Conference Bulletin 6* (1967), 36–40; idem, "The Plaquemine and Mississippian Occupations of the Upper Tensas Basin, Louisiana," (Ph.D., diss., Harvard University, 1972); Jeffrey P. Brain, "Winterville: A Case Study of Prehistoric Culture Contact in the Lower Mississippi Valley" (Ph.D. diss., Yale University, 1969), "The Archaeology of the Tunica: Trial on the Yazoo (Preliminary Report of Investigations Conducted by the Lower Mississippi Survey)," and "Late Prehistoric Settlement Patterning in the Yazoo Basin and Natchez Bluffs Regions of the Lower Mississippi Valley;" Jeffrey P. Brain and Stephen Williams, "Archaeological Survey in Southwest Mississippi," *Mississippi Archaeological Association Newsletter* 6:3, (1971), 6–10; Ian W. Brown, "Archaeological Investigations at the Historic Portland and St. Pierre Sites in the Lower Yazoo Basin, Mississippi, 1974" (M.A. thesis, Brown University, 1975), "Excavations at Fort St. Pierre," "The Portland Site (22-M-12), an Early 18th Century Historic Indian Site in Warren County, Mississippi," "Early 18th Century French-Indian Culture Contact in the Yazoo Bluffs Region of the Lower Mississippi Valley," (Ph.D. diss., Brown University, 1979), and "Functional Group Changes and Acculturation: A Case Study of the French and the Indian in the Lower Mississippi Valley;" and Alan Toth, "Early Marksville Phases in the Lower Mississippi Valley: A Study of Culture Contact Dynamics" (Ph.D. diss., Harvard University, 1977).

[30] Ian W. Brown, "Settlement Patterns in the Bluff Area of the Lower Mississippi Valley" (Honors thesis, Harvard College, 1973); Brown and Brain, "Archaeology of the Natchez Bluffs;" Vincas P. Steponaitis, "The Late Prehistory of the Natchez Region: Excavations at the Emerald and Foster Sites, Adams County, Mississippi" (Honors thesis, Harvard College, 1974); idem, "Plaquemine Ceramic Chronology in the Natchez Resion;" Brain, "Late Prehistoric Settlement Patterning;" and Brain et al., *Archaeology of the Natchez Bluffs.*

[31] Primary sources of information were Joseph V. Frank, III, Robert Prospere, and John Frank. See Joseph V. Frank, "A European Trade Bead from the Anna Mounds Site, Adams County, Mississippi," and "The Rice Site: A Natchez Indian Cemetery."

[32] Julian H. Steward, "The Direct Historical Approach to Archaeology," *American Antiquity* 7 (1942), 337–43.

[33] Roland B. Dixon, "Some Aspects of North American Archeology," *American Anthropologist* 15:4 (1913), 549–77; Nels C. Nelson, *Pueblo Ruins of the Galisteo Basin, New Mexico,* American Museum of Natural History Anthropological Papers 15, pt. 1 (New York, 1914); William D. Strong, *An Introduction to Nebraska Archeology,* Smithsonian Institution Miscellaneous Collections 93, No. 10 (Washington, D.C., 1935); idem, "From History to Prehistory in the Northern Great Plains," in *Essays in Historical Anthropology of North America,* Smithsonian Institution Miscellaneous Collections 100 (Washington, D.C., 1940), 353–94; Waldo R. Wedel, *The Direct-Historical Approach in Pawnee Archaeology,* Smithsonian Institution Miscellaneous Collections 97, No. 7 (Washington, D.C., 1938); idem, "Culture Sequence in the Central Great Plains," in *Essays in Historical Anthropology of North America,* 291–352; and Henry B. Collins, Jr., "Outline of Eskimo Prehistory," in ibid., 533–92.

[34] Steward, "Direct Historical Approach to Archaeology," 337.

[35] David A. Baerreis, "The Ethnohistoric Approach and Archaeology," *Ethnohistory* 8:1 (1961), 51–52; for problems in determining ethnicity of sites see: Ronald J. Mason, "Ethnicity and Archaeology in the Upper Great Lakes," in *Cultural Change and Continuity: Essays in Honor of James Bennett Griffin,* ed. Charles E. Cleland (New York, 1976), 351–52.

[36] Examples are: James B. Griffin, *The Fort Ancient Aspect* (Ann Arbor, 1943); Phillips et al., *Archaeological Survey Lower Mississippi Alluvial Valley,* 345–421;

Jeffrey P. Brain, Alan Toth, and Antonio Rodriguez-Buckingham, "Ethnohistoric Archaeology and the De Soto Entrada into the Lower Mississippi Valley," *Conference on Historic Site Archaeology Papers* 7 (1974), 232–89; R. Mason, "Ethnicity and Archaeology Upper Great Lakes;" and Stephen Williams, "Armorel: A Very Late Phase in the Lower Mississippi Valley," *Southeastern Archaeological Conference Bulletin* 22 (1980), 105–110.

[37] David J. Hally, "The Archaeology of European-Indian Contact in the Southeast," 61–63.

[38] Brain et al., "Ethnohistoric Archaeology and the De Soto Entrada;" Marvin T. Smith, "European Materials from the King Site," *Southeastern Archaeological Conference Bulletin* 18 (1975), 63–66, "The Route of De Soto through Tennessee, Georgia, and Alabama: The Evidence from Material Culture," *Early Georgia* 4:1 and 2 (1976), 27–48, and "The Early Historic Period (1540–1670) on the Upper Coosa River Drainage of Alabama and Georgia," *Conference on Historic Site Archaeology Papers* 11 (1977), 151–67; George E. Lankford, III, "A New Look at De Soto's Route through Alabama," *Journal of Alabama Archaeology* 23:1 (1977), 10–36; Jerald T. Milanich and Samuel Proctor, *Tacachale: Essays on the Indians of Florida and Southeastern Georgia during the Historic Period* (Gainesville, 1978); Chester DePratter, Charles M. Hudson, and Marvin T. Smith, "Juan Pardo's Explorations in the Interior Southeast, 1566–1568" (Paper delivered at the Society for American Archaeology Meetings, Philadelphia, Pa., 1980); John A. Walthall, *Prehistoric Indians of the Southeast: Archaeology of Alabama and the Middle South* (University, Alabama, 1980), 246–75; and Jeffrey P. Brain, "Introduction," in John R. Swanton, *Final Report of the United States De Soto Expedition Commission,* Smithsonian Institution Classics in Anthropology Series (Washington, D.C., in press).

[39] Jeffrey P. Brain, *On the Tunica Trail,* Louisiana Archaeological Survey and Antiquities Commission, Anthropological Study no. 1 (Baton Rouge, La., 1977), "The Archaeological Phase: Ethnographic Fact or Fancy?" in *Archaeological Essays in Honor of Irving B. Rouse,* ed. Robert C. Dunnell and Edwin S. Hall, Jr. (The Hague, 1978), 311–18, *Tunica Treasure,* Papers of the Peabody Museum of Archaeology and Ethnology 71 (Cambridge, Mass., 1979), "Archaeological and Electronic Survey of the Trudeau Site," Report Submitted to Office of State Parks, Department of Culture, Recreation and Tourism, Baton Rouge, Louisiana, mimeographed (Cambridge, Mass., 1980), "Ceramics of the Eighteenth Century Tunica," *Southeastern Archaeological Conference Bulletin* 20, in press, and "Tunica Archaeology," in *Traces of Prehistory: Papers in Honor of William G. Haag,* ed. Frederick H. West and Robert W. Neuman, (Geoscience and Man 22, Baton Rouge, Louisiana, 1981).

[40] Iberville recorded the village names of the Théloël tribe as follows: Nachés, Pochougoula, Ousagoucoula, Cogoucoula, Yatanocha, Ymacacha, Thoucoue, Tougoula, and Achougoucoula. The Nachés name eventually became the label for the entire group. Tougoula, which means "Tioux people," is the only one of Iberville's village names to continue into the eighteenth century. The villages mentioned most often in confrontations between the French and Natchez were the Grand Village, Flour, White Apple (or White Earth), Jenzenaque (Walnuts or Hickories), Grigra (or Gris), and Tioux: Swanton, *Indian Tribes,* 45–48; Richebourg G. McWilliams, *Iberville's Gulf Journals,* 72–73.

[41] Ian W. Brown, "The Location of the Historic Natchez Villages" (Paper delivered at the 7th French Regime Symposium, Natchez, Mississippi, 1978); and Brain et al., *Archaeology of the Natchez Bluffs.*

[42] Ian W. Brown, "The Portland Site," "Historic Aboriginal Pottery from the Yazoo Bluffs Region, Mississippi," "Early 18th Century French-Indian Culture Contact," and "Functional Group Changes and Acculturation;" and Brain, "Archaeology of the Tunica: Trial on the Yazoo."

French Fortification at Fort Rosalie, Natchez

SAMUEL WILSON, JR.

•

IN A WORK CALLED *Le Voyageur Français* (The French Traveller), edited by the Abbé Delaport and published in Paris in 1769, the traveller, in a letter on Louisiana, states that La Salle "took possession of the country in the name of Louis XIV, called it Louisiana in honor of this prince and constructed a fort there; the Spaniards would have built a church; the English a tavern."[1] The building of forts was indeed the principal interest of the French, for their occupation of Louisiana and the Mississippi Valley was primarily for the miliitary purpose of preventing the westward expansion of the British colonies from the Atlantic coast or the encroachment of the Spanish from Mexico.

The first of these forts was built by La Salle in the upper Mississippi Valley in 1680 and 1682, with his ill-fated Fort St. Louis being built on the Texas Gulf Coast in 1685. The building of this fort is described in the journal of Henri Joutel, who accompanied La Salle, and a crude drawing indicates the arrangement of buildings within it.[2] This was followed by Iberville's Fort Maurepas on Biloxi Bay in 1699. Iberville's journals and the drawing, probably made by his engineer Remy Reno, provided the basis for the reconstruction of the fort near the original site at Ocean Springs, Mississippi, by the Mississippi Bureau of Recreation and Parks. Then in 1700 came Iberville's Mississippi Fort, sometimes called Fort La Boulaye, whose actual site on the river below New Orleans was identified some years ago. Fort Condé in Mobile followed and in 1714 came Fort St. Jean Baptiste de Natchitoches, a replica of which has been recently completed near the original site by the Louisiana Office of State Parks.[3]

Fort Rosalie at Natchez followed in 1716, although the site had been seen and admired by Pierre Le Moyne d'Iberville, who visited the Grand Village of the Natchez in 1700, and André Pénicaut, who accompanied him, noted that "of all the savages, they are the most civilized nation."[4] The English cartographer Thomas Jeffreys attributes the naming of Fort Rosalie to Iberville who, he states,

> entered the Mississippi by the sea, sailed up as high as the country of the *Natchez,* and found it so delightful and advantageously situated that he concluded it the fittest place that could be found for erecting a metropolis of the whole colony. Wherefore he drew the plan of a city, to which he gave the name *Rosalie,* after the lady of the chancellor *Pont Chartrain.* This project appears not to have been carried into execution, though the name of this city is retained in most maps, and particularly by *d'Anville* is called *Fort Rosalie.*[5]

Jérome Phélypeaux, Comte de Pontchartrain, was Minister of the Navy under Louis XIV from 1699 to 1715.[6] His wife, from whom Fort Rosalie derived its name, was Hélène Angélique Rosalie de Laubespine de Verderonne, Comtesse de Pontchartrain.[7] The Louisiana historian François Xavier Martin also credits Iberville with selecting Natchez as the proper place for the principal establishment of the colony. On his 1700 visit, says Martin, Iberville "selected a high spot which he laid out for a town, and called it Rosalie, in honor of the Countess of Pontchartrain."[8] Martin also states that it was on this spot chosen by Iberville for a town that Fort Rosalie was built sixteen years later.[9]

Natchez as a French settlement had its origins when Louisiana was under the regime of Antoine Crozat, who was given a trading monopoly by Louis XIV on September 14, 1712.[10] Lamothe Cadillac was then governor of Louisiana and on February 20, 1714, wrote to the Minister Pontchartrain that "M. Crozat has made an agreement with M. de La Loire in order to establish the Natchez [post]. The former binds himself to have him given ten men and a sergeant for this garrison [from Fort Louis, Mobile]."[11] Cadillac declined to give up these men unless Crozat could replace them with the same number. Again on March 20, 1714, Cadillac wrote that the de La Loire brothers were declining to go to Natchez and had presented him with a petition in which they stated that "The Sieurs Marcantoine de La Loire des Ursins and Louis Auguste [de La Loire] Flaucourt, brothers, humbly represent to you that being in the impossibility of being able to form an establishment at the Natchez as they had agreed with Mr. Crozat," they asked to be returned to France at Company expense.[12] Cadillac, however, persuaded the brothers to continue on to Natchez. According to Pénicaut, they had arrived at Mobile on the frigate *La Dauphine* in April 1713 and were sent by Cadillac "to the Natchez with twelve persons in two boats to take them there with their personal belongings, because it had been decided to establish a trading office there."[13] A warehouse was erected for Company merchandise and one of the brothers, de La Loire des Ursins, was still in Natchez in 1729 and died in the massacre that November.[14]

By 1716 it had been decided to have a fort built at Natchez and Fort St. Jerome on the Wabash River. Jean-Baptiste Le Moyne, Sieur de Bienville, King's Lieutenant under Cadillac, was to build these two forts after Englishmen had been found on the Mississippi trading with and making friends with the Indians. Bienville and Cadillac did not agree on priorities, and on January 2, 1716, Bienville wrote to Pontchartrain that Cadillac had tried "to persuade me that I must not build any fort at all at Rosalie, that that would be a useless expense . . . that the Natchez were a very docile nation."[15]

Pénicaut relates that in the year 1714 a group of four Frenchmen on their way up the river with merchandise to trade in the Illinois country were robbed and murdered by several Natchez Indians whom they had hired to help them "as the current on the river was very rapid at that time."[16] On hearing of this outrage, Cadillac sent Bienville with a force from Mobile to exact vengeance. The murderers were caught and executed and peace with the Natchez was restored on terms that required them "to build a fort in their village at their expense, on the spot that M. de Bienville would mark for them in the manner that he would wish, with the necessary quarters and magazines within the fort for the convenience of the officers and soldiers that would stay there."[17] The peace terms were accepted, and according to Pénicaut:

> M. de Bienville chose a spot on a height close to the village for the site of the fort, which they commenced the very next day after he had prescribed the form of it and had had the *enceinte* marked off. A few days later he returned to the fort of the Tunicas, leaving M. Pailloux with twelve Frenchmen to carry on the work of the fort. It took a full six weeks to finish it; and as soon as it was finished, M. de Bienville was notified and he came there. . . . As soon as he got there he ordered still more officers' quarters and more soldiers' barracks inside the fort, and magazines [storehouses] to hold munitions and food supplies and the merchandise belonging to the Company. . . . This fort was named Rosalie by M. de Bienville.[18]

In a letter of June 23, 1716, Bienville wrote to Cadillac that "I have decided to make peace with the Natchez on conditions as advantageous as I could hope for." Among other things, "that they build us a fort of the size that will be laid out for them. . . . I laid out the fort for them and I left there M. de Pailloux with some soliders to make them plant the piles in a straight line."[19] On May 10, 1717 Bienville wrote to the Regency Council of the success he had had "in obliging, with thirty soldiers, the Natchez nation of a thousand men to deliver to me the chief and the other accomplices who had had a part in the murder of five Frenchmen. . . . I also forced the nation to build and construct for me a fort with four bastions among them free of cost and to return to M. de Crozat's agents all the merchandise that they had pillaged."[20] Thus it would appear that the first Fort Roaslie was built for Bienville by the Natchez in 1716 rather than 1714 as indicated by Pénicaut, who was often inaccurate in his dates. In that same year, 1716, Cadillac was replaced as governor by the Sieur de L'Épinay, and from October of that year until L'Épinay's arrival in March 1717, Bienville was in command of Louisiana.[21]

Little detailed information has been found in official records or drawings of this first Fort Rosalie of Natchez. It was described as a fort of four bastions, of palisades, with several buildings inside. It may be surmised that it was not unlike Fort St. Jean Baptiste at Natchitoches that was begun in 1714. Marcel Giraud, in his *Histoire de la Louisiane française,* Volume 2, says:

> The aide-Major Pailloux de Barbezan went there with two soldiers to seek the most favorable site for the erection of this fort Rosalie which would consecrate the military occupation of the region. He chose for this purpose a hill that dominated the Mississippi at a short distance above the Natchez landing place, and having brought from Bienville's camp the necessary tools, axes, spades, pickaxes, ironworks, he engaged without delay in the works of construction. The natives were employed to cut and to cart the acacia stakes, to prepare the bark intended to cover the buildings. Assisted by a dozen soldiers, they rapidly erected the quadrangular palisade of the fort, in the interior of which were established a *corps de garde,* a powder magazine, a warehouse and some barracks. Begun in the course of the month of June 1716, the works were completed at the beginning of August in the presence of Bienville who had rejoined the aide-major. . . . In fact Fort Rosalie was reduced to a simple *standing palisade,* formed of *stakes as thick as a leg,* and furnished with four angle bastions, and it remained in this state until the year of its destruction [1729]. . . . The double slope by which the "little mountain" on which it stood dominated the Mississippi, was itself relatively accessible. Broutin noted that it *could be entered flat-footed from all sides.* As to the buildings that it contained, they looked, from the corps de garde to the barracks, only like "wretched huts." For the moment, however . . . this rudimentary structure seemed to guarantee the occupation of the territory.[22]

Perhaps the most detailed description of Fort Rosalie is that given by François Benjamin Dumont de Montigny, who had come to Louisiana in 1719 as a sub-lieutenant on the ship *La Marie*[23] and whose memoirs were subsequently published. Dumont wrote:

> To the west of this [Grand] village, the French built a fort elevated on a hill and named it Fort Rosalie. This was only a small

land of twenty-five *toises* [150 feet] long by fifteen [90 feet] wide, enclosed with palisades, without any bastion. Inside, towards the gate of the Fort was placed the *corps de garde* and at three *toises* [18 feet] along the palisades were the barracks of the soldiers. At the other end, opposite the gate, a cabin had been erected to serve as lodging to the officer who was on guard, and on the right on entering was the powder magazine. The Company maintained in this post a company of soldiers with an ensign, a sublieutenant, a lieutenant and a captain commandant.[24]

In September of 1729 there had arrived in Louisiana the engineer-architect Ignace François Broutin in command of the troops of the Belle Isle-d'Asfeld-LeBlanc-de La Jonchère concessions. These four were high officials in France, d'Asfeld being director of fortifications, the successor to the Maréchal de Vauban, the great military engineering genius of Louis XIV. Pierre Le Blond de La Tour, engineer-in-chief of Louisiana, arrived in Louisiana in December 1720 and was also director of the d'Asfeld-LeBlanc concession. On September 24, 1722, Broutin received orders from La Tour "to go up to Natchez, to draw up a map and to take cognizance of the concession of the *Terre Blanche* [White Earth] that the company of the Indies had established there and . . . to make the acquisition of it in the name of Msgr. Le Blanc and the administration: this the Sr. Broutin did in the sweat of his brow and at the expense of his health and his youth."[25] Broutin remained in Natchez until the death of La Tour on October 14, 1723, required his return to New Orleans.

While in Natchez, Broutin, besides working on maps of the area, had an opportunity to inspect Fort Rosalie, the palisades of which he found entirely rotted.[26] This was reported to the Council at New Orleans by Charles Henri Joseph Tonty, called Desliettes, former commandant at Natchez, when on March 25, 1725, he stated that

> it is very necessary to have another fort built at the said place of the Natchez because the one that is there is completely decayed; that it would be advisable to have it made of earth because it would last longer; that more than six months ago he informed the

Council of it and that M. de Pauger, chief engineer, had written him that he would go to the spot to see in what way it would be re-established; that it would be very necessary to make a road for the transportation of the goods from the bank of the river along the hill. These will be of little expense according to M. Broutin. [marginal note: To determine whether this road must lead to the fort.][27]

On July 12, 1725, Broutin was ordered by the Council to take over the command of the Natchez post,[28] where he "commanded six or seven months while waiting for M. Dutisné to come down from the Illinois." In the meantime, Pauger died in New Orleans on June 11, 1726, and Broutin requested the Company of the Indies to either make him engineer-in-chief or commandant at Natchez, where, he said, "I will also charge myself with building the fort, buildings and surveys of the said place."[29] At about the same time, in a letter to the Abbé Raguet, Father Raphael, the Capuchin superior at New Orleans, wrote that he had visited Natchez and that

> there is a fort on the first eminence with a garrison of about thirty men, if however, an enclosure of poor piles, half rotten, that permit free entrance almost everywhere can be called a fort. There are several pieces of cannon but very useless because this would-be fort, being at a distance from the edges of the eminence, cannot command any of the approaches, and if it were attacked, the enemy would be at the palisade before a shot could be fired at him. I think that they are going to have work done to put themselves in a position of greater security.[30]

On August 24, 1726, the Directors of the Company of the Indies in Paris issued a commission of commandant at Natchez to Broutin, to do "everything that he shall judge necessary and appropriate for the glory of the King and the good of the service of the Company."[31] In March 1727, Étienne de Périer arrived in New Orleans, succeeding Bienville as commandant, and preferred to have Broutin remain in New Orleans. In a letter of May 6, 1727, Broutin explained this to the Directors of the Company in thanking them for naming him as commandant at

Natchez. In the same letter he discussed the plan of Fort Rosalie, which he sent together with specifications for the work to be done there. He then planned to visit Natchez in the fall with Périer and perhaps at that time to begin the rebuilding of Fort Rosalie.[32] Broutin felt strongly that buildings in Louisiana should be built of brick and Périer agreed, but there was a lack of masons in the colony. Périer therefore requested the Directors of the Company to send some, which they agreed to do at their meeting in Paris on June 3, 1729. At the same meeting, "his plan to build the fort of the Natchez of bricks has been approved."[33]

In the meantime, on November 22, 1728,[34] there arrived in New Orleans a naturalist, Pierre Baron, who had been named by the Royal Academy of Sciences to do natural history studies in Louisiana.[35] He soon found favor with Périer, who made him King's Engineer in place of Broutin, whom he then sent back to Natchez. On his various visits to Natchez, Broutin did several surveys of the area, showing the two principal concessions, St. Catherine and Terre Blanche, as well as Fort Rosalie.

Among the maps sent by Broutin is one of "the Environs of Fort Rosalie at the Natchez,"[36] based on surveys that he made in 1723 but not drawn until May 1727 when it was finished by his draftsman, Gonichon. With his letter of December 23, 1726, Broutin sent another map of the area, "the map of this post, with the two concessions of Messrs. LeBlanc and Colly [Kolly] and the grand village of the Natchez Indians. As I drew this map two years ago, I have not yet been able to have time to make a copy of it."[37] Dumont de Montigny also made several maps of the area in his crude, naive style, one of which was engraved and used as an illustration in his *Mémoires Historiques*.[38] Most of the maps, however, were drawn up after the tragedy of November 28, 1729, when the Natchez Indians revolted and massacred the French and destroyed Fort Rosalie as well as all the plantations and other French properties in the area. This horror was blamed on the actions of an irresponsible and drunken commandant who had succeed Broutin at Natchez and attempted to drive the Indians from their White Apple village.

Figure 1. Partial tracing of Broutin's "Carte Des Environs du Fort Rosalie des Natchez et du Fort Provisionnelle."

According to notes on one of Broutin's finest maps of the area, Fort Rosalie at the time of the massacre was in miserable condition and none of the plans for its rebuilding had been accomplished. This undated map (Fig. 1) is apparently based on Broutin's earlier surveys and shows Fort Rosalie as a nearly square palisade enclosure with bastions at each corner, though one of them seems to have been abandoned and cut off by a palisade partition. This beautifully drawn map, in color, is entitled "Map of the Environs of Fort Rosalie of the Natchez and of the Provisional Fort built since the destruction of this post happened on the 28 November 1729 between 8 and 9 o'clock in the morning, by the Indians." The dilapidated fort, (A), is described as "Fort Rosalie where there were not 100 palisades when the Indians destroyed this post, entered from every side, flat-footed." Within the palisade four buildings are shown, all described as miserable or wretched huts, one, (B), where an officer sometimes slept; another, in two parts, (C), which served as barracks; (D) which served as a *corps de garde;* and (E) in one of the bastions served as powder magazine. A note on the map states that "Fort Rosalie has never been anything other than a palisade standing all around only."[39]

Following the Natchez massacre, Governor Périer raised an army, attacked the Indians, and rescued the French women and children who had been made slaves by their captors. Among Périer's officers were the two engineers, Broutin and Baron, the latter incurring Périer's displeasure and subsequently being sent back to France. The Natchez were defeated, driven from the area, and the entire tribe scattered.[40]

With the aid of Baron's draftsman, Alexandre de Batz, Broutin then drew up plans for a new fort, probably in a slightly different location, to which the name of Fort Maurepas was to be given. A provisional fort was also constructed in 1730. In a letter to the Comte de Maurepas, who had succeeded his father the Comte de Pontchartrain as Minister of Marine, Périer wrote on December 10, 1731 that "the wood of this country is not suitable for building forts of stakes in the ground. If they should be undertaken, they would cost more for repairs in four or five years than to do them in masonry." He added that he was sending the plan of the Natchez fort which, he said, "is only of earth until Your Highness might order its revetment in masonry."[41] Broutin's plan of Fort Maurepas showed a pentagonal structure without bastions, a fort that maintained the French presence in the Natchez area until the French regime ended with the transfer of that part of its Louisiana colony east of the Mississippi, except the Isle of Orleans, to England following France's defeat in the French and Indian War.

On June 30, 1732, the Intendant Edmé Gatien Salmon wrote to the Minister, "In regard to the French fort of Natchez . . . M. de Pradel, Captain, who has been in command there since the month of December last . . . has had an earthwork fort built in this place which it is expedient to revet in brick. The Sr. de Batz draftsman at New Orleans, who is at the same time a good architect, has gone by my orders and has drawn up the plan of this fort which I have the honor of sending you with the estimative specification of what it will cost."[42] The name Maurepas was apparently forgotten and the fort continued to be known as Rosalie.

Le Page du Pratz gives a slightly different version of the rebuilding of Fort Rosalie and mentions the forts built by the Indians which are shown on several maps of this period. Le Page says:

M. de Loubois . . . gave his orders to have a terrace fort constructed. This manner of building a fort is much better for defense than that which had formerly been followed. The forts were made only of stakes in the ground of the thickness of the fattest part of the leg, without moats outside, without banquettes inside; also the soldiers there had contrived breaches by which they escaped without being obliged to pass in front of the sentinel. It is true that there were three cannons but without gun carriages, one of the three was spiked: as to the rest, what would gun carriages have served since there were no embrasures for placing the cannons.

When the terrace fort was constructed the general left there M. le Baron de Crenet, Lieutenant of the King of the Colony, to command there; he gave him a hundred twenty men as garrison, some cannon and some munitions. . . . The Natchez, as I have already said, had abandoned their fort; it was demolished and its stakes burned. . . . the fort that was constructed near the old one, having need of being completed with proper materials for covering the buildings in order to lodge the garrison. For this purpose they sent to a cypress swamp about a league and a half below the fort, in order to there make cypress bark shingles. In order to do this operation, cypress trees are cut down in the time of budding, encircled every six feet, then the bark is lifted at least a foot wide which is easily done because this bark is thin and supple. At the rate that they are lifted they are applied on an expressly made bed and they are stacked so as to hold them overlapping one over the other. When the roofing is done they are lined up like tiles and they are held with large laths of the same wood, nailed with iron pins.[43]

Natchez never recovered from the effects of the 1729 massacre. The great French plantations were never reestablished and only the fort remained, and even it was allowed to fall into a sad state of disrepair. On June 23, 1760, the Intendant Rochemore at New Orleans wrote to the French court that "the redoubt Rosalie of the Natchez and all its appurtenances are, it is said, at a point of perishing which would indispensably demand to be rebuilt anew . . . an infinity of repairs have been obliged to be made, so costly as much due to the distance of the place as to the scarcity of workmen."[44]

The engineer Broutin had died in 1751 and Bernard Deverges, who had come to Louisiana in 1720 as Le Blond de La Tour's draftsman, had become Engineer-in-Chief of Louisiana. On October 22, 1760, he issued orders to his assistant, Louis Antoine Andry, to direct the works for the completion of the fort at Pointe Coupée and then to go to Natchez to check the work of contractors that had been authorized by M. Gourdon, captain commanding there. His orders were "to measure exactly the length of the enclosure of the *enceinte*, both of the fort and the forward fortifications, [he] shall enumerate the palisades" and make sure that requisitions dating from February 19, 1758, and subsequently were not for the same work for which requisitions were issued on March 3 and 22 and July 31 of 1759. It was stated that these were for items "not possibly requiring to be redone so soon without entailing very strong presumptions that the works of their initial repair could not have been other than very incompetent. . . . The new road made along the bluff, from the fort of the first high ground to the river landing, with the intention, it is said, of avoiding floods, also seeming extremely useless, since the post had got along well without it until this innovation." Deverges' orders to Andry contain many interesting details of the construction of the fort and strong implications of fraud or excessive charges in these repairs. These orders were approved and Andry was ordered to proceed to Pointe Coupée and Natchez by Governor Kerlérec and Intendant Rochemore on December 22, 1760.[45]

With the end of the war in 1763, Fort Rosalie was surrendered to the British and its name changed to Fort Panmure in honor of a British minister of war.[46] The French had abandoned the ruinous fort as soon as the terms of the Treaty of Paris of February

3, 1763, became known. The British Major Robert Farmar was advised by Governor Kerlérec that if he wished to take possession of Fort Rosalie he should "be sure to send workmen to build barracks, those which are now there being so old that we were obliged to evacuate and abandon them, they not being fit to be repaired."[47] Kerlérec added that "if you think proper at present to establish a post at Natchez, you ought to leave a garrison of fifty men with two officers." By April the following year nothing had been done, and Major Farmar wrote from Mobile to the British secretary of war that he was hoping to "if tis possible, take possession of the post at Natches as I find it a place of the greatest consequence, both with regard to Command the River Mississippi and [to] take possession of the whole Country of Illinois."[48] Another year passed without any action, and on August 6, 1765, the Council, in response to the governor's inquiry, "Agreed that a detachment of one captain, two subalterns and fifty men should be sent to take possession of the post at Natchez."[49] By June of 1766 this had finally been accomplished with a detachment of sixty men sent from Mobile.[50]

It was probably with this detachment and other British troops going up to the Illinois country that the British Captain of Engineers Philip Pittman arrived at Natchez in August 1765. He made the following remarks about the area and Fort Rosalie:

> The fort is about six hundred and seventy yards from the river's side. The road to it is very bad, on account of a steep high ground which is at a small distance from the landing-place, very difficult to ascend, and almost impracticable for carriages; a small distance from this high land is a hill, on the summit of which stands the fort, and the road becomes much better, ascending with a gradual slope. The trouble of going up is recompensed by the sight of a most delightful country of great extent. . . . The breadth of the river at this place is exactly eighteen hundred and seventy feet, and the fort stands one hundred and eighty feet above the surface of the water. It is an irregular pentagon, without bastions, and is built of plank of five inches thick; the buildings within the fort are a store-house, a house for the officers, a barrack for the soldiers, and a guard-house. These buildings are made of framed

timber, filled up with mud and barbe Espagnole (a kind of moss which grows in great abundance on all the trees in Louisiana) and in this country that manner of building houses is very common. The barbe Espagnole (which much resembles a black curly beard) is also made use of for stuffing mattresses.

The ditch is partly made and partly natural; the bottom is in most places nineteen feet from the top of the rampart, and in many twelve and thirteen from the top of the counterscarp; on the north side of the fort there is no ditch at all, but it is fenced with pickets, to prevent any enemy getting under the cover of the counterscarp or into the ditch. The rampart is nearly the same height above the pickets as it is in other parts above the bottom of the ditch. The fort received the name of Rosalia in honour to Mad. la duchesse de Pontchartrain, whose husband was minister of France when it was built.[51]

The buildings of framed timber "filled up with mud and moss" are the same type of *columbage-bouzillage* construction used by the French in Louisiana, probably the type indicated in the De Batz drawing for rebuilding Fort Rosalie in 1732.[52]

Pittman also made a map of the fort and the Natchez area as it was in 1765, probably a most accurate representation (Fig. 2). His map shows the road up from the landing to the fort. It also shows the pentagonal fort and the buildings he mentioned in his text. In addition, within the fort, Pittman indicates a powder magazine, while outside surrounding the fort are a bake house, stable, and two large "gardens belonging to garrison." Also shown is an "outwork of stockades partly burnt down." No private houses nor any indications of a town or settlement are shown, nor does Pittman make any mention of anything in the area except the fort.

In a lengthy report to the Lords Commissioners of Trade and Plantations written from Pensacola on November 22, 1766, the Council and Assembly of West Florida recommended that "Fort Natchez ought to be put on a very respectable condition, as well for pushing the settlements in those parts which are so perfectly adapted for corn, wine and oil as for keeping the Choctaws in subordination." An estimated sum of £4,000 was

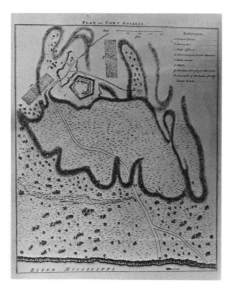

Figure 2. Pittman, "Plan of Fort Rosalia." Published courtesy of Mississippi Department of Archives and History.

included in the report for "the works proposed . . . to complete the Fortifications at Natchez."[53]

After losing the eastern part of Louisiana to England, France's King Louis XV gave the rest of the colony, including New Orleans, to Spain. During the American Revolution the Spanish, under Governor Bernardo de Galvez, friendly to the American cause, attacked and captured the British forts at Manchac and Baton Rouge. With their capitulation, Natchez was also surrendered to Spain. The fort was garrisoned by Spanish troops but retained the name Panmure. About 1792 the town of Natchez was laid out on the bluff near the fort, and in 1798 it passed to the United States when the boundary between the American and Spanish territories east of the Mississippi was set by treaty at the thirty-first parallel.[54] A plan of the fort and the town was made by the surveyor Barthelemy Lafon in 1814 and included in an atlas of forts in the Louisiana Purchase territory.[55] The fort appears on this map much as it was rebuilt during the French colonial period, a pentagon with outer fortifications. It was soon abandoned and all traces of it eventually disappeared, only its name Rosalie being recalled by Peter Little's great mansion built near the site in 1822.

Notes

[1] Abbé Delaport, ed., *Le Voyageur Français ou la Connaissance de l'Ancien et de Nouveau Monde*, 10:6.

[2] Samuel Wilson, Jr., "Gulf Coast Architecture," 92.

[3] An account of most of these early French forts is contained in Samuel Wilson, Jr., "Colonial Fortifications and Military Architecture in the Mississippi Valley." The firm of Koch and Wilson Architects of New Orleans designed the replica of the Natchitoches fort and was associated with Fred Wagner, architect, of Bay St. Louis for the Fort Maurepas replica.

[4] Richebourg Gaillard McWilliams, *Fleur de Lys and Calumet, being the Penicaut Narrative of French Adventures in Louisiana*, 28.

[5] Thomas Jeffreys, *The Natural and Civil History of the French Dominions in North and South America*, Part 1, 145.

[6] Dunbar Rowland and A. G. Sanders, *Mississippi Provincial Archives: French Dominion* 2, 20 (hereafter cited as *MPA:FD*).

[7] Marcel Giraud, *Histoire de la Louisiane Française* 4, 444.

[8] François Xavier Martin, *History of Louisiana* 1, 102.

[9] Ibid., 190.

[10] Maggs Bros. Catalogue No. 8, *The French Colonization of America*, 30.

[11] Paris, Archives Nationales, Archives des Colonies, série C13A, 3, fol. 436 (hereafter cited as AC, C13A).

[12] AC, C13A, 3, 465.

[13] McWilliams, ibid., 159.

[14] Fr. Mathurin Le Petit, *The Natchez Massacre*, 40.

[15] *MPA:FD* 3, 193; AC, C13A, 4, 765.

[16] McWilliams, ibid., 167.

[17] Ibid., 180.

[18] Ibid., 182.

[19] *MPA:FD* 3, 213; AC, C13A, 4, 694.

[20] *MPA:FD* 3, 218; AC, C13A, 5, 59.

[21] *MPA:FD* 3, 12 and 215.

[22] Giraud, *Histoire* 2, 151, translation mine.

[23] A. L. Dart, "Ship Lists of Passengers Leaving France for Louisiana, 1718–1724," *Lousiana Historical Quarterly* 15 (1932), 455.

[24] François Benjamin Dumont de Montigny, *Mémoires Historiques sur la Lousiane*, 62.

[25] Heloise Cruzat, "Records of the Superior Council of Louisiana," *Lousiana Historical Quarterly* 20 (1937), 238.

[26] AC, C13A, 10, 4–6.

[27] *MPA:FD* 2, 421; AC, C13A, 9, 83v.

[28] AC, C13A, 10, 10.

[29] AC, C13A, 10, 4.

[30] *MPA:FD* 2, 525; AC, C13A, 10, 49.

[31] AC, série B, 43, 628.

[32] AC, C13A, 10, 276.

[33] *MPA:FD* 2, 649; AC, C13A, 11, 347.

[34] AC, C13A, 12, 412.

[35] Paris, Service Hydrographique de la Marine.
[36] Paris, Bibliothèque Nationale, GE-002982 (No. 8834).
[37] AC, C13A, 10, 4.
[38] Dumont de Montigny, ibid., 94.
[39] Paris, Archives Nationales, Section Outre Mer, La. No. 35A.
[40] Le Page du Pratz, *Histoire de la Louisiane* 3, 318.
[41] AC, C13A, 13, 75.
[42] AC, C13A, 15, 152.
[43] Le Page du Pratz, ibid. 3, 295.
[44] AC, C13A, 42, 118.
[45] AC, C13A, 42, 86.
[46] Dunbar Rowland, *Mississippi Provincial Archives, 1763–1766, English Dominion* 1, 9.
[47] Ibid., 56.
[48] Ibid., 117.
[49] Ibid.
[50] Ibid., 514.
[51] Philip Pittman, *The Present State of the European Settlements on the Mississippi*, 78–81.
[52] Washington, D.C., Library of Congress, Maps Division.
[53] Clinton N. Howard, *British Development of West Florida, 1763–1769*, 113.
[54] J. F. H. Claiborne, *Mississippi as a Province, Territory and State*, 106.
[55] Barthelemy Lafon, "Atlas of the 7th Military District."

The English Bend: Forgotten Gateway to New Orleans

CARL J. EKBERG

•

WHEN ROBERT CAVELIER DE LA SALLE and his party of explorers descended the Mississippi River to the Gulf of Mexico in the spring of 1682, they became the first Frenchmen to pass through the section of the lower river that would later be named the English Bend. Amongst La Salle's exploratory group was the Recollect priest Zenobius Membré, who recorded the party's journey on the river and provided the first description of the area of the English Bend. After planting the Christian cross and the royal arms of France at the mouth of the Mississippi on April 9, 1682, La Salle and his party began to reascend the river. According to Membré, they lived "only on potatoes and alligators, [for] the country is so bordered with canes, and so low in this part, that we could not hunt, without a long halt."[1] Forty years later, when French colonists began to settle the area of the English Bend, they raised other foodstuffs and ceased to subsist on potatoes and alligators, which were not normal components of French colonial cuisine. The low banks of the Mississippi at the English Bend continued to plague the Frenchmen, however, and this inhospitable geography affected the colonial establishments in the area, including the fortifications. This is a study of a French fort and plantation at the English Bend.

When in 1943 H. Mortimer Favrot published his study, "Colonial Forts of Louisiana," he gave the English Bend short shrift. Favrot merely quoted from a letter of the Baron Hector de Carondelet, Spanish governor of Louisiana in 1795: "The English Bend is an elbow of the river, which from this port [i.e. New Orleans] to the sea makes several windings. This point was formerly chosen by the English to defend the entrance of the river, and two small forts had been erected; but the Spaniards

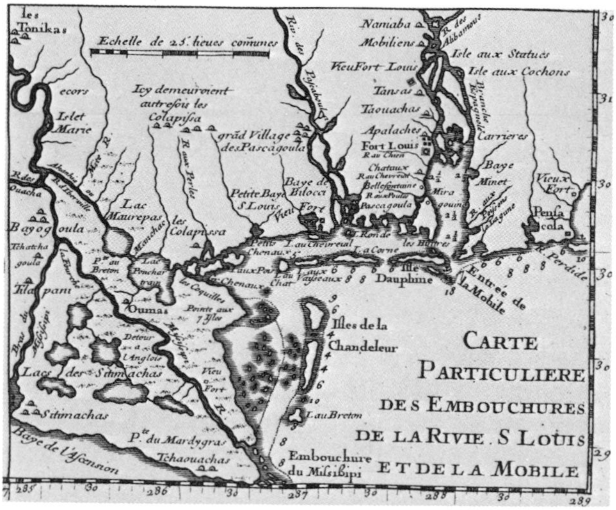

Figure 1. Map showing the mouths of the Mississippi and Mobile rivers shortly before New Orleans was founded in 1718 (inset in Guillaume Delisle, 1718). The English Bend, Détour à l'Anglois, is clearly designated. Map printed courtesy of the Cornell University Library, Ithaca, New York.

have abandoned them, and have chosen a better position twenty miles lower, called the Bend of Plaquemines."[2]

Favrot's neglect of the English Bend in his article on early Louisiana forts was unfortunate, for he thus skipped over an area that once served as the defensive keystone for French Louisiana and he presented a quotation from Carondelet that is inaccurate and misleading (England never built forts at the English Bend). Favrot's neglect of the English Bend is also ironic, for it would seem that he was of the same family as one of the early French commandants at the Bend; in 1746 Governor Vaudreuil posted Lieutenant Claude Favrot to command the garrison at the Bend.[3]

But before these issues are examined, the odd name, English Bend, for a French colonial locality must be explained. Eighteenth-century French manuscripts that mention the Bend present the appellation in four different forms: Détour à l'Anglois (Fig. 1), Détour aux Anglois, Détour de l'Anglois, and Détour des Anglois. The Frenchmen could not seem to decide whether the Bend was *to* the English or *from* the English. In any case, the French names have been translated variously as English Turn, English Reach, and English Bend. Although the first form is the most widely used, it would seem, for reasons explained below, that the last form is the most accurate and thus to be preferred.

The origin of the name English Bend almost certainly derives from an encounter in 1699 on the lower Mississippi River between Jean-Baptiste Le Moyne, Sieur de Bienville, who would become the first royal governor of Louisiana, and the captain of an English ship named Bond. Bienville's brother, Pierre Le Moyne, Sieur d'Iberville, described the incident in his journal for 1699:

> A group of English with ten cannons commanded by Captain Louis Bank [Bond] had entered the Mississippi and ascended twenty-five leagues, where my brother Bienville encountered him anchored and waiting for the right winds to go further up. My brother dispatched two men to talk to him and tell him to leave forthwith, . . . or we would be forced to make him do so; he complied after having talked to my brother, whom he knew. . . .[4]

Henri de Tonti, La Salle's trusted and loyal lieutenant, who unlike Iberville was in Louisiana at the time of Bienville's confrontation with the English ship, gave a somewhat more precise and less dramatic account of the international incident that provided the English Bend with its name: "A small English vessel ascended the river 30 leagues, August 3, 1699. M. de Bienville ordered the captain, in the name of the king to withdraw, which he did, saying, however, that he would come back to establish himself on the river."[5] The accounts of Iberville and Tonti are probably responsible for the notion that the name English *Turn* derived from the location on the river where the Englishmen *turned* tail and fled in the face of *force majeure*.

The early historian of Louisiana, Le Page du Pratz, offered a more picturesque explanation for the origin of the name. He explained that as the English ascended the Mississippi from the Gulf the wind failed them as they entered the English Bend.

Observing besides, that the Mississippi made a great turn or winding, they despaired of succeeding; and wanted to moor at this spot, for which purpose they must bring a rope to land: but the Indians shot a great number of arrows at them, till the report of a cannon fired at random, scattered them, and gave the signal to the English to go on board, for fear the Indians should come in greater numbers, and cut them to pieces. Such is the origin of the name of this Reach.[6]

Du Pratz was wrong about Indians having driven off the Englishmen but was correct in emphasizing how the name for the area derived from the bend in the river. Surely the appellation English Bend is preferable to English Turn, for the name simply comes from the bend in the river where the Englishmen were encountered by Bienville (not Indians). The French *détour* signifies bend or detour, not turn in the sense of turn around. In any event, after Captain Bond and his crew sailed down and out of the Mississippi the only English presence on the lower river for years to come was the peculiar place name, *Détour aux Anglois* or English Bend.

Virtually all eighteenth-century observers of the lower Mississippi commented upon the great difficulty of bringing a ship upriver through the English Bend; it was a century when men were alive to the requirements of sailing ships. The English Captain Philip Pittman, who visited the region in the 1760s, remarked that "at the Detour the river forms almost a circle; so that vessels cannot pass it with the same wind that conducted them to it, and are obliged to wait for a shift of wind."[7] This difficulty presented by the Bend may have been one reason why in 1718 Governor Bienville selected the site he did for establishing the city of New Orleans; it afforded the city some protection from potential enemies coming upstream from the Gulf because the Bend was located five and one half leagues (about eighteen miles) below the city.

The royal French engineer, Adrien de Pauger, explained this point in 1724, at which time there was some talk about relocating New Orleans closer to the Gulf. Pauger wrote to the directors of the Company of the Indies, which controlled the colony of Louisiana at that time:

> You have been told that because New Orleans is above the English Bend that ships require a considerable amount of time to get there from the mouth of the river and that if the city were below [the Bend] they could get there in twenty-four hours with a favorable wind. I used to agree with this argument, but experience has made me see that precisely the contrary is true. . . . If an enemy vessel with a good wind behind it could get past the batteries at the mouth [of the Mississippi], . . . it could push on as far as New Orleans to loot and burn the storehouses if it were not stopped by the English Bend.[8]

Pauger was thus the first person explicitly to articulate this special virtue of New Orleans' emplacement, that it was protected from enemy ships because it was located upriver from the English Bend. It would seem, however, that Bienville probably considered this issue when he selected the site in 1718, although there is no direct evidence that he did.

It is not known precisely when the Company of the Indies, which controlled land policy in Louisiana from 1717 to 1731, granted its first concessions in the area of the English Bend; probably the first concessions were made about the same time that New Orleans was founded, 1718, but conceivably they were made even a bit earlier. In any event, a map of ca. 1723 reveals an almost continuous string of concessions and dwellings from the newly established city downstream through the English Bend (Fig. 2). By 1727 Roman Catholic authorities in New Orleans felt that the settlement at the English Bend was large enough to warrant a church and a rectory.[9] The civil community at the Bend was apparently flourishing under the French regime in Louisiana, but its military importance is what made the Bend prominent in the eighteenth century and what makes it of interest to historians in the twentieth century.

The decision to fortify the English Bend thrust that particular locality prominently into the written records of colonial Louisi-

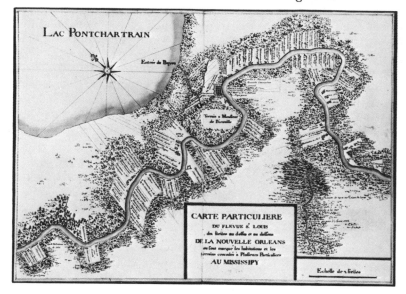

Figure 2. Concessions on the lower Mississippi. Map printed courtesy of the Newberry Library, Chicago, Illinois.

ana, and thus permits the student of the colony to reconstruct some of the history of the area. French authorities considered fortifying the Bend as early as the 1720s, for the strategic value of the site was apparent.[10] The European powers were co-existing more or less peacefully at that time, however, and nothing came of these first considerations. The pressure of warfare during the mid-eighteenth century finally brought to a head the issue of fortifying the Bend, and thus the Bend was brought into focus for the historian.

In 1740 the War of the Austrian Succession erupted in central Europe when Frederick the Great of Prussia invaded the Austrian province of Silesia. Almost immediately this central European affair swept across the Continent and the Channel and brought archrivals, England and France, into the war on opposite sides; and once this had occurred it was inevitable that the French and English colonies in North America would also be dragged into the hostilities. In 1743 Pierre de Rigaud, Marquis de Vaudreuil, was appointed royal governor of French Louisiana and thereby acquired the responsibility of maintaining the defensive fortifications of the province.[11] The capital, New Orleans, was the most important place to defend in the colony, and the city was most vulnerable to possible enemy incursions up the Mississippi from downriver. The fort of the Balize, which was located on an island at the mouth of the river, had been since the early 1720s the principal defensive barrier preventing enemy ships from entering the Mississippi and ascending to New Orleans. But the Balize was unsatisfactory for several reasons: its low-lying location at the mouth of the river made it vulnerable to high winds and pounding seas and it had constantly to be rebuilt; its great distance from New Orleans (more than 100 miles by water) meant that communications were awkward and slow and that its garrison could not handily be reinforced from the city. Thus Vaudreuil, good governor that he was, began casting about for an alternative strong point to defend his capital city.

Vaudreuil began to reconnoitre the lower Mississippi in the spring of 1746 and by September of that year he had made this decision. He wrote to the commandant at Mobile: "I have returned from the Balize to think over the situation of our passes [from the Gulf into the Mississippi]. I have decided to fortify the English Bend."[12] One reason Vaudreuil was a good governor was that he carefully protected himself from the consequences of possible slips in judgment by waiting a prudent period of time before informing the royal government in Versailles of his decisions. Thus he decided to fortify the English bend in September, 1746; he had the work in progress by mid-October; but he did not write to Versailles about it until November.[13] By that time Vaudreuil was persuaded that he had made the right decision and he could present it to the Minister of the Navy and the Colonies as a *fait accompli*.

In his letter to Maurepas of November 1746, Vaudreuil presented a comprehensive account of his work and his plans for the Bend: He would place ten eighteen-pound guns on either side of the river at the beginning of the Bend because the "southwesterly or westerly winds" necessary for sailing vessels to enter the Bend were rare during the period from August to January, which was the best time for any potential invader to come up the Mississippi because the river was low then and the current less difficult to work upstream against. The guns would be mounted behind earthworks contained by revetments of wattle and fascines, although Vaudreuil advocated that the gun shoulders *(épaulements)* be covered as soon as possible with masonry "to protect them from damage by high water." While the eighteen pounders would be placed to sweep the river, smaller guns, four and six pounders, would protect the emplacements from the landward side; this side was swampy in any case, and was not much to worry about.[14]

Vaudreuil had appointed Bernard Devergès engineer for the project, and the labor was to be done by black slaves, both those owned by the government *(nègres du roy)* and those levied from all the slaveholders of New Orleans and its environs, each owner supplying twenty percent of his slaves for a six-week period of time. Vaudreuil and his *commissaire-ordonnateur,* Sebastien-François-Ange Lenormant de Mézy, hoped to have the earthworks completed and the artillery mounted by the end of the year.[15]

Minister Maurepas back at Versailles did not even hear of all this activity until well on into the year 1747. When he sent his formal approval in September, 1747, Maurepas noted that Plaquemines Bend, which was closer to the mouth of the Mississippi, would have the advantage of protecting *all* of the French settlements along the river below New Orleans and not just those above the English Bend. But the minister deferred to Vaudreuil's judgment and approved of the decision to fortify the English Bend. Maurepas even promised Vaudreuil that he would try to send him some additional artillery for the project, although the king (Louis XV) had baulked at the request to face the batteries with masonry; such expensive work would have to be postponed "until peace arives."[16] Peace, temporary though it was, did in fact arrive in 1748 (Treaty of Aix-la-Chapelle), but the royal government never did see fit to build masonry works

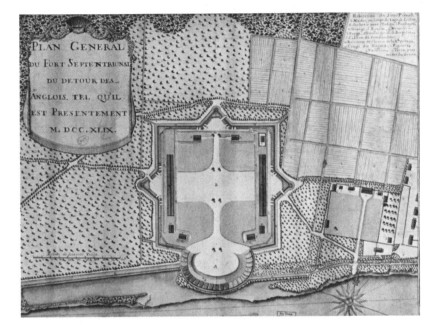

Figure 3. Map printed courtesy of the Map and Cartographic Division of the Library of Congress, Washington, D.C. This map was first printed in an article by Samuel Wilson, Jr., "Louisiana Drawings by Alexandre De Batz," *Journal of the Society of Architectural Historians* 21 (May 1963): 86.

at the English Bend; the earthen works were merely repaired and improved.

The fort on the right bank of the Mississippi (going downstream) was at first called simply "Fort Septentrional," the North Fort, to distinguish it from the fort that was located on the left bank at the Bend. Later the forts became, respectively, Fort St. Léon and Fort Ste. Marie. Fort St. Léon on the right bank is the focus of this study, and the site upon which it was built made up part of a plantation that had been established well before Governor Vaudreuil decided to fortify the Bend. Sieur Jean-Baptiste Prévost, who was an agent of the Royal Company of the Indies, had a concession at the Bend that extended for seventy-six arpents (about 14,595 feet) along the river and had a depth back from the bank of forty arpents (about 7,685 feet).[17] Vaudreuil built the North Fort on the downriver flank of Prévost's concession, and the plan of the area drafted in 1749 by the engineer Alexandre de Batz shows the fort in relation to Sieur Jean-Baptiste Prévost's adjacent plantation and the surrounding swampy hinterland (Fig. 3). The "Grand Battery" faced the river and there were two barracks (V) for the resident garrison. Samuel Wilson, Jr., has observed that the fort had a "curious Baroque character,"[18] but given its location and function (to cover the river) the fort appears simple and rigorously utilitarian in De Batz's plan of 1749.

The North Fort was built on Prévost's concession, and his plantation was used as a logistical base during the construction of the fort. A controversy developed about how much to indemnify Prévost for his losses of land and materials caused by the construction, and the colonial authorities in New Orleans sided with Prévost against the parsimonious officials at Versailles.[19] The Royal Minister of the Navy and Colonies finally decreed, however, that the land itself belonged to the crown by right of eminent domain and that Prévost would be paid only for his "provisions, his fences, the rent of his house, and the loss of his pirogue."[20] Prévost was an important man, but once the royal minister had spoken he was obliged to suffer his losses in silence.

Alexandre de Batz' meticulous rendering of the Prévost plantation is valuable because it gives an unusually detailed view of such early Louisiana establishments (Fig. 4):

Legend

a.	main house	j.	[left out]
b.	kitchen	k.	sheepfold
c.	indigo dryer	l.	commandant's cabin
d.	hen house	m.	fences and road to New Orleans
e.	barn		
f.	stable	n.	slave camp
g.	cabinet-maker's shop	o.	fig orchard
h.	forge	p.	dairy barn
i.	bakery	q.	planting land

Jean-Baptiste Prévost died in July, 1769, and the then *commissaire-ordonnateur,* Nicolas Foucault, ordered an inventory made of the entire Prévost estate.[21] Prévost had died in his town house in New Orleans, which was his principal residence, but he also maintained residences on his two river plantations, including the one at the English Bend. On the afternoon of July 14, 1769, a group of officials led by the Chief Clerk of the Provincial Council travelled to the English Bend to compile their inventory of the late Prévost's real and personal property there.[22] The configuration of the plantation had changed somewhat between 1749 and 1769, but the main house, slave cabins, dairy barn, and hen house were all still in place. The house was described as "forty feet in length by thirty feet in width, containing five rooms *(apartements)* on the ground floor, glazed windows and doors with many panes missing, gallery on the front, and constructed of vertical posts with bricks between. . . ." Prévost had clearly been neglecting this plantation and there were only three black slaves in residence, as opposed to forty-six at his plantation closer to New Orleans.

The contents of the main house at the English Bend reveals a lifestyle not unlike that of an eighteenth-century country gentleman of modest means in France: a four-poster bed, a card table, brass candelabra, pewter pots, crystal salt-cellars, and serge

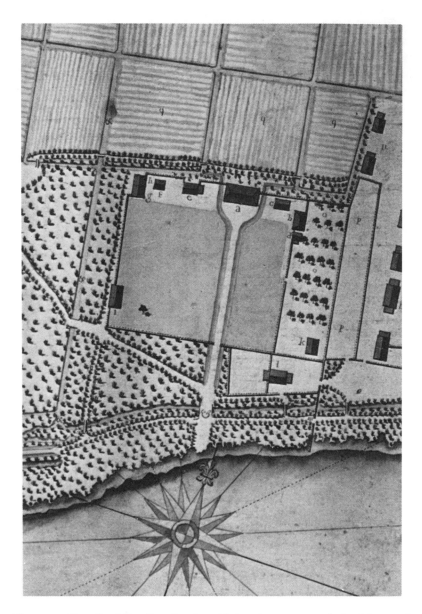

Figure 4. Detail of De Batz's plan. Printed courtesy of the Map and Cartographic Division of the Library of Congress, Washington, D.C.

curtains. The wooden furniture (armoire, bedstead, chest of drawers), however, was made of North American woods, cypress and walnut. Indeed, the room in the house with the most valuable inventory of items and goods, 600 livres, contained amongst other odds and ends much equipment for working wood: "six double bolts and hinges, eight large bolts with springs, six large frame saws, forty-six saw blades, six pit-saws, ten fixtures and hooks for glass doors, a shoulder of mutton. . . ." Louisiana's abundance of fine lumber—cypress, cedar, oak, walnut—for house-construction, ship-building, and furniture-making was one of the colony's most attractive attributes to eighteenth-century Frenchmen, for they came from a country where good wood was in short supply.

When the War of the Austrian Succession ended in 1748 and an uneasy peace settled over Europe and European colonies, the French forts at the English Bend lost their immediate importance as defensive outposts for lower Louisiana. Late in the year 1749, the new *commissaire-ordonnateur* (intendant) of the colony, Honoré Michel de Rouvillière, asked Governor Vaudreuil to remove the garrisons from the forts at the Bend in order to save money, which was always scarce in Louisiana.[23] Vaudreuil obliged the intendant; he placed the artillery at the Bend in storage, pulled the troops out of the forts, and left the defense of the lower Mississippi to the small garrison at the Balize in the mouth of the river.

The removal of the garrisons from the Bend left the barracks there vacant and occasioned a policy that provides us with an interesting vignette of life in Louisiana for French colonists. Vaudreuil and Michel struck upon the efficient notion of using the vacant barracks at the Bend to house the married colonial soldiers newly arrived from France, together with their wives and children. This policy would give the new colonists "time to adjust, to care for their sick, and to make arrangements" for settling down more permanently in Louisiana. The colonial government would supply the families with certain "indispensable items" such as cooking kettles and mosquito nets. The soldiers themselves would receive the usual military rations of food, and the women and children rye flour "so that they can subsist."[24]

Not a very pleasant welcome to Louisiana: oppressive heat (it was August, 1750), clouds of mosquitoes (including of course the malaria-bearing variety), and rye bread or gruel to eat. Frenchmen were not accustomed to such conditions, for crushing heat and mosquitoes are almost unknown in France; the newcomers had probably never seen a mosquito net before arriving in Louisiana. It is no wonder that the colony had a bad name in France and that the royal government had great difficulty in finding settlers willing to emigrate there.

By the spring of 1751 Vaudreuil was about to regarrison the forts at the English Bend with four companies of soldiers, and by August, 1751, new quarters were being built for the officers.[25] According to the inventory of artillery compiled in April, 1753, the English Bend was far and away the most heavily armed post in French Louisiana, boasting thirty eighteen-pound guns, and four each of eights, sixes and fours.[26] These guns would have been apportioned evenly between the forts on either side of the Mississippi, with the heavy pieces bearing upon the river and the lighter pieces protecting the landward sides of the forts. Apparently these fortifications were not as formidable as the bare inventory suggests, however. In January 1753, Louis Billouart de Kerlérec replaced Vaudreuil as governor of Louisiana. At this changing of the colonial guard, the two men conducted an inspection tour of the forts at the English Bend, after which Kerlérec reported to France that though the fortifications themselves appeared to be in good shape the artillery was both deficient in quantity and defective in quality.[27]

As the Anglo-French rivalry again heated up during the mid-1750s, Kerlérec worked to maintain and improve the forts at the Bend, for the course of events in Europe always dictated the level of funding and activity in the colonies. Thus it was during the Seven Years' War (French and Indian War), 1756–1763, that the forts at the Bend reached their high point of development, strength, and importance.

In February, 1759, Governor Kerlérec was preparing himself for an inspection trip to Mobile and, fearing an English ascent of the Mississippi, he drafted a set of instructions for his subordinate in New Orleans, Sieur de Belle-Isle.[28] In these instructions Kerlérec described the batteries of artillery at the Bend as being in "perfect condition, the cannons well-mounted, equipped, and supplied with requisite munitions." The muster rolls from 1759 of the two forts at the Bend, Fort St. Léon and Fort Ste. Marie, show the forts each to have had garrisons that averaged three officers, two non-coms, and twenty to twenty-five enlisted men throughout the year.[29] Nonetheless, Kerlérec was worried about shortage of manpower and not deficiency of equipment. He instructed Belle-Isle to levy Negroes from the neighboring settlements to use in a variety of ways: to build fire rafts for potential use against English warships; to strengthen the defensive posture of the two forts by improving the forward works; and, finally, Belle-Isle was to "select and assign . . . a quantity of handy Negroes to assist with the artillery." The history of black men's involvement in eighteenth-century warfare has yet to be written, but it is clear that the French were counting upon their black slaves to help defend Louisiana during the Seven Years' War. In any event, the colony was plagued at the end of the French regime with the same problem that had plagued it at the beginning—lack of able-bodied men for both civil and military enterprises.

We do not know precisely when the French removed the garrisons from the forts at the Bend and left the posts to fall into desuetude. France first ceded Louisiana to Spain at Fontainebleau in November 1762, and the Treaty of Paris (February, 1763) ended the Seven Years' War and divided Louisiana into English and Spanish sections. Spain received the territory on the west side of the Mississippi south as far as the Iberville River, and from there down to the Gulf of Mexico got both banks of the Mississippi, including New Orleans and the English Bend.

The period from 1763 to 1769, when the Spanish monarchy finally dispatched the decisive General Alexandro O'Reilly to take command in New Orleans, was chaotic for Louisiana.[30] Several English army officers and engineers ascended the Mississippi from the Gulf through the Bend to New Orleans during this disorderly time, and it is to Captain Philip Pittman that we

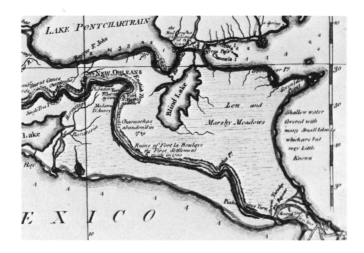

Figure 5. Detail of Lieutenant John Ross's map (1765), "Course of the Mississippi River from the Balize to Fort Chartres," printed in Thomas Jefferys, *The American Atlas* (London, 1778), #26. Notice the two forts, St. Leon and St. Mary's, just down-river from New Orleans.

owe our best description of the forts at the Bend during the mid-1760s. The captain commented upon the fragile nature of the structures themselves, "only enclosures of stockades," but he also noted that "the batteries on each side, which are ten twelve-pounders, are more than sufficient to stop the progress of any vessel."[31] It seems apparent that when Pittman visited the forts, 1764–65, the artillery was still in place but the garrisons were gone; there was no effective government in New Orleans either to supply or maintain such garrisons (Fig. 5).

In 1769 the artillery was removed from the forts at the Bend and shipped to New Orleans in preparation for transport to "Old France," as an English officer expressed it.[32] By the end of that year, O'Reilly was in full command in New Orleans, having moved effectively to quash the French revolt against Spanish rule in Louisiana and execute the ringleaders of the revolt.[33] O'Reilly wrote to one of the French commissioners charged with effecting the transfer of power and summed up conditions at the English Bend during that pivotal period:

With regard to the buildings at the English Bend. You know their bad condition and that Monsieur Aubry [the last French governor of Louisiana] is, like myself, persuaded of the uselessness of that post, which was abandoned long ago. . . .[34]

Thus the desolate prospect of the English Bend at the beginning of the Spanish regime in Louisiana.

We owe our last description of the decaying French forts at the English Bend to another English officer, Lieutenant Thomas Hutchins, who was an engineer and cartographer in the British royal army. He visited the area in 1773 and included the following description of the Bend in his report to General Thomas Gage, British commander in North America at the time:

At the English turn were formerly two Batteries one on each side of the River, with a large Stockaded Fort in the rear of each of them, that on the East side mounted ten, and the one on the West side twelve thirty-two Pounders, these Batteries were made of Earth 12 feet thick, faced with squared timber, and from their advantagious situation at a turn which Vessells cannot passe with the same Wind that conducted them to it, were able to stop the progress of any Vessell that might attempt to passe them—These Forts and Batteries are now in ruine and their Cannon sent to Old France—With some labour and expense these Batteries may be made very respectable. . . .[35]

Although the Spanish colonial government in Louisiana surely knew as well as Hutchins that the English Bend could be rehabilitated and used as a defensive post, they never rebuilt or refortified the forts there, preferring instead to rely upon forts further downriver, at the Plaquemines Bend and the Balize, for defense of the lower Mississippi and of New Orleans.[36] For half a century the English Bend had no military significance whatsoever.

Spain retroceded Louisiana to France by the Treaty of San Idelfonso in 1800. France's second possession of the colony was, however, short-lived and only nominal, for in 1803 President Thomas Jefferson acquired Louisiana for the United States.

Like the French, the American government viewed the English Bend as an important strategic location, and between 1807 and 1813 the first masonry fort was built there.[37] In 1814 Andrew Jackson visited the Bend, and the American troops garrisoned there participated in the defense of New Orleans against the British in December, 1814, and January, 1815, although the fort itself was not directly involved in the action. After the War of 1812, the War Department and the U.S. Corps of Engineers rejected the English Bend in favor of the Plaquemines Bend as the best site for river fortifications, and Fort Jackson was built at the latter location during the 1820s.

By the 1820s the strategic value of the English Bend was being undermined by other developments in any case. The Bend's original importance had stemmed from the extreme difficulty that sailing vessels met in trying to ascend the Mississippi through that tortuous stretch. By the second decade of the nineteenth century steam was replacing wind as the driving force of shipping on the lower river, and steamboats had no difficulty in navigating the Bend. During the Civil War the English Bend was of no military significance, and when Admiral David C. Farragut came up the Mississippi with his Union flotilla in April 1862 he easily swept through the English Bend with his steam-powered frigates.[39]

The English Bend had reached its highest level of strategic importance one hundred years before the Civil War, in the era of sailing ships and when the English had had enemies other than Americans in Louisiana. But the French fortifications at the English Bend were never tested, for the English did not attempt to ascend the Mississippi during the Seven Years' War. The interest of the history of the English Bend during the eighteenth century lies not in the battles fought there but rather in the fact that the preparations for battle taken at the Bend made it the gateway to French New Orleans.[40]

Notes

[1] Zenobius Membré, "Narrative of La Salle's Voyage," in John G. Shea, *Discovery and Exploration of the Mississippi Valley*, 174.

[2] H. Mortimer Favrot, "Colonial Forts of Louisiana," 749.

[3] Vaudreuil to Favrot, Oct. 3, 1746, *Favrot Papers* 1, 131.

[4] Pierre Margry, *Découvertes et établissements* 4, 395. For a view of the incident from the English side see Verner W. Crane, *The Southern Frontier*, chap. iii.

[5] Jean Delanglez, "Tonti Letters," 215. Footnote 1, p. 215, provides full details on the incident.

[6] Antoine Simon Le Page du Pratz, *The History of Louisiana*, 157.

[7] Philip Pittman, *The Present State of the European Settlements on the Mississippi*, 8.

[8] Pauger to Directors, May 29, 1724, Archives des Colonies, série C13A, 8, 53.

[9] Father Raphael to Abbé Raguet, April 10, 1727, AC, C13A, 10, 324.

[10] Company of the Indies to the Council of Louisiana, Dec. 13, 1722, abstract in Rowland and Sanders, *Mississippi Provincial Archives: French Dominion* 2, 256.

[11] On Vaudreuil's career as governor of Louisiana see Guy Frégault, *Le Grand Marquis*.

[12] Vaudreuil to Louboey, Sept. 26, 1746, Huntington Library, MS Loudoun 9, Letterbook III, 221.

[13] Vaudreuil to Maurepas, Nov. 24, 1746, ibid., I, 98.

[14] Ibid.

[15] Vaudreuil and Lenormant to Maurepas, Nov. 26, 1746, AC, C13A, 30, 7.

[16] Maurepas to Vaudreuil, Sept. 30, 1747, Loudoun 103, 1.

[17] The inventory of the Prévost estate describes the plantation at the English Bend as "seventy-six arpents along the river with the usual depth." Henry P. Dart and Edith Dart Price, "Inventory of the Estate of . . . Prévost," 496. Forty arpents was the usual depth of the concessions along the river.

[18] Samuel Wilson, Jr., "Colonial Fortifications and Military Architecture in the Mississippi Valley," 118.

[19] Vaudreuil and Lenormant to Maurepas, March 26, 1748, AC, C13A, 32, 4.

[20] Maurepas to Vaudreuil and Lenormant, Nov. 25, 1748, Loudoun 156, 1.

[21] Dart and Price, "Inventory of the Estate of . . . Prévost," 411–98.

[22] Ibid., 452–55 in English translation, 493–96 in the original French.

[23] Michel to Minister, Jan. 27, 1750, AC, C13A, 34, 303.

[24] Vaudreuil and Michel to Minister, Aug. 20, 1750, AC, C13A, 35, 56.

[25] Vaudreuil to Rouillé (who had replaced Maurepas as minister), April 28, 1751, Loudoun 281, 3.

[26] Inventory of artillery, April 24, 1753, AC, C13A, 37, 47.

[27] Kerlérec to Minister, March 8, 1753, AC, C13A, 37, 35.

[28] Kerlérec to Belle-Isle, Feb. 25, 1759, AC, C13A, 40, 18–20.

[29] Archives des Colonies, série D2C, 52, 211-235.

[30] See John P. Moore, *Revolt in Louisiana*, chap. x.

[31] Pittman, ibid., 9.

[32] Charles Aubry, the last French commandant in New Orleans, certified the shipment of the guns to New Orleans in November 1769. See AC, C13A, 49, 1. Thomas Hutchins used the phrase. See "Report of Lieutenant Thomas Hutchins in consequence of His Excellency General Gage's Instructions," May 1, 1773, Clements Library, Gage Papers 138, 21.

[33] See Moore, ibid., chap. x.

[34] O'Reilly to Bobé Descloseaux, Dec. 26, 1769, AC, C13A, 49, 169.

[35] Hutchins, "Report."

[36] Baron Hector de Carondelet, "Military Report on Louisiana and West Florida," 315-19.

[37] See *American State Papers, Military affairs* 1, 236, 246, 311, 383.

[38] Ibid., 2, 713, 715.

[39] See the excellent account of Farragut's campaign up the lower Mississippi in Alfred T. Mahan, *Admiral Farragut*, (New York, 1908), 115–76.

[40] The author wishes to thank Dr. Kathleen Gilmore of North Texas State University, who provided, in association with the U.S. Army Corps of Engineers, New Orleans District, funding for much of the research in this paper.

Bibliography

Guides and Calendars

Fortescue, J. W. (ed.). *Calendar of State Papers, Colonial Series, America and West Indies . . . Preserved in the Public Record Office*, 40 vols. (Reprinted Vaduz, Lichtenstein: Kraus Reprint, 1964).

Surrey, N. M. Miller, *Calendar of Manuscripts in Paris Archives and Libraries Relating to the History of the Mississippi Valley*, 2 vols. (Washington: Carnegie Institution, 1926).

Published and Manuscript Documents and Contemporary Accounts

Adair, James. *The History of the American Indians* (London: Edward and Charles Dilly, 1775).

American State Papers: Military Affairs, 7 vols. (Washington: Government Printing Office, 1832–1838).

Anderson, Melville B. (trans.). *Relation of the Discoveries and Voyages of Cavelier de La Salle from 1679 to 1681* (Chicago: The Caxton Club, 1901).

Anderson, Melville B. (ed. and trans.). *Relation of Henri de Tonty, Concerning the Explorations of La Salle from 1678 to 1683* (Chicago: The Caxton Club, 1898).

Barcia Carballido y Zúñiga, Andrés Gonzáles de. *Barcia's Chronological History of the Continent of Florida* (Gainesville: University of Florida Press, 1951).

Beverley, Robert. *The History and the Present State of Virginia, In Four Parts* (London: R. Parker, 1705).

Brasseaux, Carl A. (ed. and trans.). *A Comparative View of French Louisiana, 1699 and 1762: The Journals of Pierre Le Moyne d'Iberville and Jean-Jacques Blaise d'Abbadie* (Lafayette: University of Southwestern Louisiana, 1981).

Bushnell, David I. "The Account of Lamhatty," *American Anthropologist* n.s. 10 (1908), 568–74.

Butler, Ruth Lapham (ed. and trans.). *Journal of Paul du Ru* (Chicago: The Caxton Club, 1934).

Carondelet, Baron Hector de. "Military Report on Louisiana and West Florida, November 24, 1794," in James A. Robertson (ed.), *Louisiana under the Rule of Spain, France, and the United States, 1785–1807*, 2 vols. (Cleveland: Arthur H. Clark Co., 1911).

Charlevoix, Pierre François Xavier de. *Histoire et description générale de la Nouvelle France avec le Journal Historique d'un Voyage fait par ordre du Roi dans l'Amérique Septentrionale*, 6 vols. (Paris: Rollin fils, 1744).

Cox, Isaac J. (ed.). *The Journeys of René Robert Cavelier, Sieur de La Salle*, 2 vols. (New York: Allerton Book Company, 1922).

Coxe, Daniel. *A Description of the English Province of Carolana, By the Spaniards call'd Florida, And by the French La Louisiane*, ed. William S. Coker (1722; facsimile Gainesville: The University Presses of Florida, 1976).

Cross, Marion E. (ed. and trans.). *Father Louis Hennepin's Description of Louisiana* (Minneapolis: University of Minnesota Press, 1938).

Dart, Henry P., and Edith Dart Price (ed. and trans.). "Inventory of the Estate of Sieur Jean Baptiste Prévost, Deceased Agent of the Company of the Indies, July 13, 1769," *Louisiana Historical Quarterly* 9:3 (1926), 411–98.

Davenport, Frances Gardiner, and Charles O. Paullin (eds.). *European Treaties Bearing on the History of the United States and its Dependencies*, 4 vols. (reprint Gloucester, Mass.: Peter Smith, 1967).

Delanglez, Jean (ed. and trans.). *The Journal of Jean Cavelier: The Account of a Survivor of La Salle's Texas Expedition* (Chicago: Institute of Jesuit History, 1938).

Delaporte, Abbé (ed.). *Le Voyageur français ou la Connaissance de l'ancien et de nouveau monde*, vol. 10 (Paris, 1769).

Documents relative to the Colonial History of the State of New-York Procured in Holland, England and France, 14 vols. (Albany: Weed, Parsons and Co., 1856–1883).

Dumont de Montigny, François Benjamin. *Mémoires Historiques sur la Louisiane*, 2 vols. (Paris: Cl. J. B. Bauche, 1753).

Falconer, Thomas. *On the Discovery of the Mississippi, and on the South-Western, Oregon, and North-Western Boundary of the United States* (1844; reprint Austin: Shoal Creek Publishers, 1975).

French, Benjamin F. *Historical Collections of Louisiana*, 5 vols. (New York: Wiley and Putnam, 1846–1853) and *Historical Collections of Louisiana and Florida*, 2 vols. (New York: J. Sabin and Sons, 1869, and Albert Mason, 1875).

Gómez Raposo, Luis. "Diario del descubrimiento que hizo el Capitán Don Andrés del Pez," ed. Capitán de Corbeta D. Luis Cebreiro Blanco, *Colección de diarios y relaciones para la historia de los viajes y descubrimientos*, vol. 4 (Madrid: Instituto Histórico de Marina, 1944), 111–50.

Higginbotham, Jay (ed. and trans.). *The Journal of Sauvole* (Mobile: Colonial Books, 1969).

Jefferys, Thomas. *The Natural and Civil History of the French Dominions in North and South America*, Part I (London: Thomas Jefferys, 1760).

Joutel, Henri. *Joutel's Journal of La Salle's Last Voyage, 1684–7*, ed. Henry R. Stiles (Albany: Joseph McDonough, 1906).

Knight, Vernon J., and Sherée L. Adams. "A Voyage to the Mobile and Tomeh in 1700, with notes on the interior of Alabama," *Journal of Alabama Archaeology* 27:1 (1981), 32–56.

La Salle, Nicolas de. *Relation of the Discovery of the Mississippi River*, trans. Melville B. Anderson (Chicago: The Caxton Club, 1898).

Lawson, John. *A New Voyage to Caroline*, ed. Hugh T. Lefler (1709; Chapel Hill: University of North Carolina Press, 1967).

Le Clercq, Chrestien. *Premier Établissement de la foi dans la Nouvelle France*, 2 vols. (Paris: Amable Auroy, 1691).

Leonard, Irving A. (ed. and trans.). "The Spanish Re-Exploration of the Gulf Coast in 1686," *Mississippi Valley Historical Review* 22 (1936), 547–57.

Leonard, Irving A. (ed. and trans.). *The Spanish Approach to Pensacola, 1689–1693* (1939; reprint New York: Arno Press, 1967).

Le Page du Pratz, Antoine Simon. *Histoire de la Louisiane*, 4 vols. (Paris: De Bure, 1758).

————. *The History of Louisiana or of the western parts of Virginia and Carolina* (London: T. Becket, 1774).

Le Petit, Mathurin. *The Natchez Massacre*, trans. Richard H. Hart (New Orleans: Poor Rich Press, 1950).

Margry, Pierre (ed.). *Découvertes et établissements des français dans l'ouest et dans le sud de l'Amérique septentrionale*, 6 vols. (Paris: Maisonneuve, 1876–1886).

McWilliams, Richebourg Gaillard (ed. and trans.). *Fleur de Lys and Calumet, being the Penicaut Narrative of French Adventures in Louisiana* (Baton Rouge: Louisiana State University Press, 1953).

———— (ed. and trans.). *Iberville's Gulf Journals* (University: University of Alabama Press, 1981).

Minet. "Voiage fait du Canada par dedans les terres allant vers le Sud dans l'anné 1682." Manuscript MG 18, B 19, Archives françaises, Public Archives Canada, Ottawa.

Morfi, Fray Juan Augustin. *History of Texas, 1673–1779*, trans. and ed. Carlos Eduardo Castañeda, Quivira Society Publications 6 (Albuquerque: The Quivira Society, 1935).

Pease, Theodore C., and R. C. Werner. *French Foundations, 1680–1693*. Collections of the Illinois State Historical Library 23, French Series 1 (Springfield: Illinois State Historical Library, 1935).

Pichardo, José Antonio. *Pichardo's Treatise on the Limits of Louisiana and Texas*, trans. Charles W. Hackett, Charmion C. Shelby, and Mary R. Splawn, vol. 1 (Austin: University of Texas Press, 1931).

Pittman, Philip. *The Present State of the European Settlements on the Mississippi*, ed. Frank H. Hodder (Cleveland: A. H. Clark, 1906).

Rowland, Dunbar (ed.). *Mississippi Provincial Archives: English Dominion*, 1 vol. (Nashville: Brandon Printing Co., 1911).

Rowland, Dunbar, and A. G. Sanders (ed. and trans.). *Mississippi Provincial Archives: French Dominion*, 3 vols. (Jackson: Mississippi Department of Archives and History, 1927–1932).

Shea, John Gilmary. *Discovery and Exploration of the Mississippi Valley* (New York: J. S. Redfield, 1852).

Sibley, John. "Historical sketches of the several Indian tribes in Louisiana south of the Arkansas River, and between the Mississippi and the River Grand," in *Travels in the Interior Parts of America,* by Captains Lewis and Clark, Doctor Sibley and Mr. Dunbar (London: Richard Phillips, 1807), 40–53.

Thomassy, R. *De La Salle et ses Relations inédites.* (Paris: Charles Dounoil, 1859).

Thwaites, Reuben Gold. *The Jesuit Relations and Allied Documents,* 73 vols. (Cleveland: The Burrows Brothers, 1896–1901).

Woodward, Thomas S. *Woodward's Reminiscences of the Creek, or Muscogee Indians* (Montgomery: Barrett and Wimbish, 1859).

WPA Historical Records Survey. *The Favrot Papers,* 9 vols. Transcriptions of Manuscript Collections of Louisiana 1 (WPA, 1940–41).

Secondary Works

Albrecht, Andrew C. "The Location of the Historic Natchez Villages," *Journal of Mississippi History* 6 (1944), 67–88.

———. "Indian-French Relations at Natchez," *American Anthropologist* 48:3 (1946), 321–54.

Alessio Robles, Vito. *Coahuila y Texas en la época colonial.* (México: Editorial Cultura, 1938).

Atkinson, James R. "A Historic Contact Indian Settlement in Oktibbeha County, Mississippi," *Journal of Alabama Archaeology* 25 (1979), 61–82.

Baker, J. N. L. *A History of Geographical Discovery and Exploration* (London: George G. Harrap & Co., 1937).

Baker, Vaughn B. "Les Louisianaises: A Reconnaissance," in James J. Cooke (ed.), *Proceedings of the Fifth Meeting of the*

French Colonial Historical Society, 1979 (Washington: University Press of America, 1980), 6–15.

Bancroft, George. *History of the United States from the Discovery of the Continent,* 6 vols. (1859–1882; reprint ed. New York, 1924).

Bancroft, Hubert H. *History of Mexico, 1600–1803.* The Works of Hubert H. Bancroft, vol. 11 (San Francisco: The History Company, 1887).

———. *History of the North Mexican States and Texas.* The Works of Hubert H. Bancroft, vol. 15 (San Francisco: The History Company, 1886).

———. *History of Mexico, 1861–1887.* The Works of Hubert H. Bancroft, vol. 14 (San Francisco: The History Company, 1887).

Bolton, Herbert Eugene. "Location of La Salle's Colony on the Gulf of Mexico," *Mississippi Valley Historical Review* 2 (1915), 165–82.

Boston, Barbara. "The De Soto Map," *Mid-America* 23 (n.s. 12, 1941), 236–50.

Boucher, Philip. "French Images of America and the Evolution of Colonial Theories, 1650–1700," in Joyce D. Falk (ed.), *Proceedings of the Sixth Annual Meeting of the Western Society for French History* (Santa Barbara: ABC-Clio, 1979), 220–28.

Brain, Jeffrey P. "The Natchez 'Paradox'," *Ethnology* 10 (1971), 215–22.

———. "The Archaeology of the Tunica: Trial on the Yazoo," *National Geographic Society Research Reports* (Washington: National Geographic Society, 1975).

———. "Late Prehistoric Settlement Patterning in the Yazoo Basin and Natchez Bluff Regions of the Lower Mississippi Valley," in Bruce Smith (ed.), *Mississippian Settlement Patterns* (New York: Academic Press, 1978), 331–68

Brain, Jeffrey P., Ian W. Brown, and Vincas P. Steponaitis. *Archaeology of the Natchez Bluffs* (Cambridge: Peabody Museum, forthcoming).

Brasseaux, Carl A. "The Image of Louisiana and the Failure of Voluntary French Emigration, 1683–1731," in Alf Heggoy and James J. Cooke (eds.), *Proceedings of the Fourth Meeting of the French Colonial Historical Society* (Washington: University Press of America, 1979), 47–56.

Brinton, Daniel G. "On the Language of the Natchez." Paper read before the American Philosophical Society, Philadelphia, December 5, 1873. Copy in the Tozzer Library, Cambridge, Massachusetts.

Brookes, Samuel O., and John Connaway. "Archaeological Survey of Clay County, Mississippi," report on file, Mississippi Department of Archives and History, Jackson.

Brown, Calvin S. *Archeology of Mississippi* (Oxford, Mississippi: Mississippi Geological Survey, 1926).

Brown, Ian W. "Exavations at Fort St. Pierre," *Conference on Historic Site Archaeology Papers* 9 (1975), 60–85.

———. "The Portland Site (22-M-12), an Early 18th Century Historic Indian Site in Warren County, Mississippi," *Mississippi Archaeology* 11:1 (1976), 2–11.

———. "Functional Group Changes and Acculturation: A Case Study of the French and the Indian in the Lower Mississippi Valley," *Midcontinental Journal of Archaeology* 4:2 (1979), 147–65.

———. *Salt and the Eastern North American Indian: An Archaeological Study.* Lower Mississippi Survey Bulletin 6 (Cambridge: Lower Mississippi Survey, Peabody Museum, 1980).

———. "Historic Aboriginal Pottery from the Yazoo Bluffs Region, Mississippi," *Southeastern Archaeological Conference Bulletin* 21 (in press).

Brown, Ian W., and Jeffrey P. Brain. "Archaeology of the Natchez Bluffs Region, Mississippi: Hypothesized Cultural and Environmental Factors Influencing Local Population Movements in the Natchez Bluffs Region," *Southeastern Archaeological Conference Bulletin* 20 (Memphis, in press).

Brown, Ian W., and Stephen Williams. "Archaeological Investigations at Seven Historic Sites in the Natchez Bluffs Region, Mississippi: 1981 Season," *Natchez Project, Research Notes* 1 (Cambridge: Lower Mississippi Survey, Peabody Museum, 1982).

Brown, Philip M. "Early Indian Trade in the Development of South Carolina," *South Carolina Historical Magazine* 76 (1975), 118–28.

Byington, Cyrus. *A Dictionary of the Choctaw Language.* Bureau of American Ethnology Bulletin 46 (Washington: Government Printing Office, 1915).

Calderón Quijano, José Antonio. *Fortificaciones en Nueva España* (Sevilla: Publicaciones de la Escuela de Estudios Hispanoamericanos de Sevilla, 1953).

Caldwell, Norman W. "The Chickasaw Threat to French Control of the Mississippi in the 1740s," *Chronicles of Oklahoma* 16 (1938), 465–92.

Caruso, John Anthony. *The Mississippi Valley Frontier* (Indianapolis: Bobbs-Merrill, 1966).

Chabot, Victorin, "Journal inédite relatant les expéditions de Cavelier de La Salle," *The Archivist* 8 (1981), 8–9.

Chesnel, Paul. *Histoire de Cavelier de La Salle* (Paris: Maisonneuve, 1901).

Claiborne, J. F. H. *Mississippi as a Province, Territory and State* (Jackson: Power & Barksdale, 1880).

Conrad, Glenn R. "L'Immigration alsacienne en Louisiane, 1753–1759," *Revue d'histoire de l'Amérique française* 28 (1975), 565–77.

———. "Emigration Forcée: A French Attempt to Populate Louisiana, 1716–1720" in Alf Heggoy and James J. Cooke (eds.), *Proceedings of the Fourth Meeting of the French Colonial Historical Society* (Washington: University Press of America, 1979), 57–66.

Cotter, John L. "Stratigraphic and Area Tests at the Emerald and Anna Mound Sites," *American Antiquity* 17:1 (1951), 18–32.

———. "The Gordon Site in Southern Mississippi," *American Antiquity* 18:2 (1952), 110–26.

Crane, Verner W. "The Tennessee River as the Road to Carolina: The Beginnings of Exploration and Trade," *Mississippi Valley Historical Review* 3 (1916), 4–5.

———. "The Southern Frontier in Queen Anne's War," *American Historical Review* 24 (1918), 379–95.

————. *The Southern Frontier, 1670–1732* (reprint ed. Ann Arbor: University of Michigan Press, 1956).

Crawford, James M. *The Mobilian Trade Language* (Knoxville: University of Tennessee Press, 1978).

————. (ed.). *Studies in Southeastern Indian Languages* (Athens: University of Georgia Press, 1975).

Cumming, William P. *The Southeast in Early Maps* (Princeton: Princeton University Press, 1958).

Cumming, William P., S. E. Hillier, D. B. Quinn, and G. Williams. *The Exploration of North America* (New York: G. P. Putnam's Sons, 1974).

Curren, Cailup B. "Prehistoric and Early Historic Occupation of the Mobile Bay and Mobile Delta area of Alabama with Emphasis on Subsistence," *Journal of Alabama Archaeology* 22 (1976), 61–84.

Debo, Angie. *The Rise and Fall of the Choctaw Republic*, 2nd ed. (Norman: University of Oklahoma Press, 1961).

Delanglez, Jean. *The French Jesuits in Lower Louisiana (1700–1763)* (Washington: The Catholic University, 1935).

————. "A Louisiana Poet-historian: Dumont *dit* Montigny," *Mid-America* 19:1 (1937), 31–49.

————. *Some La Salle Journeys* (Chicago: Institute of Jesuit History, 1938).

————. "Tonti Letters," *Mid-America* 21 (1939), 209–38.

————. "La Salle's Expedition of 1682," *Mid-America* 22 (1940), 3–37.

————. *Hennepin's Description of Louisiana: A Critical Essay* (Chicago: Institute of Jesuit History, 1940).

————. "The Sources of the Delisle Map of America, 1703," *Mid-America* 25 (1943), 275–98.

————. "The Voyages of Tonti in North America, 1678–1704," *Mid-America* 26 (1944), 255–300.

————. *El Rio del Espiritu Santo*, Catholic Historical Society Monograph Series 21 (1945).

Dickason, Olive. "The Concept of *l'homme sauvage* and Early French Colonialism in the Americas," *Revue française d'histoire d'outre-mer* 44 (1977), 234.

Dunn, William Edward. "The Spanish Search for La Salle's

Colony on the Bay of Espiritu Santo, 1685–1689," *Southwestern Historical Quarterly* 19 (1916), 323–69.

———. *Spanish and French Rivalry in the Gulf Region of the United States, 1678–1702: The Beginnings of Texas and Pensacola.* University of Texas Bulletin 1705 (Austin: University of Texas Press, 1917).

Durand, René. "Louis XIV et Jacques II à la veille de la Révolution de 1688: Les Trois missions de Bonrepaus en Angleterre," *Revue d'Histoire Moderne et Contemporaine* 10 (1908), 28–44.

Eccles, William J. *France in America* (New York: Harper & Row, 1972).

Eggan, Fred. *The American Indian: Perspectives for the Study of Social Change* (Chicago: Aldine, 1966).

Enciclopedia universal ilustrada Europeo-Americana, vol. 44. (Madrid and Barcelona: Espasa-Calpe, 1908–1930).

Favrot, H. Mortimer. "Colonial Forts of Louisiana," *Louisiana Historical Quarterly* 26 (1943), 722–54.

Faye, Stanley. "The Contest for Pensacola Bay and Other Gulf Ports, 1698–1822," *Florida Historical Quarterly* 24 (1945–6), 167–95, 302–28.

Fischer, John L. "Solutions for the Natchez Paradox," *Ethnology* 3:1 (1964), 53–65.

Fite, Emerson D., and Archibald Freeman. *A Book of Old Maps Delineating American History* (New York: Dover, 1969).

Folmer, Henry. *Franco-Spanish Rivalry in North America, 1524–1763* (Glendale, Cal.: Arthur H. Clark Co., 1953).

Ford, James A. "Outline of Louisiana and Mississippi Pottery Horizons," *Louisiana Conservation Review* 4:6 (1935), 33–38.

———. *Analysis of Indian Village Site Collections from Louisiana and Mississippi.* State of Louisiana Department of Conservation Anthropological Study 2 (1935).

Fortier, Alcée. *A History of Louisiana,* 4 vols. (New York: Manzi, Joyant & Co., 1904).

Frank, Joseph V., III. "In Defense of Hutchin's Natchez Indian," *Mississippi Archaeological Association Newsletter* 10:4 (1975), 7–11.

————. "A European Trade Bead from the Anna Mounds Site, Adams County, Mississippi," *Mississippi Archaeological Association Newsletter* 15:3 (1980), 5.

————. "The Rice Site: A Natchez Indian Cemetery," *Mississippi Archaeology* 15:2 (1980), 32–41.

Frégault, Guy. *Le Grand Marquis: Pierre de Rigaud de Vaudreuil et la Louisiane* (Montreal: Fides, 1952).

Galloway, Patricia K. "Dearth and Bias: Issues in the Editing of Ethnohistorical Materials," *Newsletter of the Association for Documentary Editing* 3:2 (1981), 1–6.

Gayarré, Charles-Étienne Arthur. *History of Louisiana*, 4 vols. (New Orleans: F. F. Hansell & Bro., 1854–1866).

Gearing, Fred. "Priests and Warriors: Social Structures for Cherokee Politics in the 18th Century," *American Anthropological Association Memoir* 93 (1962).

Gibson, Arrell M. *The Chickasaws* (Norman: University of Oklahoma Press, 1971).

Gil Munilla, Roberto. "Política española en el golfo mexicano, expediciones motivadas por la entrada del Caballero La Salle (1685–1707)," *Anuario de Estudios Americanos* (Sevilla) 12 (1955), 476–611.

Giraud, Marcel. *Histoire de la Louisiane française*, 4 vols. to date (Paris: Presses Universitaires de France, 1953–1974).

————. *A History of French Louisiana, Vol. 1: The Reign of Louis XIV, 1698–1715*, trans. Joseph C. Lambert (Baton Rouge: Louisiana State University Press, 1974).

Grant, Arthur J. *The French Monarchy (1483–1789)*, 2 vols. (Cambridge: Cambridge University Press, 1925).

Gravier, Gabriel. *Découvertes et établissements de Cavelier de La Salle de Rouen dans l'Amérique du Nord* (Paris: Maisonneuve, 1871).

Groulx, Lionel. *Notre Grande Aventure: L'empire français en Amérique du nord, 1535–1760* (Montreal, 1958).

Haas, Mary R. "The Classification of the Muskogean Languages," in Leslie Spier *et al.* (eds.) *Language, Culture and Personality* (Menasha, Wisconsin, 1941), 41–56.

————. "What is Mobilian?" in James M. Crawford (ed.),

Studies in Southeastern Indian Languages (Athens: University of Georgia Press, 1975), 257–63.

Habig, Marion A. *The Franciscan Père Marquette: A Critical Biography of Father Zénobe Membré, O.F.M., La Salle's Chaplain and Missionary Companion* (New York: Joseph F. Wagner, 1934).

Hally, David J. "The Archaeology of European-Indian Contact in the Southeast," in Charles Hudson (ed.), *Red, White, and Black* (Athens: University of Georgia Press, 1971), 55–66.

Hart, Charles W. M. "A Reconsideration of the Natchez Social Structure," *American Anthropologist* 45:3:1 (1943), 374–86.

Higginbotham, Jay. *Old Mobile: Fort Louis de la Louisiane, 1702–1711* (Mobile: Museum of the City of Mobile, 1977).

Hoese, H. Dickson. "On the Correct Landfall of La Salle in Texas, 1685," *Louisiana History* 19 (1978), 5–33.

Holmes, Jack D. L. "The Failure of French Immigration, 1700–1765: A Comment," in Alf Heggoy and James J. Cooke (eds.), *Proceedings of the Fourth Meeting of the French Colonial Historical Society* (Washington: University Press of America, 1979), 67–69.

Howard, Clinton N. *The British Development of West Florida, 1763–1769* (Berkeley: University of California Press, 1947).

Hudson, Charles. *The Southeastern Indians* (Knoxville: University of Tennessee Press, 1976).

Jaenen, Cornelius J. "Conceptual Frameworks for French Views of America and Amerindians," *French Colonial Studies* 2 (1978), 1–22.

———. "The Images of New France in the History of Lescarbot," in *Proceedings of the Sixth Annual Meeting of the Western Society for French History* (Santa Barbara: ABC-Clio, 1979), 209–19.

———. "French Views of New France and Canadians," in James J. Cooke (ed.), *Proceedings of the Sixth and Seventh Meetings of the French Colonial Historical Society, 1980–1981* (Washington: University Press of America, 1982), 1–12.

Jaray, Gabriel Louis. *L'Empire française d'Amerique, 1534–1803* (Paris: Colin, 1938).

————. "Cavelier de La Salle, Founder of the French Empire in America," trans. M. Moraud, *Rice Institute Pamphlet* 26 (1939), 1–42.

Jennings, Jesse. "Chickasaw and Earlier Indian Cultures of Northeast Mississippi," *Journal of Mississippi History* 3 (1941), 155–226.

Kellogg, Louise. "Wisconsin Anabasis," *Wisconsin Magazine of History* 7 (1924), 322–29.

Kondert, Reinhard. "German Immigration to French Colonial Louisiana: A Reevaluation," in Alf Heggoy and James J. Cooke (eds.), *Proceedings of the Fourth Meeting of the French Colonial Historical Society* (Washington: University Press of America, 1979), 70–81.

Lafon, Barthelemy. "Atlas of the 7th Military District." Historic New Orleans Collection, New Orleans.

Lauber, Almon W. *Indian Slavery in Colonial Times Within the Present Limits of the United States* (1913; reprint Williamstown, Mass.: Corner House, 1979).

Leonard, Irving A. *Don Carlos de Sigüenza y Góngora, a Mexican Savant of the Seventeenth Century*, University of California Publications in History 18 (Berkeley: University of California Press, 1929).

MacLeod, William C. "Natchez Political Evolution," *American Anthropologist* 26:2 (1924), 201–29.

Maggs Brothers. *The French Colonization of America as Exemplified in a Remarkable Collection of French Administrative Acts . . .*, Catalogue 8 (Paris, 1936).

Manucy, Albert. "The Founding of Pensacola—Reasons and Reality," *Florida Historical Quarterly* 37 (1958–59), 223–41.

Martin, François-Xavier. *The History of Louisiana from the Earliest Period*, 2 vols. (New Orleans: Lyman and Beardslee, 1827–1829).

Mason, Carol I. "Natchez Class Structure," *Ethnohistory* 11:2 (1964), 120–33.

Mooney, James. "Myths of the Cherokee," *Bureau of American Ethnology 19th Annual Report*, Pt. 1 (Washington: Government Printing Office, 1900).

Moore, Clarence B. "Some Aboriginal Sites on the Mississippi River," *Journal of the Academy of Natural Sciences of Philadelphia* 14 (1911), 366–480.

Moore, John P. *Revolt in Louisiana: The Spanish Occupation, 1766–1770* (Baton Rouge: Louisiana State University Press, 1976).

Moorehead, Warren K. "Explorations near Natchez, Mississippi," in Warren K. Moorehead (ed.), *Etowah Papers, Exploration of the Etowah Site in Georgia* (New Haven: Yale University Press, 1932).

Moraud, M. "Last Expedition and the Death of Cavelier de La Salle, 1684–1687," *Rice Institute Pamphlet* 24 (1937), 143–67.

Murphy, Edmund Robert. *Henry de Tonty: Fur Trader of the Mississippi* (Baltimore: Johns Hopkins Press, 1941).

Neitzel, Robert S. "The Natchez Grand Village," *Florida Anthropologist* 17:2 (1964), 63–6.

———. *Archeology of the Fatherland Site: The Grand Village of the Natchez*. Anthropological Papers of the American Museum of Natural History 51, pt. 1 (New York, 1965).

———. "Excavations at the Fatherland Site," *Southeastern Archaeological Conference Newsletter* 16:2 (1972), 31–2.

———. "A Doublebarreled Detective Story," in Marco Giardino, Barbara Edmonson, and Winifred Creamer (eds.), *Codex Wauchope: A Tribute Roll* (New Orleans: Tulane University, 1978).

———. *The Grand Village of the Natchez: Revisited* (Jackson: Mississippi Department of Archives and History, forthcoming).

O'Donnell, Walter. *La Salle's Occupation of Texas* (Austin: University of Texas Press, 1936).

Ogg, Frederick Austin. *The Opening of the Mississippi: A Struggle for Supremacy in the American Interior* (New York: Macmillan, 1904).

Osler, E. B. *La Salle* (Don Mills, Ontario: Longmans Canada, 1967).

Parkman, Francis. *La Salle and the Discovery of the Great West* (Boston: Little, Brown, and Co., 1908).

Paullin, Charles O. *Atlas of the Historical Geography of the United States* (Washington: Carnegie Institution, 1932).

Peebles, Christopher S. "Determinants of Settlement Size and Location in the Moundville Phase," in Bruce Smith (ed.), *Mississippian Settlement Patterns* (New York: Academic Press), 369–416.

Phillips, Philip. *Archaeological Survey in the Lower Yazoo Basin, Mississippi, 1949–1955.* Papers of the Peabody Museum of Archaeology and Ethnology 60 (1970).

Phillips, Philip, James A. Ford, and James B. Griffin. *Archaeological Survey in the Lower Mississippi Alluvial Valley, 1940–1947.* Papers of the Peabody Museum of Archaeology and Ethnology 25 (1951).

Powell, Mary Lucas. "Biocultural Analysis of Human Skeletal Remains from the Lubbub Creek Archaeological Locality," in Christopher S. Peebles (ed.), *Prehistoric Agricultural Communities in West Central Alabama,* vol. 2 (Final report to U.S. Army Corps of Engineers, 1981), 432–69.

Prator, C. H. "La Salle's Trip Across Southern Michigan in 1680," *Michigan History Magazine* 25 (1941), 188–98.

Quimby, George I. "The Natchezan Culture Type," *American Antiquity* 7 (1942), 255–75.

———. "Natchez Social Structures as an Instrument of Assimilation," *American Anthropologist* 48 (1946), 134–36.

———. "Natchez Archaeology: A Tribute to the Natchez for their Seeming Consistency in the Production of the Fictile Fabric," *Southeastern Archaeological Conference Newsletter* 3:3 (1953), 22–24.

Rubio Mañé, Jorge Ignacio. *Introducción al estudio de los virreyes de Nueva España, 1535–1746,* vols. 1 and 3 (México: Universidad Nacional Autónoma de México, 1943, 1961).

Shelby, Charmion Clair. "International Rivalry in Northeastern New Spain, 1700–1725." Ph.D. dissertation, University of Texas, 1935.

Steponaitis, Vincas P. "Plaquemine Ceramic Chronology in the Natchez Region," *Mississippi Archaeology* 16:2 (1981), 6–19.

Stern, Theodore C. "The Natchez," in Robert F. Spencer and

Jesse D. Jennings (eds.), *The Native Americans* (New York: Harper and Row, 1965), 409–19.

Surrey, N. M. Miller. *The Commerce of Louisiana during the French Regime, 1699–1763.* Columbia University Studies in the Social Sciences 167 (1916).

Swanton, John R. *Indian Tribes of the Lower Mississippi Valley and the Adjacent Coast of the Gulf of Mexico.* Bureau of American Ethnology Bulletin 43 (Washington: Government Printing Office, 1911).

———. *Early History of the Creek Indians and their Neighbors.* Bureau of American Ethnology Bulletin 73 (Washington: Government Printing Office, 1922).

———. "List of Trails," *Bureau of American Ethnology 42nd Annual Report* (Washington: Government Printing Office, 1928), 746–48.

———. "Aboriginal Culture of the Southeast," *Bureau of American Ethnology 42nd Annual Report* (Washington: Government Printing Office, 1928), 673–726.

———. "Social and Religious Beliefs and Usages of the Chickasaw Indians," *Bureau of American Ethnology 44th Annual Report* (Washington: Government Printing Office, 1928), 169–273.

———. *Source Material for the Social and Ceremonial Life of the Choctaw Indians.* Bureau of American Ethnology Bulletin 103 (Washington: Government Printing Office, 1931).

———. *Final Report of the United States De Soto Expedition Commission* (Washington: Government Printing Office, 1939).

———. *The Indians of the Southeastern United States.* Bureau of American Ethnology Bulletin 137 (Washington: Government Printing Office, 1946).

Taylor, William R. "A Journey into the Human Mind: Motivation in Francis Parkman's *La Salle*," *William and Mary Quarterly,* 3rd ser. 18 (1962), 220–37.

Tooker, Elizabeth J. "Natchez Social Organization: Fact or Anthropological Folklore?" *Ethnohistory* 10:4 (1963), 358–72.

Tucker, Sara Jones, *Indian Villages of the Illinois Country, Part I: Atlas*. Scientific Papers, Illinois State Museum, Vol. II (Springfield: Illinois State Museum, 1942).

Villiers du Terrage, Marc de. *L'Expédition de Cavelier de La Salle dans le golfe du Mexique, 1684–1687* (Paris: Maisonneuve, 1931).

————. "La Salle Takes Possession of Louisiana," *Louisiana Historical Quarterly* 14 (1931), 301–15.

Weddle, Robert S. *Wilderness Manhunt: The Spanish Search for La Salle* (Austin: University of Texas Press, 1973).

White, Douglas R., George P. Murdock, and Richard Scaglion. "Natchez Class and Rank Reconsidered," *Ethnology* 10:4 (1971), 369–88.

Williams, Stephen. "Settlement Patterns in the Lower Mississippi Valley," in Gordon R. Willey (ed.), *Prehistoric Settlement Patterns in the New World*, Viking Fund Publications in Archaeology 23 (1956), 52–62.

————. "Historic Archaeology in the Lower Mississippi Valley," *Southeastern Archaeological Conference Newsletter* 9:1 (1962), 53–63

————. "Historic Archaeology, Past and Present," in *School of American Research Annual Report for 1966* (Santa Fe: School of American Research, 1966), 23–26.

————. "On the Location of the Historic Taensa Villages," *Conference on Historic Site Archaeology Papers* 1 (1967), 3–13.

Williams, Stephen, and Jeffrey P. Brain. *Excavations at Lake George, Yazoo County, Mississippi, 1958–1960*. Papers of the Peabody Museum of Archaeology and Ethnology 74 (1982).

Williams, Stephen, William Kean, and Alan Toth. *The Archaeology of the Upper Tensas Basin*. Lower Mississippi Survey Bulletin 1 (1966).

Wilson, Baronesa de. *México y sus gobernantes de 1519 a 1910*, 2 vols. (Barcelona: Tipografía de la Casa Editorial Manucci, 1910).

Wilson, Samuel, Jr. "Colonial Fortifications and Military Architecture in the Mississippi Valley," in John F. McDermott (ed.), *The French in the Mississippi Valley* (Urbana: University of Illinois Press, 1965), 103–22.

———. "Gulf Coast Architecture," in Ernest F. Dribble *et al.* (eds.) *Spain and her Rivals on the Gulf Coast* (Pensacola: University of West Florida Press, 1971), 78–126.

Winsor, Justin. *Cartier to Frontenac, Geographical Discovery in the interior of North America in Its Historical Relations, 1534–1700* (Boston: Houghton, Mifflin and Co., 1894).

Wright, J. Leitch, Jr. *The Only Land They Knew: The Tragic Story of the American Indians in the Old South* (New York: The Free Press, 1981).

Contributors

Jeffrey P. Brain is Curator of Southeastern United States Archaeology at the Peabody Museum, Harvard University. His special interest in early European contacts with American Indians has focused on work in the lower Mississippi Valley and specifically on the early history of the Tunica. In this area his publications include "The Archaeology of the De Soto Expedition" and *Tunica Treasure*.

Carl A. Brasseaux is Assistant Director and Curator of Manuscripts at the Center for Louisiana Studies, University of Southwestern Louisiana. His most recent work on early French exploration is *A Comparative View of French Louisiana*, which includes a translation of the journals of Iberville's expeditions.

Ian W. Brown is Research Associate at the Peabody Museum and Lecturer in Anthropology, Harvard University. His work on the prehistory of Louisiana and Mississippi has included a doctoral dissertation on the excavation of the French Fort St. Pierre; he is presently engaged in a program of research and excavation of the historic Natchez Indian village sites.

William S. Coker is Professor of History at the University of West Florida. His special interest is in the history of the Spanish borderlands, specifically in the English and Spanish occupations of the West Florida area. His work on the early period of exploration has included the introduction to a recent edition of Coxe's *Carolana*, and he is Director of the Papers of Panton, Leslie and Company publication project.

Glenn R. Conrad is Director of the Center for Louisiana Studies, Professor of History at the University of Southwestern Louisiana, and editor of *Louisiana History*. His interest in the early French colonial period in North America has led to several publications in this area, including the article on "Jean-Baptiste Le Moyne" in the *Encyclopedia of the South* and an edition of La Harpe's *Journal of the Establishment of the French in Louisiana.*

James J. Cooke is Professor of History at the University of Mississippi. As a specialist in French colonial history he has published *New French Imperialism* and has served as editor of the *Proceedings of the French Colonial Historical Society* since 1978.

Louis De Vorsey, Jr. is Professor of Geography at the University of Georgia. A specialist in historical and forensic geography trained at the University of London, he has published *The Indian Boundary in the Southern Colonies, 1763–1773* and *De Brahm's Report of the General Survey in the Southern District of North America* and has served as an expert witness in several boundary cases involving southeastern states.

Carl J. Ekberg is Professor of History at Illinois State University. His interest in the French colonial history of North America began with a concern for the American repercussions of European rivalries, which he studied in *The Failure of Louis XIV's Dutch War.* He is presently engaged in researching historical documentation for French sites to provide the background for archaeological research on these sites, and has nearly completed a book-length study on the colonial history of Ste. Genevieve, Missouri.

Patricia K. Galloway is employed by the Mississippi Department of Archives and History as Administrative Assistant for Special Projects. Her interest in French colonial history has grown out of her editorship of volumes IV and V of the *Mississippi Provincial Archives: French Dominion* series and has concentrated on the early ethnohistory of the Choctaw Indians.

Jack D. L. Holmes is retired Professor of History at the University of Alabama in Birmingham. Director since 1965 of the

Louisiana Collection Series of books and documents on colonial Louisiana, Holmes was made a Knight of the Order of Isabela la Católica in 1979 by King Juan Carlos of Spain for his outstanding work on the history of the Spanish borderlands. His publications include *Gayoso: The Life of a Spanish Governor in the Mississippi Valley* and *A Guide to Spanish Louisiana, 1762–1806.*

John D. Stubbs, Jr. is a Research Associate with the Peabody Museum, Harvard University, and has conducted a survey of historic Chickasaw Indian sites in Lee County, Mississippi, for the Mississippi Department of Archives and History. He is currently serving as Scholar in Residence in Tupelo, Mississippi, under a grant from the Mississippi Committee for the Humanities.

Samuel Wilson, Jr. is a partner in the firm of Koch and Wilson Architects, New Orleans. His interest as a practicing historical architect has been sustained by archival research in France and Spain; he has contributed numerous scholarly studies of Louisiana colonial architecture and has been connected with several historic restorations, including that of Fort Maurepas on the Mississippi Gulf Coast. Founder and first president of the Louisiana Landmarks Society, he is also an advisor to the Historic Natchez Foundation.

Kennith H. York is a member of the Mississippi Band of Choctaw Indians and is presently completing a doctorate at the University of Minnesota in Education. A member of the Choctaw Heritage Council, his interest in Indian culture history and language studies has found practical application in work with the bilingual and vocational education programs for the Mississippi Band of Choctaw Indians.

Index